BARREN VICTORIES

Basil Collier

BARREN VICTORIES:
VERSAILLES TO SUEZ

The Failure of the Western Alliance,

1918–1956

DOUBLEDAY & COMPANY, INC.
GARDEN CITY, NEW YORK
1964

Library of Congress Catalog Card Number 64–11690
Copyright © 1964 by Basil Collier
All Rights Reserved
Printed in the United States of America
First Edition

Timeo Danaos et dona ferentes

PREFACE

THIS BOOK IS NOT MEANT FOR EXPERTS. IT IS OFFERED AS A PLAIN man's guide to world affairs from the end of the First World War to the Suez crisis, with special reference to the clash of ideals between the United States and Europe. Believing that readers may find it easier to see the wood if the trees are not too much thrust upon their notice, on almost every page I have dealt summarily with events about which whole volumes could be written and have been written.

The history of the period bristles with controversy, but one conclusion seems beyond dispute. When Germany asked for an armistice in 1918, the English-speaking peoples were presented with opportunities of peaceful progress such as come seldom in the lifetime of nations. Had their leaders seized those opportunities, a world which had seen Britain increase her trade sixfold in the lifetime of Queen Victoria might have witnessed a second era of expanding markets and rising standards of living for all classes, in which the lead would have come from the Anglo-Saxon nations but in which all nations could have shared. All that was needed was that British and American statesmen should sink national rivalries, pursue attainable ends, and provide their fellow citizens with the physical means of ensuring that the interests of mankind were not frustrated by self-seeking disturbers of the peace.

Their failure to do those things is the main theme of this book.

B.C.

CONTENTS

PRELUDE TO PEACE

IN THE LATE SUMMER OF 1918 THE FIRST WORLD WAR BEGAN AT last to move toward a close after nearly fifty months of deadlock on the Western Front.

That spring the Germans, seeing the need to be done with the war before the Americans arrived in strength, had tried hard to smash through the Allied line near the junction between the British and French armies. Their attempt failed, just as attempts by the Allies to break the German line had failed. Its failure left the Germans scraping the bottom of the manpower barrel as the British and the French were doing. The difference was that the Germans had no United States at their backs to feed and supply them and provide a brimming reservoir of fresh divisions.

As long ago as September 1914, when the Germans were streaming away from the Marne as fast as they could go, Field Marshal Helmuth von Moltke, then Chief of the German General Staff, had taken it for granted that the failure of his attempt to encircle the French Army in six weeks by wheeling through Belgium meant the loss of the war so far as his country was concerned. Writing to his wife on September 9, he had told her that Germany would have to admit defeat and pay for the damage she had done. When the German government of that day rejected Moltke's conclusion, appointed a new Chief of the General Staff and ordered their troops to stand fast on the Aisne, they sentenced Europe to a long-drawn agony which threatened to exhaust the belligerents on both sides without bringing a decision.

Three years and eleven months later, Moltke was proved right. On August 8, 1918, British and French troops began an advance which convinced the rulers of Germany within five days that they had no further chance of defeating their enemies in the field, and that only a diplomatic master-stroke could save them. Seven weeks later, with no master-stroke in sight, the High Command called urgently on the government to sue for an armistice while their forces were still substantially intact.

When a diplomatic offensive to save the German Army was first mooted, the government contemplated asking either the Queen of the Netherlands or the King of Spain to act as mediator between themselves and the Allies as soon as the right moment came. By September the outlook had changed so much for the worse that they could no longer afford to wait for the right moment. On September 21, after Austro-Hungary had let the cat out of the bag by publicly proposing a negotiated peace, the German Quartermaster General, General Erich Ludendorff, suggested an approach to the United States government through the Swiss government. Even with Bulgaria on the point of collapse, the High Command continued to hope that an armistice for a limited period might enable them to hold the army together through the winter and renew hostilities in the spring for long enough to improve Germany's bargaining power at the peace conference by fighting a successful defensive battle. But Ludendorff and his collaborator, Field Marshal Paul von Hindenburg, agreed by the end of the month not only that there was no further hope of victory, but that an immediate armistice was absolutely vital.

To prepare the ground for an armistice and a negotiated peace, the German government was reconstructed at the end of September on lines acceptable to the majority of the Reichstag and likely to be acceptable to enemies with marked democratic leanings. On October 4, as the sequel to further despairing messages from the High Command, a new administration under a Liberal Chancellor, Prince Max of Baden, despatched to Berne a note asking the President of the United States to "take steps for the restoration of peace."

From one point of view the choice of the President of the

United States as recipient of the German peace offer was surprising. The United States had been at war with Germany for eighteen months, had supplied the Allies with vast quantities of war material, and had lent them the best part of ten thousand million dollars. Thus the President was in no position to act as impartial mediator between the Allies and the Germans. At the same time he was divided from the scene of conflict by three thousand miles of water not yet bridged by a transatlantic telephone, so that he was not well placed to say whether an armistice was acceptable to his own side from the military point of view, or what the terms of an armistice should be if one were granted. If the Germans wanted an *immediate* respite, as they did, and if their object was to save time by reducing neutral mediation to the essential minimum, it might have seemed more logical for them to apply in the first instance to the Supreme War Council at Versailles or to the Allied Supreme Commander, Marshal Ferdinand Foch.

From another point of view the choice was not at all surprising. On the whole, American opinion, even before the United States entered the war in 1917, had always been favorable to the Allies, but it did not follow that America shared Allied war aims. Before the United States severed diplomatic relations with Germany, it had seemed quite possible that she might sever relations with Great Britain first. Throughout the years of neutrality the United States Department of State had fought the British definition of contraband of war with a tenacity equaled only by the generosity with which the United States Treasury had responded to British requests for financial aid. In 1916 Congress had sanctioned a program of naval construction which openly challenged Britain's command of the sea, obnoxious to American exporters who accepted only with reservations the British argument that an island kingdom dependent on foreign trade for the means of subsistence must keep an iron hand on her external communications and that neutrals must put up with the inconvenience of selling their goods in wartime only to the side capable of taking delivery and paying a fair price. Conversely, almost until the last moment the United States government had been at pains to avoid a breach with Germany, in spite of the loss of American lives in ships sunk

by German submarines in defiance of international custom. It
was symptomatic of relations between America and Europe that,
when the United States did enter the war on the same side as
Great Britain, France and Italy, she did so not as their ally but as
an "associated power," thus preserving her theoretical right to withdraw from the struggle without consulting them.

Then, too, the President had publicly declared, since his country
joined forces with the Allies, that he was not an enemy of the
German people, and had said much else which suggested that he
might look sympathetically on a German government claiming to
represent progressive and moderate opinion. Although he dis-
claimed the intention of "acting as arbiter in European territorial
disputes," he was known to covet the honorable role of peace-
maker, and was understood to favor a negotiated peace.

An impression in German political circles that Ludendorff was
backing the right horse when he suggested an approach to the
United States government was strengthened by similarities between some of the President's declarations and views expressed by
German politicians of the Left and Center. On July 19, 1917, for
example, the predominantly Socialist and Centrist Reichstag had
passed a resolution calling for a peace of understanding and permanent reconciliation between peoples, the strengthening of international law, the freedom of the seas, the lowering of economic
barriers and a ban on forcible annexations of territory and economic and financial penalties. All these had turned up again six
months later in the famous Fourteen Points which President
Woodrow Wilson enunciated in an address to Congress on January 8, 1918. In the following month the President had referred
specifically to the July resolution and emphasized its renunciation
of annexations and punitive indemnities.

The President's speech of January 8 was not made with a view
to the situation which developed in the following October, and
it was very nearly not made at all. President Wilson believed in
the winter of 1917–18 that there was a good chance of rallying
Liberal and Socialist opinion in Germany against a militarist government. He drew up his Fourteen Points largely because his confidential adviser, Colonel Edward M. House, had failed on a visit

to Europe to persuade the Allied governments to join the United States in making a joint declaration of war aims. Three days before the President was due to appear before Congress the British Prime Minister, Lloyd George, made a statement of British war aims to an audience of trade union leaders in London. When the President read the report of Lloyd George's speech, he felt that so little had been left for him to add that he nearly abandoned his address, but ultimately he was persuaded to deliver it without substantial alteration.

Lloyd George's immediate object when he made his speech was not so much to influence left-wing opinion in Germany as to persuade British working men to make concessions. He assured the trade unionists that Great Britain was not fighting to destroy Germany or Austro-Hungary or take Constantinople from the Turks, but that the interests of all good men demanded that Belgium and other countries invaded by the Central Powers should be freed and compensated for wrongs suffered by their citizens. At the same time he warned Turkey that, while Turkish sovereignty would be respected in regions "predominantly Turkish in race," the Allies did mean to deprive Turkey of Arabia, Armenia, Mesopotamia and Palestine. On the whole a businesslike statement, well suited to the occasion, the speech made a good impression in neutral countries, but was coolly received in Germany, where the March offensive was already in prospect. Count Georg von Hertling, the German Chancellor, complained that, while Lloyd George spoke of peace and even paid tribute to German culture, he seemed to think it his duty to sit in judgment on guilty Germany.

President Wilson's address to Congress, on the other hand, was meant to echo round the world, and it did. A master of the impassioned rhetoric which thrills millions to whom appeals to justice, equality, and the Rights of Man are always attractive even though their context may not always be quite clear, the President seldom failed to pull out all the stops at the right moment. Because his words were eloquent, because his country was felt to have no ax to grind in Europe, perhaps also because of the commanding position occupied by the United States as a great and powerful nation whose strength was still unsapped by the war, the President was openly or secretly hailed by Liberals and Socialists in many countries as a champion of enlightenment whose province transcended national frontiers, while Lloyd George's equally reassuring but more soberly pitched statement was regarded, at any rate in Germany, as that of a mere partisan.

But in January, when the German High Command was planning an all-out blow which promised to pen the British Army between the Somme and the Channel ports and drive the left wing of the French Army southward and westward to cover Paris, neither President Wilson's manifesto nor Lloyd George's lent enough weight to moderate opinion in Germany to tip the scale in favor of a negotiated peace. In October the outlook was very different. With the Allies and the Americans pressing eastward in France and Belgium, with Austro-Hungary avid for peace, with Bulgaria gone and Turkey cracking, and with Red revolution lurking round the corner, the Germans were ready to clutch at straws. In his message of October 4 to the President of the United States, Prince Max of Baden informed the President that the German government accepted the program set forth eleven months earlier in the Fourteen Points.

On September 26, 1918, the Bulgarian government, unable to stem an Allied offensive in Macedonia, asked General Sir George Milne, commanding the British forces on that front, to grant them an armistice. General Milne referred them to the local Allied Commander-in-Chief, General Louis Franchet d'Esperey. Lloyd George remarked acidly in his war memoirs that thereafter Franchet d'Esperey conducted all the negotiations without reference to the British. He soon had a great deal more provocation of the same sort to complain of.

The Bulgarian envoy reached Franchet d'Esperey's headquarters on September 28. On the same day Hindenburg and Ludendorff both came to the conclusion that they could not conceal from each other and from the civil authorities that the war was lost. Calling for an immediate reconstruction of the government on a broader basis as an indispensable preliminary to peace negotiations, the German Foreign Office gave impetus to the movement that led to the appointment of Prince Max as Chancellor.

In British governmental and official circles, the general opinion up to the last few days of September was that outright victory over the Germans was unlikely before 1919, but that dwindling reserves might make a negotiated peace advisable before the winter. Lloyd George did not conceal from the Chief of the Imperial General Staff on the twenty-sixth that he was seriously worried about the manpower situation. Sir Douglas Haig, the British Commander-in-Chief on the Western Front, declared on August 11, and repeated on September 28, that he would not have enough troops to take the offensive in 1919, and that therefore the British aim ought to be to go all out to force the Germans to make peace by Christmas. Marshal Foch was convinced that he could beat the Germans in the field, but he did not expect in August to do it before the following summer. General Jan C. Smuts, a member of the British War Cabinet, was strongly in favor of a negotiated peace. He continued until the end of the war to think that moderate peace terms would suit British interests better than an all-out victory followed by widespread social and economic upheavals in Central Europe.

The armistice convention with Bulgaria was signed at Salonika on September 29, and fighting stopped on the Macedonian front at the following midday. The effect on the minds of the Allied military leaders was profound. On the day of the Macedonian cease-fire Haig told Sir Henry Wilson that he thought the Germans would now ask for peace. A few days later Foch expressed for the first time a lively hope that Germany might crack before the winter. But no one in London, Paris or Rome knew how near Germany really was to cracking. Nor was the United States government, far away in Washington, in a position to know that Ludendorff had told his superiors on September 29 that even an hour's delay in asking for an armistice was dangerous.

On Saturday, October 5, the British, French and Italian Prime Ministers arrived at Versailles to attend a series of meetings of the Supreme War Council at which the principal topic of discussion was the situation arising from the Bulgarian collapse and in particular how the war with Turkey could be ended quickly. That afternoon, many hours before Prince Max's message reached Washington, Georges Clemenceau, the French Premier, brought the news that the Germans had asked for an armistice and had offered to treat for peace on the basis of the Fourteen Points.

No American plenipotentiary was present. The United States was not at war with Bulgaria or Turkey. In any case, there was no one in Europe who could have spoken for the United States at plenary sessions of the Supreme War Council. A high-level mission from Washington had attended meetings in the previous winter, but had afterward returned home on orders from the President. General Tasker H. Bliss, United States Permanent Military Representative at Versailles, was debarred by his position from considering any but military questions, and the experienced American diplomatist who was associated with the council after the departure of the American Mission had authority to act only as liaison officer. Where issues of crucial importance were concerned, the Allies were separated from Washington by a gulf at least as wide as the Atlantic.

Notwithstanding their early knowledge of the German note, the Allied ministers were thus unable to discuss with anyone who knew the President's mind what they thought his answer to it ought to be. At the same time they were far from confident that his answer would be satisfactory. In the first place they feared, unnecessarily as things turned out, that his handling of the affair might commit them to an armistice which would enable the Germans to improve their military position and then renew hostilities.

Secondly, and with much better reason, they feared that the armistice, the ultimate peace terms, and the Fourteen Points would become inextricably confused, and that they would find themselves bound, in advance of the peace conference, by a bargain rigidly founded on the Fourteen Points.

These seemed to all of them unsatisfactory for one reason or another. The British disliked the reference in the Fourteen Points to the freedom of the seas. British statesmen had toyed in the past with the idea of surrendering the age-old right of belligerents to search neutral as well as hostile merchant ships for contraband, in return for undertakings by other nations not to molest shipping bound for the United Kingdom; but Lloyd George's view in 1918 was that the seas would always be free in time of peace while Britannia ruled the waves, and that Britain would never agree that in wartime the Royal Navy should not do everything it could to prevent supplies from reaching hostile countries. As for France and Italy, they had territorial ambitions which were noticeably played down in the Fourteen Points. The French and Italian claims might seem to the British inexpedient. The attitudes of all the belligerents except the United States might seem to the President selfish and immoral. But there was no principle of international law or natural justice which forbade the ventilation of such claims at a conference attended by all the belligerents on both sides. Insofar as the Allies had a common viewpoint, a settlement so arrived at was bound to seem to them more attractive than one which committed them in advance to the Fourteen Points. It was equally natural that the President should wish to prevent the holding of such a conference except on his own terms.

As the basis of an honest bargain between the Central Powers and their enemies, the Fourteen Points were also open to more abstract objections which no one could call selfish. Admittedly a "provisional sketch," they outlined principles in language that did not always give a fair impression of what was feasible and practical. The President's Ninth Point, for example, called for readjustment of the Italian frontier along clearly recognizable lines of nationality. But the President's experts had reason to know that such an arrangement would not give the Italians the security they wanted, and House also knew that Italy had been promised a safe frontier on the Brenner. Again, Point Thirteen called for an independent Poland with free and secure access to the sea. Yet American as well as European experts knew that there was no way of giving Poland secure access to the sea except by driving a corridor through German territory. It might be expedient, but it could hardly be right in principle, to break a promise and leave Italy insecure rather than hand over Austrians south of the Brenner to Italian rule, yet simultaneously hand over Germans in the

Polish Corridor to Polish rule in order to give a different kind of security to Poland.

Yet another objection to the Fourteen Points as the basis of a settlement with the Central Powers was that they had already been overtaken by events when the Germans despatched their peace note. Since the President's historic address to Congress was delivered, Germany and her satellites had dictated their own peace terms to the Russians and the Rumanians at Brest Litovsk and Bucharest. Both treaties were highly favorable to Germany and highly unfavorable to other parties. The face of Europe was about to be transformed, too, by forces no longer within the President's control. During the greater part of the war the policy of the Allies with respect to the future political structure of Central Europe had been to weaken the Central Powers by fomenting internal dissension in Austro-Hungary, but at the same time to preserve the Hapsburg dynasty as a counterweight to Prussian-dominated Germany. On the accession of the Emperor Karl, who had married a French wife on Italian soil and was eager to come to terms with the Allies, the British and French governments had less reason than ever to turn the Hapsburgs out.

Admittedly tortuous and risky, the policy of threatening the Emperor with Czech and Yugoslav uprisings, but showing him a way to safety through agreement with the Allies, had been recommended to the President by American advisers, and he had accepted it. In Point Ten of the Fourteen Points he had shown his adherence to it by promising the Austro-Hungarian minorities autonomy, not independence. More recently he had dropped it with a thud, and had led the Allies on a track that was still more dangerous. In June 1918, the United States government announced that it favored complete independence of German or Austrian rule for all branches of the Slav race. In September the President recognized the insurrectionary Czechoslovak National Council as a belligerent government. In a sense the problem thus created was shelved when, to all intents and purposes, Austro-Hungary surrendered unconditionally after trying in vain to get a negotiated peace on the basis of the Fourteen Points. The fact remained that the Europe which was taking shape when the Germans drafted their peace note looked like being very different from that for which the President had legislated in his provisional sketch.

If the Allies were not unreservedly eager to make peace on the basis of the Fourteen Points, neither were the Germans. Genuinely eager for an armistice which would give a respite to their army, they were nothing like as wholehearted in their desire to make peace on terms dictated by the President. As their situation grew worse, however, a program which seemed to rule out punitive damages and economic sanctions began to look to most of them, though not to all, less unattractive than a further series of battles which were almost certain to turn out badly. Had they been confident that the battles would turn out well, their attitude would have been very different. The Fourteen Points might save them from the worst consequences of unconditional surrender, but they would not particularly favor German interests if they meant that Alsace and Lorraine were to go to France and that Germany was to make sacrifices for the benefit of Poland.

The situation that developed in October 1918 was thus absurd and illogical to a degree which would have been laughable if the sequel had been less grim. In spite of their hesitations and their reservations, in spite of their protestations that they wanted nothing so much as to go on fighting, all the European belligerents longed to end the war before they were drained of their last man and their last penny. Because they longed to end the war, they found themselves on the verge of making peace in a novel and unfamiliar way which suited none of them completely, but which did suit the President of the United States. Yet the President had sworn that his country had no desire to interfere in European affairs or impose its will on European peoples, that the Fourteen Points were only a provisional sketch, that he was quite ready to be shown that the settlements he proposed were not the best.

Writing to his confidential adviser a few months after the United States entered the war, the President had put the matter rather differently. If the Allies did not like the American peace program at the end of the war, he told Colonel House, then they could be made by economic pressure to accept it. "We can force them," he wrote, "to our way of thinking."

The Germans could not escape from the dilemma, for they were soon in no position to let slip any chance of avoiding defeat in the field and revolution at home. The Allies could have escaped from it only at the risk of quarreling, perhaps openly, with the government of a country which had not only sent its troops to fight beside theirs, but had supported them lavishly with goods and money, and was still their chief supplier as well as their chief creditor. On the day after he first heard of the German peace note, Lloyd George remarked to a group of ministers and officials that the British tended to defer too much to the United States. But some of his colleagues knew that, just as American wealth and productive capacity had enabled the Allies to carry on the struggle with Germany when their own resources were running low, so European manufacturers would soon be turning to the United States for raw materials and machinery needed to revive peacetime industries. They answered that it seemed to them essential to conciliate the President.

2

THE MEDIATORS

WOODROW WILSON HAD THE HABIT, NOT ALWAYS PRACTICED BY eminent statesmen, of composing his own replies to important letters, often with the aid of a small portable typewriter which he cherished with the ardor of a man who was loneliest in the midst of company. He received the German peace note on Sunday, October 6, 1918, and began almost at once to draft an answer. Next day he summoned his confidential adviser from New York.

Colonel House had already telegraphed to Washington suggesting that the President should not reply directly to the German offer, but should simply tell Prince Max that he was conferring with the Allies, and should then send him, Colonel House, to Paris to concoct an answer in consultation with the Allied governments. His view was that the Allies stood to gain by making peace before the winter, and ought therefore to take their full share of responsibility for the preliminary negotiations.

The colonel reached the White House on Monday evening. He found the President more than willing that he should go to Paris, but nonetheless determined to send a full reply to the German note before consulting the Allies. Knowing better than to press an argument which the President had already rejected, he abandoned the case for a noncommittal answer, but objected that the President's draft was too mild and conciliatory. The country, he said, would not approve of an answer which did not insist on guarantees that the President's peace terms would be incorporated in the final settlement with Germany.

According to House, the President was deeply impressed by demands for emphatic rejection of Prince Max's offer which were made in the Senate and the press as soon as knowledge of the German move became public property. Only a few weeks earlier Woodrow Wilson's great fear had been that the Allies would treat Germany too harshly if they won the war. Now he faced the insistence of politicians and editorial writers in his own country that her attempt to escape unconditional surrender should be thwarted by the action of his government. As he did not become aware of the new trend until Tuesday morning, and wished to have his answer ready for the newspapers by Tuesday afternoon, he had little time to make sure that the men who wanted him to turn down Prince Max's offer really represented popular opinion. As always, he wanted to do what was right. But what seemed to be expected of him was hardly consistent with his ambition to lead the nations of Europe swiftly back into the ways of peace.

On that Tuesday morning, and for many days afterward, Woodrow Wilson and Edward Mandell House could have claimed to be the two most powerful men in the world. Alone among the nations at war the United States, and to some extent Japan, still commanded huge reserves of men, money, and material resources. Two million American soldiers were already in France or about to go there, although they were not an entirely independent force since they relied on Allied help for much of their artillery and shared Allied transportation systems. The Allies had already lost many more than that number of men in killed and missing alone, and could barely keep their divisions up to strength. American credit was unlimited, while the Allies were living from day to day with their currencies artificially pegged in sympathetic markets to ward off inflation and collapse. American granaries were full where European granaries were empty. The acts and opinions of the President and his adviser would affect the destinies not merely of a hundred million Americans but of a hundred and twenty million Germans, Austrians, and Hungarians, forty million French citizens, and fifty million citizens of the United Kingdom, to say nothing of Italians, Rumanians, Serbs, and others. They would affect, too, the livelihoods of countless millions of non-Europeans of almost every race, creed, and color, among them three hundred million inhabitants of British India whose welfare was bound up with the economic prosperity of the Anglo-Saxon peoples. So close was the link with India in the second decade of the twentieth century that a bad cotton-crop in the Mississippi Basin, or a strike in Lancashire, could reduce millions of Indian peasants to a state of abject want for which the only remedy was prompt action by the much-criticized agents of British imperialism.

President Wilson was deeply conscious of his responsibilities toward his fellow men. At the same time he did not claim to be a political economist on the global scale. Even by the rather loose standards of twentieth-century democracy neither he nor his adviser was, in fact, outstandingly well qualified for the gigantic task of determining the future political and economic structure of the world before any peace conference or other gathering of international experts had even been summoned. Yet that, in effect, was the role for which he cast himself when he decided that there should be no truce between the Germans and their enemies unless both sides first accepted the program which he and House had worked out with the aid of an all-American staff of geographers, ethnographers, and lawyers.

In character and intellect Woodrow Wilson was reckoned by his admirers at least the equal of the best European statesmen. But not even the warmest of his adherents would have claimed that he rivaled them in experience, any more than they would have claimed that the accumulated knowledge of foreign affairs available in the State Department in 1918 matched that available in Whitehall and at the Quai d'Orsay. Before his election to the presidency in 1912 Wilson had spent twenty years at Princeton University and had served briefly as Governor of New Jersey. An authority on American rather than European history, he was willing to listen to chosen advisers, but disliked discussing his plans with the rank and file of his supporters, many of whom he considered his intellectual inferiors and doubtfully impartial. His temperament was autocratic, and exceptional circumstances which gave his backers control of both the Senate and the House during the greater part of his two terms encouraged him to take a firmer

line with Congress than many of his predecessors would have
dared to take. At the same time he drew his authority, as they
had done, from a system which concentrated executive power
in the hands of a First Citizen who was not bound to consult
adminstrative chiefs even about matters affecting their own departments.

These two factors, added to the material and moral resources
which he commanded in the name of the American people, gave
Woodrow Wilson powers far greater than were exercised in 1918
by any European Prime Minister or Chancellor, or even in
practice by any European sovereign. Unlike, for example, the
Prime Minister of the United Kingdom, who also wielded great
power but could take no important step unless he carried with
him a cabinet of equals, the President of the United States had no
colleagues and could give free rein to his will as long as his
supporters remained in possession of the field and did not desert
him.

President Wilson had never met any European statesmen of the
highest standing except the veteran bachelor-philosopher Arthur
James Balfour, who was about as unlike his conception of the
genus as it was possible for a man to be. Colonel House was
on good terms with many, but had never held a post in any
embassy or legation or filled any public office recognized by the
Constitution. Nor had he ever served in any army, either as colonel
or in any other rank. He was a planter and railroad speculator
whose father had left him enough money to enable him to indulge
a taste for politics and a distaste for the limelight. Before deciding
to back Woodrow Wilson as a potential President whom it might
be possible to "advise with some degree of satisfaction," he had
played a back-stage role in the politics of his native Texas, but
had never himself contested an election or burdened himself with
responsibility for measures which he urged other men to take.
Nor did he do so later. In his fifties he published a political novel
depicting the career of a young West Point graduate who leads
a rebellion against the federal government, becomes dictator,
founds an international alliance based on Anglo-Saxon solidarity,
and sponsors a new American Constitution. He was an affable,

self-effacing man whose integrity was beyond dispute and who believed, at the age of fifty-seven, that international affairs could be regulated on the lines of a party convention at which all important decisions were made in advance by the men who pulled the strings.

Convinced that the isolationist tradition bequeathed to the United States by Washington and Jefferson was out of date, House had worked hard since Woodrow Wilson's rise to power to put his country in the forefront of world politics. He had tried, and failed, to shepherd the South and Central American republics into a Pan-American Pact designed to give a new slant to the Monroe Doctrine. He had tried, and failed, to persuade Great Britain and Germany to sink their differences and join the United States in developing "the waste places of the earth," thus inaugurating an era in which, Anglo-Saxon and Teutonic solidarity having triumphed, the great powers would be able to transform their armies into "mere sanitary police." He had tried, and failed, to get the British and German governments to concede the freedom of the seas in the midst of the war by telling each in turn that they would get the better end of the deal. On the other hand he had succeeded, with some help from orthodox diplomacy, in persuading the British government to reconsider their Mexican policy in return for the repeal of a measure which illegally exempted American ships from Panama Canal tolls.

The President was urged by his adviser not to hurry and to take time off for a round of golf on Tuesday. Nevertheless he succeeded not only in finishing his answer on that day but in making it strong enough to satisfy his Private Secretary, who had hitherto been against any concession to Germany. The Germans, he wrote, must withdraw from Allied soil before he could recommend the Allies to grant an armistice. Futhermore, they must tell him whether they accepted the principles outlined in his Fourteen Points and other speeches, and wanted a peace conference merely to discuss the application of those principles. Finally, the Chancellor was asked to say whether he represented "merely the constituted authorities" who had hitherto conducted the war on Germany's behalf.

Far away in Paris and at Versailles, the Allied ministers had decided not to break up their series of meetings until they knew what the President was going to say. After settling their Near Eastern policy on Saturday, Sunday, and Monday, and after Lloyd George and Clemenceau had instructed their military experts to draw up provisional terms for an armistice with Germany, they waited all Tuesday for the crucial message from Washington. At last, on Wednesday, October 9, they received a copy of the President's answer to Prince Max after it had appeared in the newspapers.

Meanwhile the Austro-Hungarians had offered, like the Germans, to make peace on the basis of the Fourteen Points. Nearly a fortnight elapsed before the President informed them that, as the United States had recognized Czechoslovak independence and also favored independence for the Yugoslavs, he could do nothing. Brought to their knees by the age-old diplomatic weapon of delay as well as by the too-successful attempts of their enemies to scare the Hapsburgs into acquiescence, they were forced to sue for peace without being sure that the safeguards which the Germans hoped to find in the Fourteen Points would apply to them. A few weeks later the whole of the Hapsburg dominions were in wild disarray, and the Hapsburg monarchy was as dead as the Central European policy which the Allies had cherished for the greater part of the war.

The Allied ministers discussed the President's answer to Prince Max at a meeting of the Supreme War Council on Wednesday afternoon. They had read it that morning with mixed feelings. Clemenceau thought it spoke well for the President that, without consulting the Allies, he had insisted that the Germans should leave French soil. He also thought that the Allies were not formally cognizant of the correspondence, and so could not intervene. Lloyd George, who had said in an incautious moment in the summer that the Kaiser could have peace whenever he liked to accept the President's terms, did not agree. The Allies had received a copy of the President's note. In any case it had been published. If they said nothing, their approval would be assumed.

After further discussion, the statesmen agreed on a carefully worded message warning the President that the terms of any armistice would have to be decided in consultation with their military advisers. On the initiative of the British, they also asked him to send a fully accredited representative to Europe.

The Germans found the President's answer even more baffling than the Allies did. They had already told the President that they accepted his principles; what they wanted to know was whether the Allies accepted them. They were only too eager to withdraw their troops from Allied soil and regroup them behind the frontier so that, if the worst came to the worst, Germany should not enter the peace conference with nothing but the remnants of a defeated army. Without an armistice, they could not retreat much faster than they were already doing; even with one, an orderly withdrawal would take some weeks. As for the President's question about "constituted authorities," Prince Max had been appointed in the customary way, and he was supported by the Reichstag. He could hardly be expected to admit, even if it were true, that he was the mere tool of a military autocracy.

On the other hand, the Germans were ready to go a long way to save their army. In a further note to the President on October 12 they therefore reaffirmed their acceptance of the Fourteen Points, agreed that the purpose of a peace conference would be to discuss their application, and assured the President that the Chancellor spoke "in the name of the German Government and of the German people."

The President responded by putting strong pressure on the Germans to scrap their traditional form of government. In a message sent on October 14 he reminded them pointedly that "the destruction of every arbitrary power" was one of his war aims. At the same time he offered them, in effect, the choice between unconditional surrender, and a qualified surrender which would leave them dependent on the ability and willingness of their enemies to agree on a fair and impartial interpretation of the Fourteen Points. The armistice terms, he insisted, must be such as to ensure that the Allies and the Americans did not lose the military supremacy that they had won.

By the time they drafted their answer to the President's second note, the Germans faced the possibility of utter disaster. Allied and American advances would soon threaten the great escape routes for the German armies north and south of the Ardennes. Almost worse, there was talk in the factories of establishing a "dictatorship of the proletariat" on Russian lines. The government had lost faith in the General Staff and were ready to assert themselves to the point of overruling Ludendorff and ultimately forcing him to resign or be dismissed. They were also ready for electoral and constitutional reforms which the Kaiser would have no choice but to approve as his last chance of saving the monarchy. On October 20 they assured the President that henceforward no German government would rule without popular support, and agreed that the armistice terms should recognize the existing state of affairs on the Western Front.

With the despatch of this message, the affairs of Europe reached a crucial stage. On the whole, the Allied governments showed themselves extraordinarily blind to the morass in which any further abdication of their responsibilities threatened to engulf them. The French were bent on a settlement which would give them the benefits of a decisive victory without putting them to the expense of winning one. Italian eyes were focused on Austro-Hungary. The British saw the danger of a political collapse in Germany which would do no good to anyone, but were hypnotized by the fear that the Kaiser and his satellites might yet turn the tables on them. Misled by Haig's cautious opinion that the German Army was still capable of retiring to its own frontiers and holding its own there against superior forces, and by an unpromising long-term forecast which Sir Henry Wilson had sponsored nearly three months earlier, they were not at all sure that their side really had won incontestable military superiority, or that the Germans would accept the armistice terms they had in view. After reading the German note of October 20 they decided to tell the President that they thought he ought not to send any more communications to the enemy without consulting the Allies; but they did not add that swift acceptance of Prince Max's offer might be the only way of saving Germany from anarchy and the rest of the world from endless trouble.

There were many reasons for the reluctance of the Allies to put pressure on the President either to act promptly or to leave them a clear field. Apart from the awkward fact that the President held the purse strings there was, for example, the argument that (unless Haig were right) every hour's delay brought the Germans closer to a crushing defeat which, if it did nothing else, might at least teach them that aggression did not pay. There was also the argument that it might be easier to negotiate with Germany once Austro-Hungary was out of the way. At the root of all such pretexts for inaction lay, however, one inescapable conclusion to which all arguments led back. It was not possible for the Allies to make peace with Germany on the basis of the Fourteen Points unless they accepted the Fourteen Points.

Two days after the British government decided on their hint, President Wilson formally abandoned the equivocal role which he had held since the arrival of the first German note. Announcing on October 23 that he had passed his correspondence with the German government to the Allies, he ceased, in theory, to be at one and the same time head of a belligerent state, and sole mediator between the Allies and the Germans. In practice, he remained the arbiter. As between Germany and her enemies, the situation had changed significantly since October 4, inasmuch as she was not only closer to defeat, but understood for the first time how close to defeat she was. As between the Allies and the United States nothing had changed, except insofar as the stiffening of the President's demands on Germany had shown some Allied observers that the new-style diplomacy of Woodrow Wilson could be just as ruthless as the old-style diplomacy of Castlereagh and Metternich. Throughout Europe, millions of men and women longed for peace. But they would not get peace until the President's envoy reached their shores and persuaded the Allied governments to accept the Presidential program.

Colonel House reached Paris on October 26. He found almost universal agreement that there ought to be an armistice and a negotiated peace. With the possible exception of General Bliss, the only serious advocate of unconditional surrender whom he met on the European side of the Atlantic was General John J.

Pershing, who was more concerned to register a protest than to
carry his objections to the point of disagreement with Foch. Even
the French agreed that there was no point in continuing to fight
if they could get all they wanted by putting the screws on Prince
Max and the Reichstag. Nor was there any disagreement between
the Allies and the President as to the terms of the armistice.
The President was content to leave the armistice terms to the
men on the spot. The chief critics of the terms proposed by
Foch were the British, who thought them too severe but were
ready to compromise rather than prolong the war.

The stumbling block was the means by which the ground was
to be prepared for the final settlement with Germany after the
armistice was signed. Should the Germans be told that they could
have peace on the basis of the President's speeches, in accordance
with the tentative bargain which they had struck with the United
States government, but which did not yet bind anyone since the
Allies had not formally assented to it? Or should the Allies openly
declare, at the risk of seeing the United States make a separate
peace with their enemies, that they would rather enter the peace
conference with their hands free? Should they hint, at the almost
certain cost of quarreling with the President and with millions of
well-wishers on both sides of the Atlantic, that a settlement negotiated by the European belligerents without prior commitments
to anyone might suit Europe better in the long run than one
dictated by the United States, no matter how good the intentions of the United States might seem to the President to be?
Were the Germans likely, after telling the world that they trusted
the President to give them peace with honor, to take the hint
if it were offered?

For more than a week House tussled with the Allies for the
American program. At meetings of the Supreme War Council
and at informal gatherings he pressed British, French, and Italian
statesmen and officials very strongly to accept the principles outlined in the Fourteen Points and the four supplementary speeches
which formed the substance of the President's provisional bargain
with Prince Max. In the end he won, but the struggle left him
feeling that the men with whom he had been dealing were

"thoroughly unsympathetic," and he said so in a cable to the President. Although the context suggests that he had in mind only the attitude of European statesmen to the Fourteen Points and not their attitude to American aspirations in general, such a verdict from a man who was known to be as warm an advocate of the European point of view as it was possible for a loyal American citizen to be was hardly likely to give the President a favorable impression of the Allies.

How far the verdict was justified can only be a matter of opinion. At any rate the reluctance of the Allied ministers to stake everything on the Fourteen Points was understandable. Experience had taught them that political speeches made in wartime were a doubtful basis for a lasting settlement of European problems. To speak of the purpose of a peace conference as being merely to discuss the detailed application of the President's principles was to invest those principles with a comprehensiveness which they did not seem to European diplomatists to possess. Besides territorial adjustments which threatened to raise formidable strategic and economic issues, the President promised the belligerents such abstract benefits as impartial justice and the right to determine their own destinies. His words were lofty and inspiring, but what precisely did they mean? What was their bearing, for example, on the problem of whether a community of Polish-speaking Protestants, more than half of whom professed German sympathies while the rest either considered themselves Poles or were too young to have opinions, should be left under the rule of Protestant Prussia or be transferred to that of Roman Catholic Poland?

As for those of the President's promises which did appear specific, a commentary circulated to the Allies by House himself showed all too clearly that some of them could be interpreted by one set of men in ways which might seem to another set of men anything but compatible with impartial justice. "The removal, so far as possible, of all economic barriers," for example, did not mean to American jurists that the United States would foreswear tariffs, or that the Allies and the United States would not be free to discriminate against the trade of any country which they chose to exclude from the proposed League of Nations. Nor did disarmament "to the lowest point consistent with domestic safety" pledge the successful belligerents to reduce their armaments by a single gun unless "some kind of international commission of investigation" should hit on a hitherto-undiscovered means by which disarmed nations could protect themselves against invasion and enforce treaties. The President's principles did not of themselves ensure, and were not meant to ensure, that everyone on the winning side received everything that some of the Allies considered part of the just rewards of victory. But neither did they safeguard the losers against the penalties of defeat, although the Germans, who had not seen Colonel House's commentary, may have thought they did.

But House was in a strong position. If they turned down the Fourteen Points, he told the Allied statesmen, then the United States might have to make a separate peace with the Central Powers. Should that happen, the Allies would be left to fight alone if they went on fighting, perhaps be deprived of American credit and raw materials if they stopped fighting. To reinforce the warning, the President armed his envoy with a specially cabled message threatening to make his disagreement with the Allies public. But House did not need to show the cablegram. The Allies had their own means of knowing that the President held most of the cards and meant to play them. On November 4 they formally accepted the President's principles with two reservations. The British refused point-blank to concede the freedom of the seas without conditions, at the same time agreeing to discuss the matter later. The French insisted that the Germans should be told that they would have to pay for damage done to Allied civilians and their property. The Italians also suggested reservations, but reluctantly withdrew them in face of the argument that their claims did not apply to the settlement with Germany but only to that with Austro-Hungary. The great thing, according to House, was not to burden the President with too many exceptions, or give the impression that the Allies intended to make difficulties.

Within an hour or two a message informing the President that the war of words on the Versailles front had ended with a substantial victory for Colonel House was on its way to Washington.

But the end of the more immediately damaging hostilities which had cost the British alone well over a hundred thousand casualties since August was still a week away. Before anyone could order the cease-fire the Germans had to be told that, if they wanted an armistice, they must send accredited representatives to Allied General Headquarters. On November 7 the duly accredited German Armistice Commissioners received orders to leave the headquarters of the High Command at Spa, take the road through Chimay, La Capelle, and Guise, and present themselves at the Allied lines under the protection of a white flag. On November 8 they were shown armistice terms whose effect would be to strip their country of the means of resuming hostilities, and were given seventy-two hours to accept or reject them. Staggered by their severity, they asked permission to send one of their number back to Germany for fresh instructions. Even with the war on its last legs, fire from the German trenches was so heavy that their envoy could not get through his own lines, had to spend the night at a French divisional headquarters, and reached his destination only on the ninth.

The immediate outcome of this procedure was that, by the time the armistice convention was signed in a railway carriage at Rethondes on November 11, Prince Max and the Kaiser had both been swept away by a Communist and Socialist revolution; the Red flag was flying on the palace of the Hohenzollerns; and the nearest approach in Germany to the popularly elected government with which the President wished to treat was an agreement among a number of left-wing leaders to combine for the purpose of restoring order. A long-term consequence was that German historians were able, after the war, to reproach the Allies and the United States with having exposed their country, under the guise of willingness to make concessions, to most of the consequences that would have flowed from the crushing military defeat which they claimed not to have suffered.

The President also had his troubles. The same month as saw the Emperors of Germany and Austro-Hungary toppled from their thrones saw his own position severely shaken. On the eve of the Congressional elections in November he appealed to the American public to strengthen his hand at the peace conference by voting for the Democratic party. The American public responded by returning the Republican party to power with majorities of 49 to 47 seats in the Senate and 237 to 191 in the House. At the same time, the President lost ground with progressive Republicans who had hitherto been sympathetic. As no peace treaty would bind the United States unless at least two-thirds of the Senate approved of it, there could be no doubt that he had suffered a grave setback almost at the very moment when the triumph of the Fourteen Points brought him what House called a diplomatic victory.

3

DESTINATION VERSAILLES

IN DECEMBER 1918 WELL OVER A THOUSAND DELEGATES AND plenipotentiaries from more than thirty countries began to assemble in Paris to discuss the treaties that were to end the war. The gathering they attended was not the peace conference contemplated in the pre-armistice negotiations with Germany. Nor was it meant to replace that conference. Its official designation was the Preliminary Peace Conference of Paris. Its purpose was to give the Allied and United States governments an opportunity of agreeing on tentative proposals which would then be discussed with representatives of the Central Powers at the peace conference proper. Had that intention been put into effect, the peace conference proper would almost certainly have been held at Versailles, and would therefore have been called the Conference, or Congress, of Versailles.

Except that German delegates attended ceremonies at Versailles at which the terms proposed by the Allied and Associated Powers were presented and accepted, but not discussed, no Congress of Versailles was ever held. The first attempt to apply the new methods which were hailed as a great advance on those of the old diplomacy thus resulted in a denial of the principle that justice must not only be done, but must be seen to be done. The armistice terms put Germany so much at the mercy of her enemies that in the long run she would almost certainly have found it necessary, in any case, to accept such terms as she was offered. The fact remained that she was promised a peace conference to discuss the detailed application of the Fourteen Points, and that no such conference took place.

Many factors contributed to this grotesque outcome of a much-heralded attempt to achieve a peace of understanding, but the root cause of failure was brutally simple: the Congress of Versailles was not held because there was no time to hold it. The preliminary discussions took so long, and disclosed so many points of difference, that nearly six months elapsed after the signing of the armistice convention before the Allies and the United States were ready to offer Germany the best settlement they could agree upon. By that time their armies were melting away, European commerce was almost at a standstill because Allied and American merchants could not legitimately trade with German firms until hostilities were formally concluded, and the French had come so near financial collapse that they had had to ask the British for an immediate loan of a few millions to see them through from day to day. Had the Allied and Associated Powers waited to haggle face-to-face with representatives of the Central Powers over every clause in the drafts they had prepared or were preparing, chaos might have come to Europe before even the first of the treaties was signed.

Instead of convening the full-scale congress of all belligerent states which they had envisaged, the Allied and Associated Powers therefore summoned the German delegates to Versailles after warning the German government that oral discussion of the terms of settlement would not be allowed. They also set a time limit within which Germany must either take the consequences of rejecting the draft treaty, or accept it with such amendments as the Great Powers might see fit to make in the light of written comments.

Appalled by this ultimatum and by the severity of the terms, the President of the new German Republic called the Treaty of Versailles a "product of hate." But it would be quite wrong to picture the Allied and United States plenipotentiaries as united in hatred of Germany. If anything united them, it was the knowledge that they would be branded as "the greatest incompetents in history" if they failed to make peace quickly after arguing among themselves for many months.

On the whole, the emotional attitudes toward Germany of the men who made the treaties were never likely to be decisive. Nor were they any more consistent than such attitudes usually are. President Wilson excused himself from visiting the devastated areas immediately after his arrival in Europe by saying that the French wanted him to see red, but that nothing could make him despise Germans more than he did already. At an earlier stage of the war he said that he did not see how any decent man could fail to be heart and soul with the Allies. He also said that he and his fellow citizens had no wish to injure Germany. When he uttered them, these words expressed his feelings as a man. Had he been a medieval sovereign, they might also have expressed his policy. As he was not a medieval sovereign but a democratic statesman, they did not: as a policy maker he was not heart and soul with the Allies. As the head of a belligerent state, he was bound to injure Germany.

Similarly, Georges Clemenceau had seen the victorious Prussians enter Paris in 1871, and had no cause to love them. But he was too cynical and disillusioned a man to believe that Prussians were always wrong and Frenchmen always right. He did not need to hate Germany to know that there were nearly two Germans to every Frenchman and that Germany, even if disarmed, could make new weapons faster than France could.

Again, Lloyd George was long reckoned in Germany the archenemy of the German people. He knew that Germany had planned, if she won the war, to make Belgium a vassal state, appropriate the Briey coal mines, and extract a huge indemnity from the Allies. He once said that Germany would be crushed out of existence if justice were done to her. Some of his supporters spoke of making Germany pay to the last farthing and of squeezing the German orange until the pips squeaked. But Lloyd George also knew that it would not pay the British people to be too hard on the Germans. He was against transferring two million or more Germans to Polish rule. He urged his fellow statesmen not to discriminate against German trade after the war, to do all they could to put Germany on her feet again, and to admit her to the League of Nations as soon as peace was signed.

If Lloyd George's recommendations had been adopted, if time had been allowed for German delegates to discuss the settlement face-to-face with Allied delegates, and if care had been taken so to frame the reparation clauses of the treaty as not to humiliate Germany or do unnecessary damage to her credit, she would have had no cause to complain, so far as the treaty was concerned, that she did not receive fair treatment from her enemies. At the same time the Allies would have received a better long-term bargain, and would have stood at least as good a chance of collecting a substantial part of the reparations which Germany had already pledged herself to pay.

From the hundreds of thousands of words that have been written about the Treaty of Versailles, one conclusion stands out clearly. The harshness of the treaty was not due to any conspiracy or agreement among the principal treaty makers to punish Germany. On the contrary, some of its worst features were due to the difficulty they had in reaching prompt agreement about anything. Responsibility for the treaty rests chiefly on Wilson, Lloyd George, and Clemenceau. Since none of the three was a trained diplomatist, and since at least two of them despised diplomatists and their ways, perhaps it is not surprising that all three showed themselves deficient in the readiness to make concessions while preserving principles which is the essence of diplomacy.

In the end, of course, they did have to make concessions. But in doing so they sacrificed their principles, and lost so much time that the formality of oral discussion between all the belligerents on both sides had also to be sacrificed. In a secret memorandum Lloyd George argued strongly for leniency toward Germany as a contribution to European concord. Yet he abandoned his case rather than repeat his arguments in the House of Commons and risk falling out with France, although he was a master of parliamentary oratory and could legitimately have pressed the essentially logical and clear-minded French to take a longer view. Clemenceau's great object was to avoid exposing France to a third Franco-

Prussian war, yet he approved of clauses in the treaty which were bound to feed Germany's desire for revenge. President Wilson attached great importance to the lowering of economic barriers between nations, yet the treaty forbade Germany to discriminate against the trade of the Allies and the Americans, but did not forbid the Allies and the Americans to discriminate against German trade.

The incredible slowness with which the treaty took shape was itself an indictment of the principal negotiators. The armistice convention put the duration of the armistice at thirty-six days, with option to extend. To make peace within that time would have been a formidable undertaking, but there was no reason why the Allied Foreign Ministers and Colonel House should not have made an immediate start in that direction, except that they were not encouraged to do so. Plenary sessions of the Supreme War Council had made summit conferences so much the fashion that it scarcely occurred to the Allied Prime Ministers that negotiations could begin without them, and perhaps even be completed without them. President Wilson, who looked forward to an "intellectual treat," also insisted on attending the proceedings, although House and others advised him not to do so.

One consequence was that more than two months elapsed before the leading plenipotentiaries could be brought together. Another was that the gathering did not have the severely professional and technical character of a meeting between trained diplomatists accustomed to work to a carefully planned timetable. It became a sort of international circus which no ambitious camp follower of the great could afford to miss.

The sheer size of some of the delegations was a handicap. As compared with the staff of fourteen which Viscount Castlereagh had taken to the Congress of Vienna in 1814, the British delegation numbered nearly two hundred, exclusive of clerks and typists, the whole filling five hotels. The American delegation was almost as big, the Italian not much smaller. One result was that groups of delegates and experts tended to work in watertight compartments, often with little or no guidance from their chiefs.

Where the delegates did receive guidance, it was sometimes

incomplete or misleading. American opinion was deeply distrustful of the secret treaties in which the Allies had agreed to support each other's claims to certain territories if they should win the war. President Wilson, on the way to Europe, fed these suspicions by telling his subordinates that he and they would be the only disinterested people at the conference, and that the men they were going to meet did not really represent their countries. He did not add that the secret treaties were no secret as far as the United States government was concerned, since the British government had voluntarily given a full account of them as soon as America entered the war. Nor did he add that he had in his possession a written proposal from the French government that the Allies should scrap the secret treaties and make a fresh start, with the Fourteen Points as point of departure for a reasoned scheme of settlement.

Sometimes lack of co-ordination from the top led to paradoxical situations in which members of the same delegation pulled in opposite directions. For example, Norman H. Davis, Bernard M. Baruch, Vance C. McCormick, and Thomas William Lamont, the four American members of the commission appointed to consider reparations problems, were unanimously of the opinion that the treaty should name a sum which Germany must pay, and which she could pay. Colonel House thought likewise. So also did the British economist, John Maynard Keynes, whose influence stood high with Lloyd George at one stage.

Yet it was an American lawyer and future Secretary of State, John Foster Dulles, who suggested that, on the contrary, no sum should be mentioned in the treaty, and that a permanent reparation commission should consider after the treaty was signed what Germany should pay for and when she should pay. Lloyd George and Clemenceau jumped at the proposal because it saved them the embarrassment of telling their supporters that there was no chance of collecting the astronomical sums expected by the public. But its adoption severely damaged Germany's standing in the international money market, since no one, unless he had ulterior motives or was exceptionally kindhearted, was likely to be eager to lend money to a debtor whose liabilities were unknown.

Disunity and mutual suspicions also hampered the Allied and Associated Powers in their handling of day-to-day affairs. Even with millions of men still under arms, they had nothing like the number of trained troops needed to police the whole of the vast territories nominally under their control, especially as the Russian revolution had robbed them of Russian help at the same time as it posed new problems for them. It was therefore very important that they should maintain their moral ascendancy by showing a united front, scrupulously observing their pledges to friends and enemies, and abstaining from threats and promises which they were in no position to make good. These things they failed to do.

For example, when drawing up the armistice terms the Allied and Associated Powers had come to the conclusion that it would be almost impossible for them to ask their troops to start fighting all over again once the armistice was signed. They had therefore decided that, until the peace treaty came into force, they must reserve the right to blockade Germany as the only practical means of enforcing their authority. At the same time they had agreed that Germany must be fed. As things turned out, the failure of British and American statesmen to reach prompt agreement as to how the feeding should be done contributed to delays which enabled the Germans to claim that the Allied and Associated Powers could not be trusted to redeem their promises. The Germans refused, except after a long argument, to put their ships at the disposal of the Allied and Associated Powers so that they could be used to carry food to Germany. In spite of these delays, Germany was better fed in the winter of 1918–19 than in the winter of 1916–17. But the full benefit of the British and American cargoes which began to arrive in the spring was not immediately apparent to the German public. The Weimar government, either because they were genuinely afraid of a breakdown of peace negotiations which might cut off supplies, or because it was their policy to put the Allied and Associated Powers in a bad light, insisted on hoarding a good deal of the food sent to them. The result was that hatred of the Allied and Associated Powers was fostered in Germany at the very moment when, if the experience of past wars was any guide, the successful belligerents ought to have been doing everything they could to reconcile the Germans to defeat.

Their handling of the Russian problem, too, was notably unsuccessful. Two logical and consistent courses were open to them. They might have acted on the assumption, as the French were inclined to do, that Communism was an evil to be resisted at all costs, although probably they would not have succeeded in defeating the Bolshevists outright unless they had allowed the German Army to do it for them. Alternatively, they might have taken the line that the new masters of Russia were free to do as they liked in their own country. As it was, they did neither. Their policy of handing out arms and money to almost anyone, except the Germans, who would undertake to fight the Bolshevists, while at the same time some of them made more or less shamefaced attempts to establish commercial relations with Russia, did nothing to prevent Communism from becoming a new force in world politics. All that the Allied and Associated Powers succeeded in doing was to give an impression of duplicity and hypocrisy.

Again, in Central Europe the Allied and Associated Powers failed conspicuously either to placate their enemies or to show that they were masters of the situation. Having gone further than they first meant to do in encouraging Czechs and Yugoslavs to rebel against their lawful masters, they were forced to acquiesce in the creation of two potentially troublesome new states. Worse still, they had to choose between a Czechoslovakia with an indefensible northern frontier, and a Czechoslovakia whose fourteen million inhabitants included more than four million Austrian Germans, Magyars and Ruthenians who could be relied upon, at some future date, to serve the Czechs as the Czechs had served the Hapsburgs. At the same time Austria was reduced to a country with a splendid capital but no means of livelihood, since she was forbidden to make the best of a bad bargain by allying herself politically or even economically with Germany. Hungary was left without an effective government or an army of occupation strong enough to save her from the Communist leader Béla Kun. The Allied and Associated Powers were able to comfort themselves for their failure to achieve either an immediate or a lasting settlement in Central Europe with the reflection that they were morally bound to support the Slav minorities whose disruption of the Austro-Hungarian Empire they had fostered, and that it was beyond the power of mortal man to prevent the less amenable of the Central European peoples from quarreling over the spoils. The fact remained that their Central European policy could not fail to appear to Germans and Magyars as one of punishing loyalty and rewarding treachery.

But the most spectacularly disastrous of all the attempts made by the Allied and Associated Powers to regulate the affairs of the world on a basis of justice and fair dealing was their handling of the Near Eastern problem. Their failure to impose a just peace, or any sort of peace, on Turkey saddled the Near East with a new war which lasted intermittently for more than three years, caused untold suffering, brought down a British government, and gave the modern world its first successful dictator in the person of Mustafa Kemal, surnamed Atatürk.

Almost from the start of the First World War it was perhaps inevitable that, sooner or later, the French and British should fall out over Syria. From the moment when the United States became a belligerent, or even earlier, it was perhaps also inevitable that bad blood between Europe and America should result from efforts made by the Allies to lessen their dependence on American raw materials by staking out claims to parts of the crumbling Turkish Empire where there might be oil and where cotton was or might be grown. What was not so easy to foresee was that the end of the war in Europe would see France and Great Britain making common cause with the United States against their ally Italy.

The immediate cause of the breach between the United States and Italy was that the Italians, determined that control of the Adriatic should be one of the rewards of victory, laid claim to Fiume, the chief port of Yugoslavia, on the ground that its population was predominantly Italian. On April 23, 1919, President Wilson, unable to shake Vittorio Orlando and Baron Sonnino, the Italian Prime Minister and Foreign Minister, appealed over their heads to the Italian people to renounce the claim. A wave of indignation swept through Italy, Orlando left Paris, and for the time being the Italian delegation took no further part in the conference.

Although the Italian claim to Fiume was hard to defend, Lloyd George's first feeling was that the President had behaved badly toward Orlando. He did his best to provide consolation by suggesting that Italy should receive concessions in the Caucasus. At the same time it did not escape anyone that matters went faster without the Italians. Less than a week after the date first fixed for the arrival of the German delegates, the draft Treaty of Versailles seemed near enough to completion for them to be summoned to Versailles to receive it, although in the outcome it was not ready for another week. Yet only a few weeks earlier a serious split between the plenipotentiaries of the leading Allied and Associated Powers had seemed imminent. Toward the end of March and early in April, Americans in Paris were openly canvassing the prospects of a separate peace, Foch was almost as openly accusing the Americans of exploiting Europe under the flag of victory, and Lloyd George was able to patch up a working arrangement with the President only by threatening to insist on exclusion of the Covenant of the League of Nations from the draft treaty if the American delegation did not agree to postpone discussion of the freedom of the seas until after the treaty was signed. Moreover, the President was known to have made provisional arrangements to leave Paris and return to the United States.

If the absence of the Italians during the last week in April and the greater part of the first week in May helped President Wilson, Lloyd George, and Clemenceau to forget some of their differences or thrust them out of sight, it also gave scope for some close work on the Near Eastern problem. By the Treaty of London, under which Italy had agreed, in April 1915, to enter the war on the side of Britain, France, and Russia, the Italians had been promised "a just share of the Mediterranean region adjacent to the province of Adalia." In the abortive Treaty of Saint-Jean-de Maurienne, which was never ratified by Russia and was therefore only morally binding on France and Britain, that share was defined as an immense tract of southern Anatolia, including Smyrna and its hinterland. Since February 1919 the Greek Prime Minister, Eleutherios Venizelos, had, however, been pressing a claim to Smyrna, which he based on the large number of Greek merchants and settlers there and in the neighborhood, and on the principle of self-determination. With Orlando out of the way, he pressed it harder. Lloyd George and Clemenceau had backed him from the start. After the withdrawal of the Italians, President Wilson was persuaded, against the wishes of his expert advisers and without their prior knowledge, to back him also.

The consequence was that, on May 15, 1919, Greek troops landed at Smyrna, where they massacred a number of Turkish inhabitants. As a result Mustafa Kemal, a Turkish officer who had been sent by the authorities at Constantinople to make sure that Turkish troops in Anatolia observed the armistice terms, was able to engineer a nationalist rising, defy both the Allies and his own government with the help of Russian arms and credits, and make himself dictator of a new and militant Turkey with its capital at Ankara.

As soon as it became apparent that Kemal's movement was a serious threat to the Allies and that he might even send troops across the Dardanelles, a storm of protest arose from critics who regarded the Greek landing at Smyrna as the outcome of a private bargain between Lloyd George and Venizelos, possibly with the connivance of the notorious dealer in arms, Sir Basil Zaharoff. But the Greek landing was not, in fact, the outcome of a private bargain between Lloyd George and Venizelos. The decision to put the Greeks ashore at Smyrna was a joint decision reached by President Wilson, Lloyd George, and Clemenceau in Paris on May 6. If there was an element of privacy, and even of secrecy, in that decision, it arose from the coyness which led the trio first to reach agreement behind the backs of the Italians, who had announced their intention of returning to Paris for the presentation of the draft treaty to the Germans and were already on their way; secondly to ride roughshod over the President's advisers; and thirdly to brush aside a warning from the British Chief of the Imperial

General Staff that to put the Greeks into Anatolia would mean "starting another war."

The immediate outcome of the decision taken by the President and the two Prime Ministers on that Tuesday in May was that, while a summary of the peace terms about to be presented to the Germans was being read to the plenipotentiaries of the Allied and Associated Powers in the conference chamber, and while the printers were working feverishly to complete the draft treaty in time for its presentation on Wednesday afternoon, British, American, and French service chiefs were reluctantly carrying out orders to concert plans with Venizelos for the landing of either one or two Greek divisions at Smyrna. In spite of the disapproval of the British and American Chiefs of Staff, Sir Henry Wilson and General Bliss, who "thought the whole thing disgraceful, dangerous, and ungentlemanly," the officers concerned were warned to say nothing to the Italians until the afternoon before the expedition sailed. When it was found later that the Italians already knew what was in the wind, the three statesmen decided that they should not be prevented from going ashore at the same time as the Greeks if they wished to do so, and on May 12 the Supreme War Council formally authorized Italian landings at Adalia.

The Smyrna expedition was thus a joint enterprise by the Allied and Associated Powers, in which the Italians reluctantly acquiesced. The shipping used to carry the troops was largely Greek, but British, American, and French warships supported the landing with the express approval of the statesmen of all three countries. Contrary to popular belief, the decision of the Big Three to underwrite the venture was not based solely on Lloyd George's sympathy with Greek claims or his regard for Venizelos. One reason for using the Greek Army in Anatolia was that the Allies were short of suitable troops in the absence of the Russians, who were to have occupied part of Turkey-in-Asia until the Bolshevist Revolution put them out of court. But the overriding motive which Lloyd George did not hide from his intimates was that he and the President and Clemenceau were determined to prevent the Italians from staking out an inconveniently wide claim under the Treaty of Saint-Jean-de-Maurienne.

The cure, however, was worse than the disease. So far as the French and the British were concerned, the expedition was just within the letter of the armistice convention with Turkey, although a contravention of the spirit of it. The American contribution, on the other hand, would seem to have been unmistakably illegal. The Americans were not at war with Turkey and could scarcely be entitled, therefore, to assist in putting troops ashore on Turkish soil. The United States government was not, however, responsible for a later decision to pit the Greek Army against Kemal's Nationalists, which could presumably have been justified in international law, had anyone thought the attempt worth while, by the argument that Kemal was an outlaw against whom it was the duty of the occupying powers to protect the Sultan as best they could.

Against this background of chicanery and unprovoked aggression, the statesmen of the Allied and Associated Powers proceeded in the spring and summer of 1919 with their healing task. The French plea for a political reconstruction of Germany which would weaken Prussia's hold on her neighbors was rejected as impractical, and the French were persuaded to accept instead a guarantee of American support against aggression. This was backed by a similar guarantee by Britain, conditional on ratification of the American guarantee. General Bliss warned the Allies on March 31 that President Wilson had no authority to promise such support, and that neither the Senate nor the American people would endorse his action. But the President and House seemed so confident that somehow the Senate would be induced to accept the guarantee and the peace treaty that the Allied ministers, who were accustomed to ratification as a mere formality in their own countries, paid no attention to such warnings.

On May 7 the draft treaty was handed to the principal German delegate, Count von Brockdorff-Rantzau. Brockdorff-Rantzau was slightly lame. Unlike some of the plenipotentiaries, he was also an experienced diplomatist. He knew, therefore, that delegates at international conferences did not usually stand up to address their colleagues. By delivering a truculent speech from a seated position he went far to confirm President Wilson's impression that the Germans were a tiresome people.

On June 28, after the Allied and Associated Powers had made a number of concessions, the Germans signed the treaty, which stripped them of most of their navy and all their overseas possessions, pledged them to reduce their army to seven infantry and three cavalry divisions, and saddled them with an indeterminate debt for reparations at the same time as it reduced their earning power by depriving them temporarily or permanently of important commercial assets. They were also obliged to confess, against their deepest convictions, that they were at least morally responsible for all the loss and damage suffered by the Allied and Associated Powers in consequence of the war.

Whether these terms were morally justifiable in view of the enormous suffering inflicted on the world by German aggression can only be a matter of opinion. Possibly they were. Whether they were consistent with the spirit of President Wilson's speeches, on the basis of which the belligerents had contracted to make peace, is also debatable. From a practical standpoint there can be no doubt that they did not conduce to the welfare of Germany, of the Allies, or of Europe. An opinion widely held at the time was that almost their only merit was that Article 19 of the Covenant of the League of Nations, which stood in the forefront of the treaty, provided for revision by consent of settlements found to be unworkable.

Responsibility for the admitted severity of the treaty was generally attributed to the firm resolve of the French government to weaken Germany. But the rule was that all decisions had to be unanimous. If Clemenceau was answerable for the harshness of the terms, so also were Woodrow Wilson and Lloyd George. Indeed, the President's responsibility can be fairly assumed to have been greater than Clemenceau's or Lloyd George's. Great Britain and France were deeply in debt to the United States, and were also dependent on the United States for future supplies of food and raw materials. In international as well as private affairs, the man who pays the piper can usually be assumed to call the tune.

Immediately after the signing of the treaty and the British and American guarantees to France, the President left for the United States. At a parting interview Colonel House, who was never again to see the man who had been his intimate friend and partner for nearly a decade, urged the President to meet the Senate in a conciliatory spirit. The President replied that all his life he had had to fight for anything worth having.

He soon found that he was fighting a losing battle. His opponents were particularly angry with him for having allowed Japan to take over a German concession at Shantung, but the Covenant of the League of Nations and the guarantee to France were also sharply criticized. Although an ample staff had accompanied him to Paris, he was unable to provide the Senate Foreign Relations Committee with comprehensive or detailed records of his transactions. On August 19 he faced a grueling interview with the committee, which left him visibly shaken. In the course of it he testified that he knew nothing of the secret treaties until after he reached Paris in December 1918. His statement, which was utterly at variance with the facts, can be explained only on the assumption that he was already suffering from the mortal illness which struck him down soon afterward.

The President's advisers urged him to invite the Senate to accept the treaty with reservations, but he refused all concessions. On September 3 he left Washington on a country-wide tour for the purpose of defending the treaty before the American public. After he had made thirty-seven speeches in twenty-eight cities in three weeks, he collapsed on September 25 at Pueblo, Colorado. He was quickly rushed back to the White House, where, on October 2, his physician, Dr. Grayson, announced: "The President is paralyzed."

On November 19 the Senate refused, at one of the most exciting sessions in its history, to ratify the treaty either unconditionally, or with fourteen reservations already adopted by the Senate in committee. Further attempts to carry the treaty through the Senate in the next few months were also unsuccessful. With the final defeat of a proposal for ratification with fifteen reservations on March 19, 1920, all hopes founded on the President's promises of American participation in the League of Nations and the maintenance of frontiers fixed by the treaty crumbled. Farseeing Europeans faced the knowledge that, unless they succeeded in pulling themselves out of their troubles by their own efforts, they might well have another devastating war on their hands as soon as the rising generation in Germany grew to manhood.

4

AFTERMATH

WHEN SIGNOR ORLANDO LEFT PARIS IN DUDGEON IN APRIL 1919, President Wilson, Lloyd George, and Clemenceau hastened to put into the Treaty of Versailles a clause providing that ratification by three signatories should suffice to bring it into force. An unlooked-for consequence was that the abstention of the United States did not kill the treaty. In due course three ratifications were obtained, and on January 10, 1920, the treaty became part of the public law of Europe. Thus the Allies were left with a settlement which seemed satisfactory to none of them, while at the same time they were deprived of the American participation which had induced them to put up with its imperfections in the first place.

European commentators tended, on the whole, to blame the United States Senate for this outcome. Senators who led the opposition to the treaty were roughly handled by European critics. But the Senate had the duty, as well as the privilege, of accepting or rejecting treaties. They would not have performed it very well if they had accepted one of which they did not approve in order to please a President whose views they did not share and who had taken little trouble to consult them. Before leaving for Paris, Woodrow Wilson had promised them that they should "know all that he did." When it came to the point, they had had to drag essential information out of him by cross-examination.

In any case, there was no reason to suppose that American adherence to the treaty would have made it satisfactory. Its coming into force brought hostilities between Germany and the Allies to a formal close, but it did not bring peace in any real sense. Before there can be peace at the end of a great war, there has to be a settlement which the winners are willing to impose and the losers, however reluctantly, to accept. The Germans were not willing to accept the Versailles Treaty, and there was no sustained and un-divided will among the Allies to impose it. Hence there was no peace in Europe. Ratification by the United States might have made the Allies readier to impose the Versailles settlement on Germany, but it would not have made the Germans readier to accept it.

In the sequel, Europe had to wait another five years for the simultaneous emergence in Britain, France, and Germany of statesmen both willing and able to strike a bargain more or less acceptable to all parties. The men who then came to the fore were not necessarily wiser or more intelligent than the general run of democratic statesmen. But at least they saw, and were able to make others see, that the hardships inflicted on Europe by the failure of their forerunners to make peace in 1919 had gone beyond all bearing, and that peace must now be made. Thus a peace of un-derstanding was made not at Versailles in 1919 but at Locarno in 1925. But by that time such damage had been done to the Euro-pean polity that the new Concert of Europe proved too frail a ves-sel to withstand the winds of circumstance that soon beat upon it from more than one direction.

By 1920 seven Great Powers had succeeded to the roles filled before the war by Austro-Hungary, France, Germany, Great Brit-ain, Italy, and Imperial Russia. They were France, Germany, Great Britain, Italy, Japan, Soviet Russia, and the United States. The outcome of the Paris Conference was a bitter disappointment to all of them, with the possible exception of Soviet Russia, whose avowed object was the destruction of capitalist-imperialist society.

At any rate on paper, even the Russians had some reason to feel dissatisfied when they looked back from the standpoint of 1920 on the experiences of the past twelve months. In the early part of 1919 the Soviet government faced a far from negligible challenge to their authority from no less than four self-styled provisional governments, each of which had a footing on Russian soil and was receiving help from the Allies. In March of that year they offered, in a memorandum handed to William C. Bullitt of the American delegation in Paris, to make peace with the provisional governments, enter into diplomatic and commercial relations with the Allied and Associated Powers, and assume joint responsibility with the provisional governments for Russia's external debts. Their terms were that each government should keep the territory it held, and that the Allied and Associated Powers should give no further help to anti-Soviet governments and should withdraw their own troops from Russian soil. Probably the Soviet government would not have made such an offer if they had expected it to be accepted. But that made it all the more unfortunate that the Allied and Associated Powers turned down the Russian proposal without bringing it into the light of day and giving honest reasons for rejecting it. Lloyd George, meeting Bullitt after his return from Russia, expressed great interest in the Soviet memorandum and suggested that it should be published. President Wilson, on the other hand, vetoed publication. Thereupon Lloyd George went out of his way to give a false impression by telling the House of Commons that no authentic overtures from the Soviet government had reached the Paris Conference.

Again, in January of the same year, the Soviet government gave a qualified acceptance to an invitation from President Wilson to meet representatives of the provisional governments and the Allied and Associated Powers on the island of Prinkipo in the Sea of Marmara. The project failed not because the Soviet government preferred to go on fighting, as Lloyd George asserted in another of his disclosures to the House of Commons, but because the provisional governments did.

These evasions left Western statesmen with a legacy of trouble where their relations with Soviet Russia were concerned. A question which they never succeeded in answering to the satisfaction of their critics was whether they had really meant to treat with the Communists or not. If they were determined from the start to have no truck with the Communists, then why, it was asked, did Presi-

dent Wilson launch the Prinkipo project after discussing it with
Lloyd George and Clemenceau, and why was the Bullitt Mission
ever sent? Alternatively, if they did want to come to terms with
the new Russia, then why did they refuse to meet the Soviet leaders after making overtures to them?

But for every critic who found fault with the handling by
Western statesmen of this issue, there were dozens who found
fault with the inclusion of the Covenant of the League of Nations
in the peace treaties. That President Wilson should have pressed
for it was understandable, for his country had no precedent for intervention in European affairs in peacetime, so that presumably
he needed both a pretext for intervention and a means of
persuading American voters that isolationism was dead. But when
the United States repudiated the League, it seemed to many
Europeans to have lost its purpose. Even statesmen who did not
object to the League in principle, but thought that its formation
could well have been left until European concord was restored,
complained of the illogicality and hypocrisy of an arrangement
which put the safeguarding of the peace of Europe ostensibly into
the hands of a body without fleets or armies, and without power
to compel member states to use their fleets and armies in support
of its decrees. Regarding the League as an expensive debating
society conducted chiefly for the benefit of the small, weak powers
created by the war, the Great Powers preferred to conduct their
business at conferences which did not pretend to draw their authority from Geneva or defer to its opinions. The only major question referred to the League during its first few years of existence
was the interpretation of the results of a plebiscite in Upper Silesia
at which fourteen communes voted for attachment to Germany
and seven for attachment to Poland. The league's decision, which
awarded the most valuable communes to Poland, did nothing to
enhance its reputation.

From the points of view of individual nations, there were at
least as many objections to the peace settlements as there were
Great Powers. France had poured out lives and money during the
war to honor her obligations to Imperial Russia and drive the
Germans from her soil. At the end of it all she hoped for a treaty

which would at least safeguard her against a fresh invasion. She obtained, apart from territorial gains which did not solve her strategic problem, only demilitarization of the Rhineland and the abortive American and British guarantees. Ultimately she found a partial substitute for the guarantees in a series of treaties which bound Poland, Czechoslovakia, Rumania, Yugoslavia, and Belgium to her for a great part of the period between the wars. But the war left her finances in a deplorable state. Within a few years of the armistice she claimed to have spent twelve hundred million pounds on her devastated areas. It was therefore inevitable that, as long as French statesmen saw any chance of holding Germany to her promise to make reparation in cash or kind for the damage she had done, they should press for integral performance of the Versailles Treaty, imperfect instrument though it was.

To the Germans, the treaty seemed a great wrong and an intolerable affront. Germany had asked for peace because she had no choice but to do so. Nevertheless she had been promised impartial justice, and had stipulated in the pre-armistice negotiations that nothing should be required of her which was irreconcilable with German honor. The outcome was an imposed settlement almost as severe as that which she herself would have imposed if she had won. Germans of all classes felt humiliated by the treaty. For years after the war many professional men and office workers had to wear patched suits, either because they were too poor to buy new ones or because their country was too poor to import textiles. Even if their impoverishment was due partly to financial jugglery practiced by German statesmen to cheat the French of their blood money, it was still true that the reparations clauses damaged German credit, and that most Germans confidently attributed all their troubles to the malice of their enemies. Hence the treaty was quite unacceptable to Germany, and its revision was bound to figure in the calculations of her statesmen for many years.

Even in the light of its effect on Franco-German relations alone, the treaty was thus a dismal failure. The purpose of a peace treaty is to make peace. To make peace is to reconcile. Far from reconciling Germany with France and France with Germany, the Treaty of Versailles invited, and even compelled, the statesmen of the two countries to take up positions which were utterly irreconcilable, and to maintain them for more than five years. At the end of that time they were at last able to reach an understanding which did not survive the economic and social upheavals of the 1930s, themselves a more or less direct outcome of the Versailles settlement and its aftermath of fear, greed, jealousy, and hardship.

For Great Britain the treaty was a disaster. The period of economic anarchy in Europe which it ushered in was particularly damaging since it came at a time when British industry was run down after a long war. British textile factories, for example, had worked during the war almost exclusively on government account. Overseas markets had been neglected, good will had suffered, machinery had been allowed to wear out or had become old-fashioned. In some trades raw materials of the right quality, or at times of any quality, were hard to get because of shipping problems and because years of freak conditions had upset the delicate balance between supply and demand. Again, almost all Britain's surplus coal had been absorbed during the latter part of the war by France and Italy, whose normal sources of supply were cut off by the German invasion and the interruption of trade with Central Europe. These demands ceased as soon as peace returned, but that did not mean that Britain's old markets would be won back without a struggle, if at all. The essence of Britain's long-term economic and social policy before the war had been to increase the real wealth of the community by stepping up productivity without raising prices, but prices could not be kept low in inflationary conditions. As a result of heavy government spending which did not cease when fighting ceased, they soon rose to about three times those ruling in 1914. Within a few years of the Armistice, unemployment reached dimensions regarded as staggering when comparable conditions recurred ten years later. Economic and financial problems were aggravated by strikes and disturbances which were seriously thought to presage revolution. Seeing their country threatened with ruin by the economic consequences of the treaty, British statesmen were bound to press for its revision or reinterpretation in the direction of greater lenience toward Germany, even though this brought them into conflict with the French policy of integral performance.

At the same time, Franco-British relations were not helped by events in Syria, where the pro-British Emir Faisal was forcibly deposed by the French in 1920. Nor were they improved by Faisal's installation a year later as titular ruler of British-controlled Iraq.

Still worse consequences flowed from the presence of Greek troops in Anatolia, and the use made of them. By 1920 Kemal's Turkish Nationalists seemed quite likely to cross into Europe. At a meeting of British and French ministers and their military advisers at Lympne, England, in June, the Greek Army was authorized to occupy a strategic position on the Sea of Marmara, and provisional arrangements were made to send a further Greek division to Turkey-in-Asia and put it at the disposal of the local Allied commander. In the following October, Venizelos offered to drive Kemal out of Ankara and Trebizond in return for a subsidy of three-and-a-half million pounds a month for six months and a supply of warm clothing for his troops. Lloyd George remarked when these terms were reported to him that the money was the difficulty. Nevertheless means were found to keep a strong Greek Army in the field for much longer than six months. But Ankara and Trebizond remained in Kemal's hands, and the French lost patience. Renouncing the interest in the Anatolian province of Cilicia which they had claimed under the secret treaties, they decided to concentrate on Syria and the Lebanon and make their peace with Kemal. The Italians, who had likewise decided not to pursue their claims in Anatolia, also came to terms with the new Turkey. Thus the British were left in more or less reluctant opposition to their Allies as the Greek Army's sole remaining backer among the Great Powers.

As for Italy, so far as her immediate interest in the peace-settlements went she was concerned less with the Treaty of Versailles than with the Treaties of Saint-Germain and the Trianon, which purported to make peace between the Allied and Associated Powers on the one hand, and Austria and Hungary on the other. But the Treaties of Saint-Germain and the Trianon were every bit as unsatisfactory to the principal parties as was the Treaty of Versailles, and were particularly unsatisfactory to Italy.

This was not surprising, since Italy had frankly and avowedly entered the war in order to improve her lot, and had failed to improve it as much as she expected. The outbreak of war in 1914 had found her linked in a triple alliance with Germany and Austro-Hungary. Claiming that they had released her from her obligations by declaring war without consulting her, she had refused to join them. The sequel was the Treaty of London, by which she agreed in 1915 to make common cause with the Allies in return for promises of substantial gains at the expense of Austro-Hungary and Turkey if her new partners came out on the winning side.

These promises were afterward regarded by many people as immoral. Americans, especially, thought that the Allies ought not to have bribed Italy with slices of Austro-Hungary and Turkey which were not theirs to give. Nevertheless the territories of which the Allies proposed in 1915 to strip Austro-Hungary and Turkey for the benefit of Italy were far less extensive and important than the territories of which President Wilson was willing in 1919 to strip Germany and Austro-Hungary for the benefit of France, Poland, Czechoslovakia, Yugoslavia, and Rumania.

Italy's share of the spoil was afterward the subject of other agreements and understandings, but in general she entered the Paris Conference prepared to take her stand either on the Treaty of London, or on Wilsonian principles, according to which way the wind blew. Besides much else, she claimed the Adriatic region of Dalmatia. Dalmatia had cultural links with Italy. Moreover, Italy needed Dalmatia if she were to control the Adriatic. And control of the Adriatic, Italians argued, was essential to Italy in view of her geographical situation and her long coastline.

Italian claims were sweeping. Nevertheless many Europeans and Americans believed in 1919 that, if all else had been equal, it might have been no bad thing to give Italy the greater part of what she asked. Unfortunately, all else was not equal. By 1919 Dalmatia had ceased to be an Austro-Hungarian province and was claimed by Yugoslavia. And the Allied and Associated Powers felt a special responsibility toward Yugoslavia, since their actions had helped to call Yugoslavia into being.

The outcome was that Italy was allowed less than her whole claim. She received the Trentino, and the Brenner frontier. She received Trieste and Zara. Most of Dalmatia went to Yugoslavia. At the same time, the Italians were dissatisfied with the treatment given to their Turkish claims. They were incensed by the decision made by President Wilson, Lloyd George and Clemenceau behind their backs to put the Greeks ashore at Smyrna. They were outraged by Wilson's appeal to them to renounce Fiume, afterward seized on behalf of Italy by the poet Gabriele D'Annunzio. They left the Paris Conference convinced that the British, the French, and the Americans had conspired to cheat them of their just due.

Thus the peace settlements were not only the direct cause of bad blood between France and Germany and between France and Britain, they were also the direct cause of bad blood between the Italians and both the British and the French. Moreover, the economic troubles which they fostered bore hardly on Italy, with her dearth of raw materials and her large tracts of unproductive territory. By 1922 her social, economic, and financial difficulties had reached such a pitch that she succumbed easily to the dictator Benito Mussolini, who improved her internal affairs considerably but afterward led her into trouble.

Japan, unlike France, Germany, Great Britain, and Italy, emerged from the war much richer and stronger than she was when she went into it. But she suffered a loss of face at the Paris Conference which made the peace settlements unsatisfactory to her, too. In the middle of the nineteenth century she had reluctantly agreed to renounce an isolationism even more profound than that of the United States, and enter into commercial relations with the West. In little more than half a century she made such astonishing progress that by 1919 she was herself one of the Great Powers. At the Paris Conference the Japanese delegation suggested that the Covenant of the League of Nations should include a clause affirming the equality of races. The Prime Minister of Australia, William Morris Hughes, was so violently opposed to the proposal that the American delegation advised the Japanese to drop it. The Japanese never forgave the Americans for their advice, or for their criticism of clauses in the Versailles Treaty which upheld the Japanese claim to rights ceded by the Germans in the Chinese province of Shantung. So the making of peace was not only the first step toward the new European war which broke out in 1939; it was also the first step toward Pearl Harbor.

The United States, too, emerged from the war with her wealth and power enormously enhanced. No longer Europe's debtor, she had become the greatest creditor nation in the world. Yet the whole miserable affair, by the time the Paris Conference had done its work, was no more agreeable to her than it was to other nations. The peace settlements bristled with features so unsatisfactory that she showed her disapproval by repudiating the Treaty of Versailles and making, after all, a separate peace with Germany in 1921. At the same time, thinking Americans could not help knowing that their country's wartime association with Europe had done nothing to ease their relationship with the Old World or bring about the Anglo-Saxon solidarity so glowingly described by Colonel House.

From the moral point of view the United States derived no satisfaction at all from her partnership with Great Britain, France, and Italy. From 1914 to 1917 she loaded the Allies with benefits while formally protesting against their assumption that it was the duty of American exporters to ship their goods exclusively to Allied countries. She repeatedly saved the Allies from disaster by lending them huge sums of money. After 1917 she sent her citizens to fight beside theirs. The United States Army made important contributions to victory in the Saint-Mihiel salient and the Argonne, and its turn-out at the Victory Parade in Paris was considered by a good judge to put European armies in the shade. American troops took part in the occupation of Germany, and American citizens did not spare themselves to relieve distress in Europe. At the Paris Conference the rank-and-file of the American delegation, recruited largely in academic circles, made a highly favorable impression on European diplomatists who might have been expected to be critical of their amateur status. American citizens with no ax to grind did more for Europe between 1914 and 1919 than European citizens were ever likely to do for the United States. Yet, after all this, their reward was to be accused of profiting by Europe's troubles and then saddling Europe with a peace settlement so manifestly unjust, unsound, and unworkable that they themselves recoiled from it.

If there was justice in the second of these criticisms, the fault did not lie with anything done or left undone by the American people. It lay with the failure of statesmen to agree on a settlement rational and moderate enough to be tolerable and to last. Because they lived in the twentieth century and because one was a Liberal-Progressive and the other a Liberal-Radical, both Woodrow Wilson and Lloyd George thought themselves better equipped to make peace with the help of Clemenceau than their forerunners had been to make peace after the Napoleonic Wars. Yet posterity might have been well pleased with them if they had done half as well as Castlereagh and Metternich.

Two excuses often given for the failure of the trio are that Wilson's principles were too lofty for a sinful world, and that Lloyd George and Clemenceau were victims of popular prejudices which they were powerless to control.

The first does not hold water. There was nothing lofty in the Fourteen Points except the language that clothed them. Woodrow Wilson's program was to loosen the hold exercised by Prussia on Germany through the link between the monarchy and the empire, by weakening or destroying the monarchy and turning out the Kaiser; to strengthen France, but not too much, by giving her back Alsace and Lorraine; to weaken Russia, and put a barrier between her and Germany, by reviving the long defunct Polish state; to strengthen Italy, but again not too much, by extending her territory a little; to satisfy ideological objections to Hapsburg domination of Central Europe by first following, and later exceeding, the Allied policy of stirring up the Slav minorities against the Hapsburgs; and to curb Britain's high handed exercise of her sea power by stressing the freedom of the seas. This was an understandable policy for a man with no great originality of mind and little regard or liking for European institutions; but there was nothing in it that was particularly lofty, and scarcely anything that was novel. Probably its author did not foresee the economic chaos that would follow from his schemes, for his conception of states-manship was so old-fashioned that he paid little attention to economics and thought almost entirely in terms of dynasties and frontiers.

Outside the Fourteen Points, there was a good deal in Woodrow Wilson's declarations that could fairly be called lofty. He had some admirable things to say about impartial justice for friend and foe and the iniquity of punitive damages and annexations. But these principles did not square very well with the rest of his program, and he discarded them. He was shocked when Count Brockdorff-Ranzau had the courage to speak up for his country. He was will-ing to add the cost of war pensions to the German indemnity, and to strip Germany of her overseas possessions and concessions.

How far Lloyd George and Clemenceau really were victims of popular prejudice is hard to say. Both claimed that they were. Yet the line taken by Clemenceau at the Paris Conference was the line he would almost certainly have taken in any case. If it dif-fered from the program sketched in the memorandum handed to President Wilson before he left the United States, it did so chiefly in being more openly founded on national interest rather than first principles.

Lloyd George undoubtedly was hampered by his uncertain hold on the huge majority he had won at the General Election in De-cember 1918, and by pressure from his back-bench supporters and the Northcliffe press not to let the Germans off too lightly. Yet that was partly his own fault. He made no attempt to master the reparations problem until it was too late, although he had the same means of discovering the truth in 1918 as in 1919. He al-lowed the Hughes-Cunliffe Committee to circulate, without au-thoritative contradiction, the opinion that twenty-four thousand million pounds could be wrung from Germany, although he was not bound to accept their figure and had shown in the past that he was capable of overriding such opinions. He left himself a loophole in his election speeches by saying that nothing must be demanded of Germany which might harm British trade, yet he did not use the loophole when he needed it. Many of his back-bench supporters represented industrial constituencies and many had commercial interests. Would they really have been deaf to the argument that nothing could be worse for Britain than to shelve the reparations question and leave Europe in suspense?

As for the Northcliffe press, newspaper comments did not prevent Lloyd George from being one of the most persuasive talkers and orators who ever sat in Downing Street. Was it really beyond his skill to convince the public, and perhaps even journalists, that nothing would be gained by foisting on the Germans a settlement which might drive them to devalue their currency and declare themselves bankrupt, as they were reported as early as 1919 to be thinking of doing if they were pressed too hard? Even if he had failed to convert his enemy, Lord Northcliffe, would that have been fatal to him? Stanley Baldwin, who followed him as Prime Minister after Bonar Law's brief period of office, was only a moderately good speaker and lacked Lloyd George's knack of sweeping people off their feet. Yet he managed to maintain his hold on the public for many years, although he openly defied the lords of the press and called them harlots.

Criticisms and suggestions on these lines were made repeatedly in Lloyd George's hearing while the Versailles Treaty was still in draft. American as well as British delegates in Paris begged Lloyd George to tell his supporters the truth and marshal public opinion behind the policy of putting a figure in the treaty which Germany could pay. Had that been done, the question of the annuities needed to extinguish the debt within an acceptable period could still have been left open for discussion, but at least Germany's maximum liability would have been known, and the figure could always have been scaled down later if it proved too large. But Lloyd George shrank from trying to convert French opinion as well as British. No argument could convince him that it was not better to assent to a settlement which he knew to be bad than to try to educate the public.

5

VERSAILLES TO THE RUHR

THE THREE YEARS AFTER THE COMING INTO FORCE OF THE VERSAILLES
Treaty saw a steady deterioration in Anglo-French relations, cul-
minating in an open breach when the French decided in January
1923 to occupy the Ruhr against the wishes of the British government.

From one point of view all this seemed inevitable. The war had
left Germany defeated, France victorious. Britain's traditional
policy was to hold the balance of power by backing the weak
against the strong. Hence it was argued that Britain was bound
to take the part of Germany in a Franco-German quarrel such
as that which flared up over reparations.

From another point of view the trend which drew Britain and
France apart in the years immediately after the First World War
did not seem inevitable at all. It could, in fact, be argued with
considerable force that, for two reasons, Britain's traditional concern with the balance of power did not by any means compel her
to reverse the policy of friendship with France which had been
followed throughout the war and for ten years before the war.

In the first place, the emergence of Japan and the United States
as world powers made it no longer a rational proceeding after the
war to think of the balance of power in purely European terms.
British statesmen did not, in fact, think of it purely in those terms.
Lloyd George and his colleagues were well aware that the old conception, already growing out of date when the war began, had
been profoundly modified by the impetus given to American and

Japanese expansionism by wartime opportunities. They knew that in 1920 both the Japanese and the Americans were planning large additions to their navies, that both were competitors with Great Britain for world markets, and that the rivalry between them was a factor of the utmost importance in world politics. Japan did not conceal her intention of consolidating and extending her influence in China. Official and unofficial spokesmen of the United States did not deny that one of their country's chief aims was to confine Japanese ambitions within close limits, or that another was to loosen the powerful grip which Britain's naval and mercantile supremacy had hitherto enabled her to exercise on maritime trade throughout the world.

Nor was there anything surprising in all this. That Japan, with her teeming population and growing productive capacity, should seek markets and spheres of influence outside her overcrowded homeland had long been inevitable; to encourage her to find them in politically bankrupt China, where her interests conflicted least with those of other nations, had seemed to British statesmen the only answer to a problem otherwise insoluble. The United States, with her ample living space and huge domestic market, was not driven by the same compulsions; but the wartime boom had accustomed her leading citizens to an expanding economy, and competitiveness was in their blood. Nor would her naval ambitions have been hard to account for even without Japanese rivalry. In 1914 the vast majority of all American exports had been carried in foreign vessels, mostly British. Until 1917 American exporters had had to bargain with the British government for the right to sell their goods to European customers. These experiences had brought home to American industrialists, as no peacetime warnings could, the disadvantages of not possessing a large merchant fleet of their own and a strong navy to protect it. Nothing could be more natural than that they should be determined that no future United States government should overlook their claims.

Of the two nations which had come to the fore during the war as competitors with Great Britain for world markets, Japan was the weaker, the United States the stronger. Therefore, if Britain had clung to her traditional policy of the balance of power, she

would have backed Japan, to whom she was already bound by
a treaty not due to expire until 1936. Her reason for taking a
different line was not that her statesmen failed to recognize that
to back Japan was the logical thing to do, but that they were
determined not to risk a quarrel with the United States. Nevertheless there were many Englishmen who thought that their
leaders were wrong to fall in behind a Far Eastern policy which
seemed to them mistaken, and that it would have been far better
for Britain and the United States to agree to give Japan her head
in China rather than drive her into open conflict with the
whole Anglo-Saxon world. There were also many Americans who
thought that the United States would gain nothing in the long
run by challenging Britain's command of the sea or by weakening
her hold on her overseas possessions. Naval strategists in both
countries pointed out that, since the United States was primarily
a great continental power and Britain an island power, their naval
requirements could not be measured by the same standard. Political economists argued, too, that nothing had done more to create
opportunities for American enterprise than Britain's decision in
1846 to throw open her markets to the whole world, and that it
would be a mistake to risk an end to the happy state of affairs
which made it possible for the United States to ship a big share
of her exportable surpluses to Britain while defraying part of the
cost of federal government by taxing European imports.

But, even if these arguments were sound, to have acted on them
would have demanded almost superhuman forbearance on the part
of American statesmen of the 1920s. An unlucky decision by the
Allies in 1916 to threaten Germany with economic sanctions after
the war had made a powerful impression in Washington. The
harm was not undone by British assurances that the gesture was
a mere reprisal for German threats and meant nothing. Moreover,
American industrial magnates were not thinking only in terms of
trade with Britain and the British Empire, or with Europe. They
were thinking in terms of world trade, and of a possible struggle
for raw materials which might not be obtainable in domestic
markets. Rumors that American oil supplies might be near exhaustion, and that the British-controlled Middle East might be-

come the world's great oil-producing center, did not help to inspire Americans with confidence in their country's economic self-sufficiency. In the troubled postwar world, powerful vested interests combined with national pride, distrust of Japan and dislike of British arrogance to urge President Warren G. Harding's administration, as they had already urged President Wilson's, in the direction of open naval and mercantile competition with Great Britain.

Before discussing the other flaw in the argument that logic and tradition necessarily drove Britain to sever her alliance with France after the war, it will be convenient to consider how this problem was resolved in practice.

During the pre-armistice negotiations, and again at the Paris Conference, the British government had been able to shelve the awkward issue of sea power by telling Colonel House and President Wilson that they were willing to discuss it later, but would refuse to make peace with Germany on the President's terms if he insisted on discussing it at once. In 1920 they could shelve it no longer. They faced the knowledge that the United States would have substantial naval superiority by 1924 unless they either built against her, or bargained with her to stop building. They knew, too, that Japan also had a large building program.

When the Committee of Imperial Defence met to consider this stupendous question in December 1920, Lloyd George called it the most important and most difficult they had ever had to face. That was no exaggeration. Lloyd George knew that most Englishmen regarded war with the United States as inconceivable. He could reasonably assume that most Americans thought much on the same lines. But he also knew that policies which could lead to war were not framed by popular opinion; they were framed by governments. The British people had felt no particular hostility toward Germany when British and French statesmen opened the negotiations which ultimately took Britain into war on the side of France and Russia in 1914. In the final analysis, Britain had committed herself by almost imperceptible stages to war with Germany because a German government had refused to give up a program of naval construction which a British government regarded as a

threat. Was another British government now to take the same
view of an American program, perhaps with similar results? In
spite of the understanding with France, Sir Edward Grey had
done his best before 1914 to reassure Germany and keep on good
terms with both countries. Not only had he failed, he had even
been blamed for causing the war by not telling the Germans
plainly that Britain meant to fight. If Lloyd George and his
colleagues tried to keep on good terms with both Japan and the
United States while building ship-for-ship with the Americans,
would they merely be repeating Grey's mistake?

That was not the end of their problems. The country had never
yet grudged anything spent on the navy, but building ship-for-ship
with the Americans would be exceedingly expensive. The United
States had twice Britain's population and could raise twice as
much money by imposing the same rate of taxation. Even if the
government did not bring war nearer by committing the country
to an unrestricted arms race with the Americans, they might
bring ruin nearer. They were extremely reluctant to do either. Yet
they were also extremely reluctant to be the first British government in modern times to surrender the weapon of sea power without a struggle. For a time, increased use of submarines and aircraft
seemed to offer a chance of keeping control of British trade-
routes without directly competing with the American capital-ship
program; but that hope faded when a subcommittee reported that
there was no substitute for the battleship or battlecruiser.

When the picture looked blackest, they found a gleam of comfort in the recollection that the Germans had been offered a
"naval holiday" before the war but had refused it. After President
Harding moved into the White House they received indications
that he might be willing to consider some such arrangement. The
upshot was that Britain accepted an invitation in 1921 to send
a delegation to a disarmament conference due to begin at Washington in November.

Meanwhile Lloyd George made strenuous attempts to improve
relations with the United States by settling the Irish question. To
do that he had either to stamp out a powerful terrorist organization which had grown up since the beginning of the war, or come

to terms with some or all of the nationalist leaders who were competing for control of it, and whose declared aims ranged from Home Rule within the British Empire to out-and-out secession. The organization had received a certain amount of financial and other support from Germany during the war, and more recently Soviet agents had made clumsy and unsuccessful attempts at infiltration, but much of its revenue was drawn from American sympathizers. Irish independence had always had a good press in the United States. In November 1920, the British Ambassador in Washington, Sir Auckland Geddes, told a friend that anti-British feeling ran so high that he feared for the safety of his wife and children and had asked for police protection for them.

It was against this background that Lloyd George decided to risk the wrath of his right-wing supporters by making peace with the Irish if he could. In the summer of 1921 he succeeded in patching up a truce with the terrorist army, and in the following December, while the Washington Conference was sitting, he signed a treaty to which a number of Irish leaders put their names. These events did not end Ireland's troubles, but they did encourage Lloyd George to hope that he might yet persuade the United States government to reconsider their attitude to European problems.

The other flaw in the argument that a postwar break with France followed logically from Britain's concern with the balance of power was that the war did not, in fact, tip the scales decisively in favor of the French. When the cease-fire sounded in 1918, some of the most valuable industrial centers in France had been ravaged by the Germans, while Germany's industrial centers were untouched and in full production. Under the peace settlements Germany lost important industrial assets in Lorraine and Upper Silesia, while she also ceded the Saar coalfields on terms which made their ultimate restoration almost certain. But she retained the Ruhr, which was by far the richest industrial complex of its kind in Western Europe, accounting for four-fifths of her remaining output of coal, steel, and pig iron. Her population, after all adjustments had been made under the peace-treaties, was still half again as large as that of France. Once she threw off her economic and financial burdens and started to rearm, she could quickly regain her old position as the strongest Continental power. The French frontier would then lie wide open to invasion unless steps were taken to secure it.

Since Britain's aim was a peaceful Europe and hence an expanding market, it followed that her logical course was not to throw in her lot unreservedly with either France or Germany, but to reassure the French about their frontier, and at the same time see that the burden of reparations was not made so heavy as to deprive Germany of her purchasing power, drive her to bankruptcy, or weaken her to the point at which the French might be tempted to finish her off before she could recover. If the problem of French security could be solved without sacrificing Germany, then the way would be clear for an exploration of the innumerable questions left unsettled in Central Europe.

For some years after the war the difficulty of marshaling popular opinion behind any course of action which hinted at undue leniency toward Germany was a powerful handicap to statesmen who tried to follow such a policy. A still more potent obstacle was the numerical weakness of the British Army. Just as the efforts of British statesmen to avert war in 1914 by holding the balance of power in Europe had been hampered by their obvious inability to send more than a few divisions across the Channel, so also British military policy after the war was poorly aligned with British foreign policy. Three years after the Armistice, four-fifths of the Army's disposable strength was locked up in Ireland and India. With most of the remaining battalions scattered between Silesia, Constantinople, Egypt, Malta, Gibraltar, Mesopotamia, and Palestine, Lloyd George and his colleagues were not in a position to offer the French the precisely-defined help which would have appealed to them. At the same time the great mass of the British public, blissfully unconscious that economic chaos in Europe threatened their living standards and their jobs, were more interested in striking for higher pay and friendship with Russia than in reassuring the French or persuading them to be good Europeans.

Popular opinion across the Channel was even less enlightened.

The French were slow to understand that there was no way in which the Allies could extract large sums from Germany without damaging their own interests. Nor was ignorance of simple economic laws confined to the uneducated. Even well-informed statesmen and industrialists seriously believed that their country would gain more than it lost by allowing the Germans to rebuild the devastated areas with their own labor and materials, thus depriving French workers and employers of jobs and contracts.

For all these reasons, Lloyd George had an uphill task when he tried to persuade French governments to accept a settlement of the reparations problem which would not strain Germany's economy to the breaking point and thus do harm to everyone. An added complication was that the withdrawal of the Americans enabled the French and Belgians to make the Reparation Commission into an instrument of Franco-Belgian policy. The British delegate, even when supported by his Italian colleague, could always be outvoted by a combination of French and Belgian votes and the French chairman's casting-vote. It was largely on that account, and not solely because of his alleged passion for the limelight, that Lloyd George made so many attempts to rescue the reparations problem from the clutches of the commission and discuss it at international conferences where British and German representatives were sure of a hearing and where only unanimous decisions counted.

Hence it was doubly unfortunate for Lloyd George that his distrust of experts, reinforced by his sometimes excessive confidence in his own powers of persuasion, made these attempts at settlement by direct negotiation less successful than they might have been. Lord Curzon, who had succeeded Balfour at the Foreign Office in October 1919, was not immediately attracted by the reparations problem. Observing Lloyd George's confident handling of facts and figures, he was often a silent spectator of his chief's tussles with French statesmen. With all his weaknesses a superb negotiator where his interest was aroused, he might have helped Lloyd George to win more points if he had grasped from the first what was at stake.

Nor did the Germans do much to help. When Lloyd George

made his first attempt to drag the problem into the light of day at the San Remo Conference in April 1920, he was able to counter French insistence on the full machinery of the Reparation Commission and the Versailles Treaty by suggesting that the Germans should first be given a chance of making an "honest proposal." It was therefore vital from the British point of view that the Germans should be on their best behavior when, at the Spa Conference in the following July, they met Allied statesmen face-to-face for the first time since the signing of the treaty. They were not on their best behavior, and they did not make a good impression. Asked when they proposed to deliver the coal promised to the French as reparations in kind, they took up a truculent attitude reinforced by shouts of defiance from the incorrigible industrialist and press magnate Hugo Stinnes. Yet they climbed down when confronted with an ultimatum. There could hardly have been a more convincing demonstration of the strength of the French case that the Germans were an untrustworthy people from whom no honest proposal could be expected and who understood no argument but force.

When at last the Allies did have a German proposal to consider after a further delay of many months, the outcome was no more successful. Dismissing the offer as wholly unacceptable, the French proposed an immediate occupation of the Ruhr. Lloyd George and Curzon immediately nailed their colors to the mast by protesting against a move so damaging to German credit, but almost as promptly tore them down again by agreeing that Duisburg, Düsseldorf, and Ruhrort should be occupied. Allied troops moved into the three Rhine ports on March 8, 1921, only to find that their action was illegal since the Reparation Commission had not declared the Germans technically in default. The failure of the British to spot the oversight in good time and make the most of it was a tactical blunder which they would not have committed if Curzon had mastered the reparations problem before attending conferences on the subject, instead of waiting until a spell of sick leave in the spring of 1923 gave him leisure to turn his mind to it.

The next round found Lloyd George and Curzon still uneasily

poised between the rival disadvantages of giving the French their heads and trying to curb them.

In April the Reparation Commission at last did something to justify their existence. They assessed Germany's liability at roughly six-and-a-half thousand million pounds. This was about half the sum which the Allies had hitherto been trying to extract from the Germans, and about four times the sum which the Germans had offered in March.

The French government was headed by Aristide Briand, at heart a moderate man but subject to pressure from less moderate supporters. Briand traveled to London at the end of the month, accompanied by Foch. He announced that "the time had come for action," declared that France was ready to "act alone" if the British were still hesitant, and proposed that an ultimatum should be presented to the Germans, threatening occupation of the Ruhr if they did not agree to issue bonds for the required sum. On May 2 he sanctioned a call-up which added 140,000 men to the French Army, and next day Foch outlined a program for occupation of the Ruhr by six French infantry divisions, two cavalry divisions, a Belgian division, and any British troops that might be available.

This would have been a good moment for Lloyd George and Curzon to point out that, while the Allies might or might not be within their rights in occupying the Ruhr if the Germans were technically in default, the French and Belgians were certainly not entitled to prejudice the claims of Germany's other creditors by "acting alone." Unwilling to quarrel with Briand and risk having to deal with a still more unreasonable successor, they missed their opportunity. As usual, Lloyd George fell back on a compromise, asking merely that the Germans should be given a fortnight's grace. For the moment the Ruhr was saved, but only because the Germans accepted the ultimatum after enquiries through diplomatic channels had convinced them that they could expect no support from Britain or the United States if they held out.

Nevertheless the Allies did not have the last word. Germany's acceptance of their ultimatum was followed by a timely fall in the value of the mark, which had stood at 224 to the £ in January, and was down to 1,020 to the £ before the year was out. By the time the Washington Conference opened in November, the French saw that they were not going to get their money by accepting German bonds backed only by a declining currency.

Under the Washington naval agreements the five leading naval powers undertook to limit the size and tonnage of their battle fleets for ten years on terms which put the United States and Britain on an equal footing, with a combined strength substantially greater than the combined strength of the other three powers. Japan came next, with three-tenths of the strength which the Anglo-Saxon powers could wield between them, France and Italy last with enough ships to give them a small margin of superiority over the Japanese in the rather improbable event of their joining forces. All five powers agreed to build no new battleships during the ten years, the Japanese and the Americans renounced their building programs, and they and the British each scrapped about half a million tons of existing ships.

These restrictions applied, however, only to battleships and battlecruisers. No limitations were placed on cruisers in face of the argument of the British that they had more extensive trade routes to defend than other powers, and therefore must have more escort vessels. The British pressed for the abolition of submarines, which the Americans proposed to allot in the same ratio as battleships; but no agreement was reached since the French refused to consider either abolition or restriction, claiming that they had already conceded more than ought to have been asked of them. In terms of power politics, the most important consequences of the Washington talks were that Britain was forced by pressure from the United States, Australia, and Canada to give up hope of renewing her Japanese alliance, and that Japan abandoned her claim to a special position in Shantung province but could not be made to give up her interest in Manchuria.

These results were outwardly hailed as a triumph of moderation, reason, and good sense. Behind the scenes they led to fierce reproaches and repinings. Admirals David Beatty and Alfred Chatfield, the British naval delegates, cited expert opinion on both sides of the Atlantic in support of the thesis that the naval holiday would saddle Britain and the United States with enormously expensive and top-heavy replacement programs at the end of the ten years, and that meanwhile they would have to spend large sums on subsidies to shipyards and on patching up old ships. The implication that American wealth and British influence gave the English-speaking peoples the right to lay down the law to the rest of the world was deeply resented, especially by the French, who regarded proposals to limit or abolish submarines as evidence of an Anglo-Saxon plot to injure France. And the Japanese henceforward nourished an active dislike of the Western peoples who had first encouraged their ambitions and then turned against them.

Thereafter Anglo-French relations were shadowed by a growing suspicion in France that the British were more interested in currying favor with the Americans than in doing justice to French claims. The French knew that the Germans had not been well received when they appealed for American support in the spring. For a time they even had a faint hope that, since disarmament was in the air, they might be able to trade reduction of their army against renewal of the American guarantee. When they found at Washington that American opinion had turned against them, and that their German policy was now regarded with disfavor, they were more inclined to blame the sinister influence of the British than to accept the obvious inference that what the Americans disliked about their policy was that it had produced nothing but a sharp fall in the value of the mark.

These undercurrents were not lost on Lloyd George or on Briand. Both saw clearly that, after Washington, a bold stroke was needed to save the Anglo-French alliance. They saw, too, that only prompt action could prevent their policies from being trampled underfoot by reactionary forces on both sides of the Channel. The reparations problem was no longer a matter merely of squeezing money from the Germans, but of averting an economic avalanche which could ruin half Europe in a month. Europe had not recovered from the war and was in no state to withstand disasters. There were two million unemployed in Britain. There was deep discontent in France. And discontent in France was apt to take the form epitomized in Raymond Poincaré, the cautious, narrow-minded, intensely patriotic lawyer and former President of the Republic who was waiting to step into Briand's shoes.

Lloyd George had a plan to meet the situation. Always hopeful, he did not despair of enlisting American support. He was already planning a world conference at Genoa, at which the United States and Russia would be brought back into the fold and all outstanding economic, financial, and strategic problems would be settled on a basis of mutual give and take.

Nevertheless it was Briand who made the opening move. At first through diplomatic channels and later by direct negotiation with Lloyd George, he proposed that Britain should renew her lapsed guarantee and should widen it to include Poland as well as the French frontier. He also asked for a military convention defining the extent of British help. Lloyd George and Curzon were at one in thinking that the British public would not support a guarantee to Poland, but they held open the possibility of a broad pact to secure the French frontier. When Lloyd George met Briand at Cannes in January 1922 to discuss, among other matters, the program for Genoa, he took with him the draft of an agreement by which Britain would guarantee the existing Franco-German frontier for ten years.

But the offer came too late. Briand already faced allegations that his delegates had failed to outmaneuver the British at Washington. Lloyd George had made himself disliked in France by concluding a commercial agreement with Soviet Russia and by his obvious reluctance to press the Germans hard. Premature publication of the news that the Russians were to be asked to Genoa raised a storm of protest, and a newspaper photograph showing Lloyd George giving Briand a golf lesson did not help. Briand was hastily recalled to Paris and forced to resign. Before he could rally his forces and form a new government the President of the Republic sent, by pre-arrangement, for Poincaré.

Poincaré did not break off negotiations for a British guarantee, but he made his terms so stiff that they were not likely to be accepted. He insisted that the defense of France must be outside

France, not on French soil; that the British, French, and Belgian General Staffs should concert plans in advance; and that the three countries should give guarantees to Poland and Czechoslovakia. He also asked that the pact should last for thirty years, or at any rate for a minimum of twenty. These proposals were rejected by the British government, who were not willing to commit the country for more than fifteen years or to back Czechoslovakia or Poland.

Poincaré went on to wreck the Genoa Conference by trying to exclude from the agenda nearly everything that Lloyd George most wanted to discuss, and then refusing to attend in person. The Americans, unwilling to be brought back into the fold, declined even to be represented. When the conference was barely a week old, the Germans took a hand in their own undoing by making a separate pact with the Russians at Rapallo. Curzon, ill in bed and disapproving as strongly as the French of his chief's Russian policy, almost openly rejoiced that Lloyd George was "alone at Genoa with no F.O. to guide him," while Poincaré seized the opportunity to brandish the familiar threat that France would "act alone."

Concluding that Europe was heading for a fresh bout of violence and that financial pressure was their best means of averting it, American statesmen then gave a new twist to the situation by announcing that they proposed to claim repayment of the huge sums lent to the Allies during the war. This was bad news for the British, who were owed far more than they had borrowed, but whose chances of recovering anything from Soviet Russia were smaller than ever after Genoa. They responded by offering to forego all claims to reparations and war debts as part of a general settlement, but the gesture was not well received in Washington or Paris. They then issued the famous Balfour Note, in which they announced their intention of claiming no more from the Allies than was claimed from them. After that proposal had had an even worse reception, a mission headed by Stanley Baldwin left for Washington to make the best settlement it could.

The effect on the French of the American demand and the British response to it was the opposite of that intended. Instead of being sobered by the threat of financial pressure, Poincaré became more bellicose than ever. Faced with the likelihood of having to find large sums to satisfy his country's creditors, he seized German funds in French banks, expelled German residents from Alsace and Lorraine, and proclaimed his intention of providing himself with "productive pledges" by appropriating German assets in the Ruhr.

Meanwhile the sands were running out for Lloyd George. In May 1921 the Allies had publicly and officially declared themselves neutral in the war between Kemal's Turkish Nationalists and the Greek Army in Anatolia. It was nevertheless an open secret that the French and the Italians were courting Kemal, while the British were generally assumed to be pro-Greek. Even when Lloyd George was overtly trying to persuade Kemal to come to terms with his opponents, he allowed the Greeks to go on thinking that Britain was tacitly behind them. A growing impression that he had backed the wrong horse from the start was strengthened when the summer of 1922 brought signs that Kemal was daily improving his position with the aid of French and Italian arms and ammunition which supplemented his supplies from Russia. In August, Kemal launched an offensive which routed the Greek Army and left nothing between him and the Dardanelles but a single line of wire, a few hundred British troops, and a small French contingent with orders not to interfere.

The reckless courage with which Lloyd George inspired the more resolute of his colleagues at this awkward juncture led directly to his downfall. Insisting that Kemal's troops should not be allowed into Europe unless they first made peace, the Cabinet not only tried to rally the Dominions and a number of Continental powers behind proposals to defend the Straits, but ordered General Sir Charles Harington, the British commander on the spot, to deliver an ultimatum threatening war unless Kemal withdrew. Backed by Sir Horace Rumbold, the British High Commissioner in Constantinople, and supported at the last moment by the French, General Harington withheld the ultimatum but nonetheless persuaded Kemal's envoy to accept an armistice. Thus war was averted, honor was satisfied, and Harington and Rumbold earned the gratitude due to men who had saved the government from themselves without sacrificing the country's interests. But the ultimatum was too much for the rank-and-file of Lloyd George's Conservative supporters, already made restive by his high-handedness, his lavish bestowal of honors in return for contributions to his political war chest, and his negotiations with the Irish leaders. As the sequel to a meeting at the Carlton Club at which Stanley Baldwin made a strong case against the Coalition government, Lloyd George was forced to resign and was driven forever from high office.

It thus fell to a Conservative government, led at first by Bonar Law, to fight the last round of the battle with Poincaré. And it was Lloyd George's critic Stanley Baldwin who became Prime Minister when Bonar Law was forced by mortal illness to retire a few months later.

The new government, fortified by a general election which gave the Conservative party a clear lead, took office on November 16, 1922, with Curzon still at the Foreign Office and Lloyd George an impotent spectator of events. Next day Curzon left for Lausanne to make a settlement with Turkey which left Kemal in possession but kept him out of the arms of Russia.

Three weeks later the Allies met in London to discuss fresh reparations proposals based on the recommendations of a team of international experts appointed by the German government. Poincaré brushed the proposals aside and reaffirmed his intention of occupying the Ruhr, appropriating German customs receipts, exploiting State mines and forests, and seizing more than half the capital of the dyestuffs industry. He then returned to Paris and arranged that the Reparation Commission should declare Germany in default with respect to deliveries of timber under the reparations clauses of the Versailles Treaty.

In conference with his advisers, Poincaré expounded his plan with all the assurance of a man who knew everything and understood nothing. The occupation of the Rhine ports two years earlier, although useful since it secured the gateway to the Ruhr, had made the Allies look and feel foolish because the necessity of strict compliance with the law had been overlooked, and because no one had remembered until the last moment to recruit the customs officials and other civilian functionaries needed to enforce sanctions. Those errors would not be repeated. Already declared in default, this time the Germans would know exactly where they stood. Not only customs officials but a band of expert technicians and administrators, the Mission Interalliée de Controle des Usines et des Mines, would form the nucleus of the expedition. Each man would know exactly what he had to do and how to do it.

Reminded by his military advisers that the Ruhr was a vast agglomeration of densely populated townships, a warren of streets, factories and houses where resistance to an occupying force could be prolonged for many weeks, Poincaré almost smiled at the simplicity of soldiers who did not understand the law and could never stop thinking in terms of skirmishes and battles. He was not going to make war on Germany. The sending of an interallied mission to seize productive pledges was no more an act of war than the sending of a sheriff's officer to execute a judgment was an act of war. Resistance would be contrary to law, and hence absurd. The Germans would be told in advance that no harm would come to them as long as the required assets were handed over in due form. Why should they put themselves in the wrong by making difficulties? A few battalions would be needed to give solemnity to the proceedings, perhaps even to punish isolated acts of violence by extremists. But essentially the affair would be a matter for civilians, not for soldiers.

When Poincaré's plan was put before the Allies at the beginning of January 1923 it met with a cool reception from the British. Bonar Law was a successful businessman whose formative years had been spent in the Glasgow metal market. He had no difficulty in understanding Poincaré's views, but he did not share them. A calm, reflective man who had lost two sons in the war and whose instinct was always to conciliate rather than provoke, the Prime Minister had no taste for violence masquerading in a lawyer's robe. Because of his commercial affiliations, and because he valued his good name and the good name of the British Empire, he was determined that no government which he headed should ever be justly accused of putting financial advantage before morality. He told Poincaré flatly that the British government could take no part in the enterprise. The Anglo-French alliance was thus tacitly dissolved, and French journalists recorded a *rupture cordiale*. Almost simultaneously the Belgians agreed to join the French, the Italians promised a few technicians, and the mark fell to 81,200 to the £.

The French were due to move on January 11, the day after the third anniversary of the coming into force of the Versailles Treaty. On January 10, General Henry T. Allen, commanding the United States Army of Occupation on the Rhine, hauled down his flag at Ehrenbreitstein and marched his troops out of the Rhineland. On the same day the American representative on the Rhineland High Commission, a civilian body which had hitherto administered the occupied zones on behalf of the United States, Great Britain, France, and Belgium as trustees for the Allied and Associated Powers, resigned his post. Outvoting the British High Commissioner, the French and Belgians took the opportunity to pass a resolution purporting to weld all the occupied zones, the Ruhr included, into a single Franco-Belgian zone. Thereupon the British government instructed their local commissioners and service chiefs to disregard the orders of the High Commission and stay firmly where they were.

On the appointed day Poincaré's debt collectors moved into the Ruhr, escorted by French and Belgian troops. Forewarned by Poincaré himself, the German directors of the Ruhr Coal Syndicate had prudently withdrawn to Hamburg to escape service of the writ. Poincaré's envoys were forced to deal with local authorities and subordinate officials who could truthfully claim that they knew nothing of international law and had no authority to hand over anything to anyone. General Jean Degoutte, commanding the French and Belgian troops, was soon obliged to ask for reinforcements. Before long a hundred thousand French and Belgian soldiers were quartered in the Ruhr, with a hostile population watching all their movements and a disapproving British Army of the Rhine commanding their communications with the French Rhineland zone. Practically the entire working population willingly obeyed orders from Berlin to down tools indefinitely rather

than do anything for the invaders, whose claim to have the law
on their side was sharply challenged in a British note which the
German authorities distributed throughout the length and breadth
of Germany. Even when a fortieth of the inhabitants had been expelled and more than two thousand killed or wounded in clashes
with the occupying troops, productive pledges were as far away as
ever.

Throughout this astonishing struggle between six million unarmed Germans and a hundred thousand armed Frenchmen and
Belgians, the policy of the British government was to leave the
world in no doubt that they regarded the occupation as a violation
of the rights of Germany's creditors, encourage the German
government to maintain their authority and self-respect, and work
for a compromise favorable to the Germans by urging them to
make proposals which would help Poincaré to climb down without too much loss of face. In spite of an unhelpful press, the incorrigible tendency of German statesmen to overplay their hand,
and other obstacles, they succeeded in keeping Germany from
sliding into Communism or dictatorship. On the other hand, they
had no power to turn the French and Belgians out. Poincaré was
therefore able to insist that passive resistance should be called off
before any proposal could be entertained, and in September the
German government agreed to countermand the general strike
and resume deliveries in kind.

It was characteristic of Poincaré that, having gained his point
but won no productive pledges, he had no solution of the reparations problem to propose. Theoretically the Ruhr was at his mercy,
but still he could think of no way of extracting a penny from the
Germans unless they offered it. "Even when Poincaré catches the
right train," said an Italian diplomatist, "he misses the right sta-
tion."

Nevertheless his barren victory did have a sequel. The problem
of reparations had always been linked, for Frenchmen especially,
with the problem of security. And security meant to Frenchmen a
frontier on the Rhine and a divided Germany. Financially worthless and economically disastrous though it was, the stranglehold on
Western Germany which French and Belgian troops had gained

in recent months might still yield a dividend in political advantage. With Poincaré's tacit consent if not with his express approval, French and Belgian agents made a series of clumsy attempts in the autumn of 1923 to set up separatist governments in the Rhineland and the Palatinate. In October and November a whole crop of autonomous republics was reported to have sprung to life in regions controlled by French and Belgian troops. That these were spontaneous movements of revolt against Prussian rule might have been credible five years earlier when the German Empire was on its deathbed; it was not credible in 1923. Within a few weeks all these outgrowths of foreign intrigue and domestic treachery withered away in face of unshakable evidence that they had been foisted on the inhabitants by the occupying armies and would never have existed if thousands of local officials who objected to them had not been dismissed or deported without reason or excuse. But they left behind them an ugly memory of the lengths to which the French had been prepared to go to weaken Germany.

In every respect, financial and economic as well as moral, the occupation of the Ruhr was thus an appalling calamity for France and Germany alike. When patriotic fervor died and the French turned to count their gains and losses, they found that there were no gains. Poincaré's assertion of their rights had brought them less than nothing, since even reparations in kind had been suspended for many months. On the other side of the ledger, it had cost them stagnation in industries trading with the Ruhr, caused a sharp fall in the value of the franc, and left them to reap a harvest of hatred such as no French statesman before Poincaré had sown even at the bitterest moments of the war.

As for the Germans, the evils they suffered, and would continue to suffer, were immeasurable. For the moment Germany was ruined financially, industrially, and economically. As a nation she was destined to win her way back to prosperity with startling swiftness, but some Germans would never be prosperous again and some assets lost in the dark days of the Ruhr would never be recovered. The mark, already tottering when the occupation began, plunged by the end of it to such depths that a whole suitcase-full of paper currency was needed to buy a loaf of bread. Thousands of small investors saw their entire capital wiped out in a few hours, so that a man who at breakfast time believed himself well-cushioned against want had nothing by the afternoon but the price of a drink to drown his sorrows. Thousands of men and women who lived on fixed incomes found suddenly that they had no incomes which would keep them in anything but matches and shoelaces. A great part of the comfortable middle-class which had hitherto given stability to the State because it had a stake in the country and was therefore a calculable factor in the electoral balance sheet was deprived at one blow of that stake and became therefore an incalculable factor. And that was a calamity not only for Germany but for the world.

6

LOCARNO

ON THE FIFTH ANNIVERSARY OF THE ARMISTICE, THE OUTLOOK FOR Europe seemed unutterably bleak. The men who promised a new world of faith and hope had labored for five years to bring forth chaos and despair. The twin problems of reparations and French security were still unsolved. Until they were solved there would be no faith and no hope.

Yet answers to both problems were found within the next two years. They were not even particularly new answers. They were foreshadowed in proposals made long before the occupation of the Ruhr. They were implicit in British policy from the moment in 1919 when Lloyd George urged the Allied and Associated Powers to do everything they could to put Germany on her legs again. If anything was remarkable about the events of the Locarno era it was not that they happened, but that the statesmen who saw that they must be made to happen took so long about their work. Given comparable resources, even the most reactionary of eighteenth-century rulers might have been expected to achieve their aims more swiftly and with less dire consequences for their subjects.

When the Germans were first threatened with occupation of the Ruhr in the spring of 1921 and appealed to the United States for sympathy, they offered to submit to expert and impartial investigation of their capacity to pay the six-and-a-half thousand million pounds demanded by the Allies. Although the reply was not encouraging, they followed up their own suggestion by themselves appointing a committee of international experts to look into their affairs. It was on the report of that committee that they afterward based the proposals which Poincaré swept aside in favor his productive pledges.

After an interval of more than eighteen months the United States government sounded a tardy echo to the German suggestion. In a speech at New Haven on December 29, 1922, Charles E. Hughes, the Secretary of State, remarked that there ought to be some way of assessing Germany's capacity to pay, and added that the Harding administration would not object to the appointment of a distinguished American citizen to a committee of enquiry composed of experts. The speech came too late to save the Ruhr, but it was not altogether wasted. When Curzon at last decided in the spring of 1923 that reparations was a subject worthy of his talents, he was reminded by Lord D'Abernon, the British Ambassador in Berlin, that a committee of enquiry might provide a better means of bringing America back into the fold than any suggested by Lloyd George. Intent on rubbing home the lesson that the Reparation Commission was not an impartial body and therefore did not fill the bill, he took the hint. At the height of the occupation of the Ruhr he strongly advised the Germans to make an offer, and eventually he induced them to state categorically that they would abide by the recommendations of an impartial committee as to how much they should pay and in what manner they should pay.

This was a triumph for British policy. To all appearances it was thrown away when Curzon failed in the following September to ward off Poincaré's demand that the Germans should renounce passive resistance before any offer could be considered. In reality it was not thrown away. As the French had no proposals to make, the German offer stood. In November, Poincaré grudgingly agreed that an impartial committee should be set up.

In spite of much that happened later, the appointment of the Dawes Committee was a turning-point in European history. At a stroke the reparations question was transferred from the council chamber to the countinghouse. It ceased to be an issue between statesmen and became a problem in accountancy. The committee was headed by a distinguished American soldier, but it took its cue from a consortium of bankers and financiers. These men were not interested in scoring debating-points or stirring up national passions. They were interested in assets, liabilities, potential markets, and the ratio between costs of production and probable returns. Above all they were interested in the financial solvency of a concern which they might be asked to underwrite or might wish to underwrite. Under their guidance Germany's affairs were expertly scrutinized for the first time from the point of view of an investor rather than a debt collector or a theoretical economist.

These investigations led to the conclusion that Germany could not be expected to pay reparations unless she were first helped to raise her income to a point at which she could afford to pay them. They showed, too, that such help was not likely to be wasted. Inflation had wiped out Germany's internal debt. No internal debt meant low taxes and a corresponding incentive to producers. A new Finance Minister, Hans Luther, had just joined forces with a new President of the Reichsbank, Hjalmar Schacht, to throw "a bridge between chaos and hope" by issuing a new unit of currency, the rentenmark, to replace the worthless mark. Ripe for a fresh start, with physical assets unimpaired and millions of diligent workers asking nothing better than steady employment after all their troubles, German industry promised good returns to men farsighted enough to risk their capital on its prospects of success.

The committee recommended that Germany should take advantage of this state of affairs by raising nearly eight hundred million pounds in foreign markets, chiefly by mortgaging her industries and the State railways. Part of the money would be used as working capital and to back the rentenmark, part to finance annual reparations payments on a scale rising from fifty million pounds in the first year to a hundred-and-twenty-five millions by 1929. At that rate two generations would be needed to pay off a capital sum of six-and-a-half thousand million pounds with accrued interest, but the chances were that the Allies would agree to cancel the debt long before the end of that time. With the prudence of their kind, the sponsors of the scheme took care to safeguard the interests of investors by insisting that the annuities should be suspended whenever payment of them threatened to depreciate the currency.

Meanwhile popular opinion in England and France was turning against the undiluted nationalism of recent years. Toward the end of 1923 Stanley Baldwin appealed haltingly to the public to desert the standard of free trade, and was defeated at the polls. In January he resigned in favor of the first Socialist government ever to rule at Westminster. Ramsay MacDonald, a pacifist and one-time member of the Second Communist International but at heart a romantic Tory like Baldwin, decided to combine the roles of Prime Minister and Foreign Secretary. Across the Channel, Poincaré fell a few months later, discredited by his Pyrrhic victory in the Ruhr, the weakness of the franc, and his reluctance to face the awkward issue of taxation. His successor, Edouard Herriot, was a tweed-clad Radical who smoked a pipe, admired the English, and had a reputation for rugged honesty and sturdy common sense. Neither MacDonald nor Herriot led a majority government, the former depending on Liberal support and the latter on a loose coalition between his party and the Socialist group led by Léon Blum.

Given a free choice among British and French statesmen, in all probability the sponsors of the Dawes Plan would not have chosen a Socialist from Lossiemouth and a Radical from Lyons to pass judgment on the plans of international finance for Germany's rehabilitation. As things turned out, they could hardly have hit upon a better combination. Determined to break with the ill-fated policy of Poincaré and his *Bloc Nationale*, Herriot joined MacDonald in welcoming the proposals. He insisted on the right to impose sanctions, but agreed that it should be exercised only in the event of willful default and after arbitration. Dr. Wilhelm Marx and Gustav Stresemann, the German Chancellor and Foreign Minister respectively, were then invited to join MacDonald and Herriot in Downing Street. They began by demanding immediate withdrawal of French and Belgian troops from the Ruhr, but ended by accepting withdrawal after twelve months and a lighter occupation in the meantime. After discussing further means of reducing tension the statesmen dispersed, well pleased to have attended the first high-level conference since the war at which real agreement between the Allies and the Germans was achieved.

In due course the bargain was ratified, and Germany awoke from a nightmare which had haunted her since the Armistice. Henceforth she could be sure that, except in the unlikely event of her being declared willfully in default, her ultimate recovery would not be impeded by threats of violence. Outside Germany, facts which had long been obvious to a few became obvious to everyone. Large numbers of Englishmen and Frenchmen saw for the first time that only a prosperous and contented Germany could serve their interests. Yet it was a pity that they saw it only after the blindness of French policy and the weakness of British diplomacy had put millions of people out of work, sown lasting bitterness in German hearts, robbed scores of thousands of Germans of their savings, and driven out of Germany more than three hundred million pounds of capital withdrawn by investors lucky enough to get their money away before the crash came.

Before the meeting in London broke up, MacDonald and Herriot discussed with Marx and Stresemann a plan to give the moribund League of Nations a new lease of life as an instrument of Franco-German conciliation. All of them welcomed the proposal, although not all for precisely the same reasons. MacDonald saw in a revived and strengthened League a means of calming French and German fears, perhaps even of persuading the French to lead the way toward a general scaling-down of armaments by reducing the peacetime strength of their own army. The French welcomed an opportunity of strengthening their ties with Central European allies who were already keen supporters of the League. For the Germans, membership of the League offered a way of escape from the isolation and exclusion from the family of nations to which they had been sentenced at Versailles. Their view was that, having paid the penalty of defeat by surrendering all their overseas possessions, one-seventh of their homeland, and the greater part of their armed forces, they ought not to be made to pay a second time by being treated as outsiders.

Except in the eyes of the smaller powers who still regarded the Covenant as their charter, the fortunes of the League had sunk to a low ebb by 1924. The League had stopped a war between Yugoslavia and Albania in 1921, but it had not stopped the Greco-Turkish war, or a war between Poland and Russia in 1920 in which the Poles had been saved from a humiliating disaster only by the timely intervention of a French military mission. Nor had it done anything to adjust a quarrel between the Poles and the Lithuanians about Vilno. Yet all these were cases in which the League might have been expected to assert its authority if it had had any.

The arrival of the British and French Prime Ministers at Geneva in the late summer of 1924 to attend the Fifth Assembly of the League was therefore an event of some importance. MacDonald made an eloquent and impassioned speech in which he urged the nations to scrap their separate treaties and disband their armies. He then interested himself in the drafting, chiefly by the Czechoslovakian Foreign Minister Dr. Eduard Benes, of a document called the Protocol of the League of Nations, which reaffirmed and amplified the obligation on member-states to go to the aid of victims of aggression. But not even Ramsay MacDonald's dialectical skill enabled him to explain how the disbandment of armies could be reconciled with world-wide obligations to make war, and in the end he did not succeed either in persuading Europe to disarm or in getting his own country to accept the Protocol.

Soon afterward MacDonald was swept from office by the backwash of a Communist scare, and Baldwin returned to power with a new determination to hold his party together through thick and thin. Relegating Curzon to a minor post, he chose as Foreign Secretary Austen Chamberlain, a loyal and disinterested supporter who could be relied upon not to split the Tory vote by raising untimely issues, as his famous father Joseph Chamberlain had done nearly twenty years earlier, and as Baldwin himself had done in 1923. Almost simultaneously Hans Luther, the former Finance Minister, succeeded Marx as German Chancellor, with Stresemann still Foreign Minister and the ablest member of the government. A typical bull-necked Prussian in appearance, and a monarchist at heart although he supported the Republic, Stresemann was a subtle and farseeing statesman who was not afraid to take a risk. "I want," he said when asked to define his policy, "to be the German who makes peace with France."

But Stresemann also wanted something more. He wanted to draw Germany closer to Western Europe, restore her lost influence, wipe out the memory of Rapallo, and thus end a situation which gave Germany nothing but the choice between utter friendlessness and an unnatural alliance with Soviet Russia. Revival of the British guarantee to France, which Austen Chamberlain was said to favor, would be worse than useless to Germany if it left her still isolated and alone. A bold step was needed to avert such a calamity, and Stresemann took it. On February 9, 1925, the German government proposed to the Allies that France and Germany should agree to respect the Franco-German frontier as defined in the Versailles Treaty, and that Britain should undertake to support either country against unprovoked aggression by the other. At the same time the Germans made it clear that, while they did not regard the Central European settlement as final, their intention was not to go to war about it but to press for revision by peaceful means.

These proposals, previously rejected by the French when they were tentatively put forward before the occupation of the Ruhr, were well received in London. For a time the French continued to hold back, suspecting a plot to detach them from their allies in Central Europe. A change of government, which put Paul Painlevé in power with Briand as Foreign Minister, was needed before they could be persuaded to attend a conference on the subject. It was not until October that representatives of Belgium, Czechoslovakia, France, Germany, Great Britain, Italy, and Poland met at Locarno to sign the pacts which convinced Europe that at last the quarrel begun in 1914 was over. Soon afterward the ironmasters and coalowners of Lorraine and the Ruhr concluded an agreement which restored their prewar association. In the following September, Germany was admitted to the League of Nations. If world peace was still a long way off, at least there seemed to be a reasonable prospect of a long spell of peace in Europe.

7

MUSIC WITHOUT INSTRUMENTS

AS LONG AGO AS THE EIGHTEENTH CENTURY FREDERICK THE GREAT RE-marked that diplomacy without arms was music without instruments. Yet diplomacy without arms was the method by which British governments found themselves promoting their foreign policies for a great part of the period between the wars.

Soon after the Armistice the Lloyd George government instructed the service departments to assume, when they prepared their estimates for the coming year, that there would be no great war involving the British Empire for at least ten years. The rule was not meant to apply to any situation except that existing at the time, but it proved so convenient a means of keeping service leaders in their places that successive governments reaffirmed it at intervals for more than a decade. Consequently there was never a time between the Armistice and 1932 when any strategic proposal, no matter how necessary or how reasonable it might seem to its sponsors and even to the government, could not be turned down on the pretext that it would take less than ten years to complete, and that therefore a start could safely be deferred. Moreover the rule, if carried to its logical extreme, would have led to the absurd conclusion that the chances of peace or war were unaffected by the strength and disposition of the armed forces and that all strategic planning was thus a waste of time.

In practice the rule was not carried so far; if it had been, its logical fallacy would have been apparent and it might have been abandoned sooner. As things were, its effect was that the last word in matters of national defense was always with the Chancellor of the Exchequer and the Treasury. Repeated emphasis on economy led to the paradoxical situation that, while British governments continued to pursue exactly the same long-term aims as their predecessors had followed in the days when national security was regarded as a first charge on the public revenue, they made the attainment of those aims impossible by refusing to carry out measures needed to make their policies effective. All responsible statesmen, irrespective of party, accepted the principle that war anywhere in the world was a threat to the country's world-wide commercial and financial interests, and agreed that the overriding aim of British policy must be to preserve peace. British governments before the war had tried to achieve that aim by making the navy overwhelmingly strong and providing only a small army to act as a fire brigade in case of accident; but the experience of 1914 had shown that a small army was not enough, and the occupation of the Ruhr by the French in spite of British protests had rubbed in the lesson. Yet all governments which held office during the next decade and more were so determined to save money on the armed forces that they robbed themselves of the means of making their diplomacy effective. In 1914 a thoroughly pacific, and even pacifist, Liberal government had failed to keep the peace in Europe although they had a formidable battle fleet ready for instant action and could order six infantry divisions and a cavalry division across the Channel at short notice. Sixteen years later an equally pacific Socialist government were in a far worse position to exercise a restraining influence on the forces of disorder. Warned by their advisers that extremist movements were on the march in Germany, and well aware that trouble had been brewing in the Far East for many years, they faced the knowledge that the navy was not equipped to fight even a second-class power, and that even to mobilize one infantry division and a cavalry brigade for a Continental war would strain the army's resouces to the utmost.

At the same time, the passion for economy had important effects on the pattern of strategic thinking. Where money was scarce, statesmen readily succumbed to the lure of cheap weapons.

When the Royal Air Force was threatened with absorption by the other services after the First World War, it owed its survival largely to the dogged vehemence with which the Chief of the Air Staff, Air Chief Marshal Sir Hugh Trenchard, urged the case for independence. But Trenchard's arguments would probably have been ineffective if he had failed to persuade his political masters that an independent air force, and especially a bomber force not tied to the army and the navy, was an inexpensive substitute for a balanced strategy. As British bombing between 1914 and 1918 was admitted even by the keenest advocates of the bomber to have achieved very little, it was fortunate for the Air Staff that they were able to point to German successes as evidence of what a bomber force could accomplish where its users thought purely in terms of immediate results.

In two daylight raids on London in the summer of 1917, thirty-six German bombers had inflicted about six hundred casualties on the civil population without losing a single aircraft. The conclusion drawn by the Air Staff was not that a country with a capital as vulnerable as London would do well to think twice before endorsing such methods, but that the ability to retaliate in kind if similar attacks were made in a future war was a prime requisite of British strategy. Reluctant to spend money on troops or ships but unwilling to take the responsibility of leaving the country altogether unprotected, Lloyd George and his successors accepted Trenchard's argument in spite of protests from orthodox strategists who pointed out that wars were not won by killing civilians and that there was no substitute for fleets and armies. Thus the country found itself committed, at a time when no scientific assessment of the value of strategic bombing had been attempted, to the theory that its future security would depend largely on the possession of a bomber force strong enough to deter a potential aggressor or at least punish him severely.

When that theory was first adopted by a British government in 1922, the only country in a position to attack Britain from the air was France. Notwithstanding differences of opinion about reparations and also about Syria, France was extremely unlikely to go to war with Britain, not only because the French still regarded the British as allies and hoped for a British guarantee, but also because a French air attack on London would have invited a devastating bombardment of French naval harbors by the relatively strong British Navy. In any case war between France and Britain seemed to the majority of Englishmen as fantastically improbable as it did to the majority of Frenchmen. Such was the fascination exercised on the minds of postwar statesmen by the almost untried weapon of air power that Trenchard was nevertheless able to persuade the veteran Arthur Balfour, whom Lloyd George had deputed to preside over a standing subcommittee of the Committee of Imperial Defence, that the existence of a French metropolitan air force of six hundred bombers and fighters put Britain in a position of dangerous diplomatic weakness.

Not entirely convinced by Balfour and Trenchard but determined in any case to keep the aircraft industry alive, the Lloyd George government agreed, in August 1922, to form a small metropolitan air force of fourteen bomber and nine fighter squadrons as a counterweight to the French Air Force. In the following year their successors, alarmed by Poincaré's truculence and the occupation of the Ruhr, decided to set a new target of thirty-five bomber and seventeen fighter squadrons by the end of 1928. The proportion of bombers to fighters in both schemes was purely arbitrary, but reflected Trenchard's view that safety in air warfare depended on the ability to hit back. The Conservative government claimed that the new scheme would give air parity with France, whose metropolitan air force was said by Trenchard to be due for a big expansion, but they did not explain how parity was to be achieved by building in five years' time as many squadrons as the French already had. Ultimately the scheme had some value as the scaffolding on which an effective system of air defense was built, but meanwhile it had the fatal effect of diverting attention from the lack of an expeditionary force, which really was a source of diplomatic weakness. Significantly, increases in air force votes during the next few years were offset several times over by reduced expenditure on both the Army and the Navy.

The response to Locarno was also characteristic of the muddled attitude to strategic questions of most British governments between the wars. The Locarno pacts reduced tension in Europe and established good relations between France and Germany for the first time since 1914, but they nonetheless saddled Britain with an inescapable obligation to send troops to the Continent in the event of a fresh dispute. Logically they ought therefore to have been the signal for a radical reorganization of the British Army in the direction of greater mobility if not of greater over-all strength. In practice they were made the pretext for further economies. No attempt was made to strengthen the Army or prepare part of it for prompt intervention in Europe, and completion of the air expansion scheme, already deferred once, was put back until 1936. Nor was anything done to awaken the public to a sense of its responsibilities. Soothed by such signs of apparent health as the swift collapse of a general strike and the winning of the Schneider Trophy, Englishmen believed themselves to be still living at the center of a powerful empire whose moral leadership of the white man's world was undisputed. In fact they had become, and would remain until they put their affairs in orders, inhabitants of a small island kingdom whose armed strength was insufficient to protect her interests and whose influence rested on diminished wealth and a declining reputation.

If the promise of Locarno partly justified statesmen in playing down the risk of war in Europe, there was no such excuse where the Far Eastern danger was concerned. The British delegation returned from the Washington Conference in 1921 convinced that the policy to which the government had committed them meant trouble with Japan. They were so obviously right that plans were made soon afterward to develop Singapore as a first-class naval base and send the main fleet there on the outbreak of war or earlier. As the voyage from home waters would take several weeks, it was essential that Singapore, and perhaps also Hong Kong, should be made strong enough to hold out for a considerable period without reinforcement. The fleet might have to fight its way to its destination, and so must reach Far Eastern waters in fighting trim. This meant that ample stocks of fuel must be held ready on the margin of the danger area and would need to be defended against naval bombardment or capture by a landing force. The result was a heavy program of capital expenditure on harbor installations, defense works and reserves of fuel oil, and an inevitable clash between strategic needs and demands for economy.

At the same time, financial barriers were not the only obstacle. Governments differed as to the urgency of the Far Eastern problem. Service experts argued interminably about the relative merits of guns and aircraft for seaward defense. The possibility of a landward attack on Singapore was not entirely ruled out, but was thought to be a negligible risk. In 1924 Ramsay MacDonald's first Socialist government held up the scheme in the hope that general disarmament might make it unnecessary. Reminded a year later that the much-publicized Locarno spirit did not apply to relations with Japan, the Conservative Foreign Secretary, Sir Austen Chamberlain, replied that trouble in the Far East was likely to be preceded by danger signs in Europe, and that Britain and America would be able to protect their interests by presenting a united front. Assured that there was no need to hurry, experts continued their debates, and ministers saw no reason to load their budgets with unwelcome additions to expenditure. It was not until 1928 that a detailed scheme of seaward defense for Singapore received final approval, and even then the decision proved not to be final, after all. Returning to power in 1929, Ramsay MacDonald and his colleagues agreed to postpone all major measures of rearmament, Singapore included, in view of a disarmament conference due to assemble at Geneva in 1932. In the same year, and again in 1930, the government reaffirmed the familiar assumption that there would be no great war involving the British Empire for at least ten years.

Reluctance to face facts was no less pronounced in Washington than in London. Disenchanted by the breakdown of the Wilsonian experiment, the American people were not inclined to take an active part in European squabbles. Both the Harding and the Coolidge administrations helped to foster an impression that America could opt out of world affairs, except insofar as a legitimate regard for her interests might compel her to keep a wary eye on European attempts to exploit her generosity. It was tempting to believe that a hundred million Americans, whose fathers had

prospered by selling their exportable surpluses to Europe and
absorbing Europe's surplus population, could live at ease behind
a dollar curtain of tariffs and quotas which kept out European
goods and reduced the flow of European immigrants to a trickle.
Shocked by the failure of European statesmen to solve the problems of the Old World as permanently and effectively as American statesmen believed themselves to have solved those of the New
World, many honest citizens of the United States genuinely
thought that nothing more was needed to cure Europe's economic
ills than that the Allies should pay their war debts, from which
a benevolent Uncle Sam had lopped five thousand million dollars
while pursuing fiscal policies which debarred the debtors from
earning the seven thousand million dollars still needed to square
the account by selling goods to the United States. Yet economic
isolationism did not prevent enterprising Americans from claiming
their share of world markets or raising the cry of colonialism
where they were threatened with exclusion. And hand-in-hand
with economic isolationism went the comfortable conviction
that the Washington Conference had settled American strategic
problems for all time by putting foreign nations firmly in their
places.

For a time the policy of America for the Americans worked
astonishingly well, at any rate so far as material progress was concerned. Stimulated by techniques of mass-suggestion unknown in
Europe, domestic consumption kept pace so well with an expanding production that economists began to speak of two cars
in the garage of every American home as an ideal attainable
within a generation. If official relations between the Old World
and the New were not particularly happy, they were not tested by
any major conflict. Deprived by the new immigration laws of the
customary outlet for the quarter of a million subjects whom she
had settled annually in the United States before the war, Italy
was driven to desperate expedients to feed her surplus population;
but her troubles did not seriously threaten American well-being,
and to keep her on the rails was a job which could safely be left to
British and French statesmen. When the United States defied international custom by extending American territorial waters nine

miles beyond the usual limits as part of her campaign against bootleggers, the nations contented themselves with the philosophical reflection that such high-handedness seemed hardly consistent with American concern for the freedom of the seas, but that apparently Prohibition, like Bolshevism, was a new factor in world affairs which had to be accepted. And what might have become a war of propaganda in the Middle East was averted when the British government bought off the American oil lobby by offering American oil companies a quarter-share in Iraqi oil as consolation for their failure to obtain a valid concession from the Turkish authorities before the war.

Meanwhile neither Americans nor Englishmen saw any inconsistency in loudly proclaiming their devotion to peace while issuing open invitations to aggressors by reducing their armaments to levels utterly at variance with their responsibilities. In 1928 the United States government proposed that the powers should subscribe to the Kellogg Pact, which bound them to renounce war as an instrument of policy and settle all disputes by peaceful means. Sixty nations signed this egregious document, the British government entering a reservation with respect to the first provision. Yet all knew that war, or at least the threat of war, was still the only ultimate sanction for international law, and that the great powers could no more afford to contract out of their obligations to go to war if the need arose than a rich man could afford to contract out of his obligation to support the police and the judiciary. Such declarations seemed to many people harmless; in reality they were not harmless, for they fostered the illusion, always prevalent in democracies, that nothing but good will was needed to silence the thunder and prevent the rain from coming through the roof.

The happy belief of all good Americans that peace and prosperity were a permanent heritage from pioneering forebears received apparent confirmation when, in that same year, the New York stock market reported an upward trend in the prices of practically all domestic holdings. Attracted by the lure of capital gains, large numbers of speculators began to play the market with borrowed funds. Borne skyward on an upsurge of boundless faith in the inevitability of progress, prices continued to spiral as more and more investors joined the scramble for easy money. Instead of discouraging immoderate speculation by restricting credit, banks lent freely to domestic borrowers in accordance with the then orthodox belief that nothing was more fatal in boom conditions than to undermine confidence by putting on the brake. Conversely, holders of foreign loans began to recall them in order to take advantage of opportunities at home, thus depressing overseas markets and so widening the gap between the quoted prices and real values of holdings in concerns whose profits were bound to depend to some extent on the state of world trade.

Clearly, such conditions could not last forever. A time was bound to come when even the most hopeful of stockbrokers would feel obliged to warn prospective buyers that certain securities would be seriously overvalued if they were marked up further. In the light of experience it seemed possible to predict the subsequent course of events with reasonable assurance. For a few days prices would fall sharply as nervous investors unloaded their holdings, they would then seesaw for a time, and finally they would become stable at a few points below the peak level. A few speculators would lose their money, a few genuine investors would profit at their expense, and everything would then go on much as it had done before the boom.

Unfortunately this boom did not work out in that way. By the time the market reached its peak, a large number of securities were so grossly overvalued that the fall, when it came, was catastrophic. In the last week of October 1929 the bubble burst. Trading on Wall Street surpassed all previous limits as scores of thousands of disillusioned plungers threw their holdings on the market in a desperate attempt to cover their borrowings before it was too late. Within a few days the average price of all securities quoted on the New York Stock Market fell by nearly half. Many speculators lost all they had, and more; an enormous number of genuine investors saw their capital reduced to a fraction of its former value.

The result was a mammoth slump which soon affected almost every country in the world. At first in the United States and later everywhere, the demand for consumer goods fell off because many people had suddenly become too poor to buy more than the bare minimum. Factories and showrooms closed, throwing millions of people out of work and still further decreasing purchasing-power. Producers were left with huge stocks of raw materials and manufactured goods which they could not sell in their usual markets and tried to dump abroad. Countries without tariffs were compelled to impose them in order to save their industries from ruin. Commodity prices fell by 1931 to levels unheard of in modern times. Withdrawal of American capital threatened Germany with bankruptcy, and a disastrous bank failure in Austria increased her troubles. The French government were willing to help, but only in return for political benefits which Dr. Heinrich Brüning, the German Chancellor, dared not grant for fear of putting himself out of power and Adolf Hitler in. In Britain the number of unemployed rose to more than two millions for the first time since the early 1920s. A big deficit on the budget was predicted, and the gold reserves fell sharply. The Socialist government gave place to a National government pledged to keep the pound on the gold standard and put through cuts in unemployment benefit and the pay of public servants. Nevertheless the drain on gold continued, a small-scale naval mutiny caused by the failure of some commanding officers to explain the reasons for the pay cuts did not help to steady the pound, and in September the gold standard had to be abandoned, after all.

Inevitably, the troubles of the West did not go unnoticed in quarters where Western statesmen had made themselves none too popular. In the midst of their perplexities, the outgoing Socialist government in Britain found leisure to reaffirm the ten-year rule for the last time. Only a few months later Japan brought a major war within measurable distance by beginning warlike operations in Manchuria. Early in 1932 Japanese troops landed on the mainland of China only a few miles from the International Settlement at Shanghai, and attacked the city without troubling themselves overmuch about foreign interests. Singapore was nothing like ready to receive the British fleet, even if the fleet could have sailed without adequate stocks of war material and with every

expectation of finding its fuel reserves in Japanese hands by the
time it reached them. The small British naval force already in
Chinese waters was at the mercy of the Japanese. Nor was there
any alternative to Singapore, for there was not a port or a naval
harbor throughout the British Empire whose seaward defenses
were not outranged by the armament of a modern cruiser. Since
the Americans, too, were unready for war, the united front predicted by Austen Chamberlain was confined to offers of mediation by the United States and an appeal to the League of
Nations by the British. The League condemned Japan as the
aggressor, but no nation was eager to risk war by threatening
sanctions. Thus the grandiose plans which stemmed from the
Washington Conference collapsed at the first hint of danger, and
the Japanese were confirmed in their opinion that the Anglo-Saxon
peoples had lost the will to resist aggression and were no longer
formidable.

8

SHANGHAI TO THE RHINELAND

NOT EVEN THE MOST HOPEFUL OF BRITISH GOVERNMENTS COULD claim, after the early months of 1932, that all was well in the Far East. In the light of experience at Shanghai the National government, led by Ramsay MacDonald with Stanley Baldwin as second in command, said a reluctant farewell to the ten-year rule, sanctioned completion of the Singapore base and its fixed defenses by 1936, and agreed that naval and air garrisons in the Far East should be strengthened in the meantime. At the same time they turned down a recommendation from the Chiefs of Staff that they should start providing for other defensive commitments without delay. Like most of their generation, and like most sensible people in all ages, MacDonald and Baldwin hated the very idea of war. Not yet ready to concede that only rearmament could enable Britain to escape war, they recoiled from the thought of spending a substantial proportion of the national revenue on weapons of destruction while there was hope that the Disarmament Conference might solve their problems.

Apart from their distaste for violence, MacDonald and Baldwin had two powerful motives for their reluctance to embark on a course of action which might stimulate international competition in armaments. One was financial, the other strategic. Unemployment benefit was costing the country as much as the three armed services put together. A dictator might have killed two birds with one stone by drafting some of the unemployed into the armed forces, but a parliamentary democracy could not hope to do so

without arousing a storm of protest from labor leaders with leanings toward pacifism.* The strategic argument seemed in some
ways even stronger. Thanks partly to Trenchard's advocacy, the
bomber aircraft was the fashionable weapon of the 1930s, and an
arms race which took the form of a struggle for air power might
put Britain in a highly vulnerable position. Some progress had
been made with the fifty-two squadron scheme of air expansion
adopted in 1923, an Air Officer Commanding-in-Chief, Air Defence of Great Britain, had been appointed in 1925, and passive
air defense, or A.R.P., had been studied behind the scenes since
the same year. The National government had, therefore, a substantial body of data on which to base their conclusion that a
fighter force which depended for early warning on old-fashioned
sound locators had no chance of intercepting hostile bombers
before they reached London. Trenchard's doctrine of defense by
retaliation was all very well, but what would happen if London
were knocked out before an effective counterattack could be
delivered? "The bomber," Baldwin confessed with an appalling
frankness which he bitterly regretted when the invention of radar
in 1935 transformed the outlook, "will always get through."

The paradoxical result was that, while the British air delegation
went to Geneva in 1932 with a strong professional bias in favor
of the strategic bomber as the basis of their claim to independence
of the other services, the overriding aim of the British government
was abolition of bombing or its restriction to tactical operations
against battlefield targets. In practice this conflict of interest did
not matter very much, for not even the sincerest advocate of abolition or restriction could hit upon any formula or system which
would prevent an aggressor from using any aircraft he might have
as bombers, or from attacking non-military targets if he felt inclined to do so. Nor was any progress made toward disarmament

* When Neville Chamberlain's government did adopt compulsory military
service in 1939, they were able to claim that they were not really introducing
conscription in peacetime, since no one in his senses could pretend that a
true state of peace existed. The nation would not have accepted that argument
in 1932. Nor would the Chiefs of Staff Committee have been likely at that
time to commit themselves to the opinion that conscription was a military
necessity.

in general. The French argued for an international force to be used by the League of Nations to punish an aggressor, but everyone acquainted with the methods of Geneva knew that a war could easily be over by the time the League decided where guilt lay and made up its mind to use force against the offender.

Meanwhile the security won at Locarno after many trials was crumbling under the impact of the economic depression which followed the Wall Street crisis. By the time the Disarmament Conference assembled at least a quarter of the working population of Germany was jobless, and the government was powerless to prevent clashes between left-wing and right-wing demonstrators. In April 1932, Dr. Brüning, who had already been threatened by the Nazi party with nation-wide disorder if he made political concessions to France in return for financial help, tried in vain to suppress the Nazi Storm Troopers. In May he resigned when President Hindenburg refused to sign decrees increasing taxation and reducing unemployment benefit. Neither the royalist Franz von Papen nor the unrepresentative General Kurt von Schleicher, who followed him, did anything effective to check the rising tide of National Socialism. In January 1933 the ageing Hindenburg was persuaded to accept Adolf Hitler and his collaborators as a lesser evil than a left-wing government supported by at least five million Communists who drew their orders from Moscow.

Almost simultaneously the Republican President, Herbert Hoover, was decisively defeated at a presidential election in the United States by the Democratic candidate, Franklin D. Roosevelt, who used his victory to give effect to a massive program of relief and public works as a cure for ills which included fifteen million unemployed, the reduction of most of the farming community to the level of bare subsistence, and an almost complete paralysis of heavy industry. In spite of appeals from the British, who had reluctantly thrown free trade overboard in 1931 by introducing a system of imperial preference, Roosevelt refused, however, to reverse a decision to raise tariffs, arguing that the slump in commodity prices had brought enough troubles to American producers and that dumping by foreign competitors was too big a risk to take.

While the political trend in France, Britain, and the United States during the 1930s was toward the left, the economic trend was thus in the direction of a conservative nationalism which contrasted markedly with the boldness of Nazi economics in the hands of the ingenious Dr. Schacht. At a World Economic Conference in London in the summer of 1933, all delegates faced the knowledge that international trade had shrunk to a third of its former volume, and that the problem was to quicken the flow of goods by restoring confidence. All the great producing countries, especially in the New World, held vast stocks of raw materials and foodstuffs which they could not sell because their customers were too poor to buy them, and would remain too poor to buy them until a fresh injection of credit revived their purchasing power. At the same time, many producers were encumbered with unsold manufactured goods which could have been traded for such commodities if the means of exchange had been available. Yet the problem of priming the pump on a global scale remained insoluble in face of fiscal barriers which testified to the refusal of the allegedly progressive democracies to surrender the smallest fraction of their economic sovereignty. A plan to give a fresh start to international commerce by stabilizing exchanges was flatly rejected by the United States, and the existence of a moratorium on international payments for which the Americans themselves had asked did not prevent the left-wing Roosevelt from insisting just as firmly as his right-wing predecessors that there would be no health in Europe until the Allies paid their debts. The Russians offered to absorb vast quantities of goods unsold by the Western powers in return for substantial credits, but they found no takers. In the Victorian era Britain had increased her trade sixfold by her readiness to do business with anyone if the price was right, but the world had grown too cautious by the fourth decade of the twentieth century to apply the lesson.

It was thus against a background of economic anarchy that the Disarmament Conference pursued its long-drawn course toward total failure. In the meantime things were going from bad to worse in Germany. Within a month of Hitler's accession to power the burning of the Reichstag, which he was widely suspected of having engineered, gave him a pretext to declare a state of emergency and clamp down on personal liberty and on freedom of speech and of the press. After arresting all Communist deputies he held elections at which his party won more than seventeen million votes as compared with the twelve million cast for parties of the left. Thus fortified, he went on to declare open war on the trade unions and the Church, as well as on Jews, Communists, and all associations claiming any part of the loyalty which, according to the Nazi philosophy, the citizen owed solely to the State.

According to his best-selling autobiography and political testament *Mein Kampf*, Hitler did not believe that Germany ought to quarrel with Britain or the British Empire. He thought that his predecessors had blundered when they aroused British suspicions before the First World War by founding colonies in Africa. The view he claimed to hold was that Germany's destiny lay in Europe, and that her demand for living space could be met at the expense of Russia. But clearly Germany could not expand eastward into Russia unless she first settled with Poland, and probably also with Czechoslovakia and perhaps Rumania. Peaceful revision of the Central European settlement under Article 19 of the Versailles Treaty was not ruled out by the Locarno pacts, but any attempt by Germany to absorb the buffer states on her eastern and southern frontiers as bases for an attack on Russia was obviously likely to involve her in war with France unless the ground were carefully prepared by diplomatic negotiations which might extend over many years. Such a war would mean that Britain would be called upon to honor her obligation to support France if Germany were the aggressor. When Germany walked out of the Disarmament Conference in October 1933 and claimed the right to rearm in defiance of the Versailles Treaty, the British government therefore made the only logical response by appointing a committee to advise them how they could best make up some of the ground lost during the supremacy of the ten-year rule.

The setting up of the Defence Requirements Committee, in November 1933, was one of the most important steps taken by a British government between the wars, and it might well have been the means of averting the disasters that followed if the committee's recommendations had been adopted. In 1933 Germany had an army of only seven divisions, no air force, and a navy utterly incapable of presenting any serious threat to France or Britain. But it was characteristic of a state of mind which persisted in the Western democracies throughout the rearmament period that the opportunity to launch a vigorous diplomatic offensive backed by realistic preparations to prevent a breach of the Locarno settlement was thrown away. It was also characteristic that, even when France and Britain were still relatively strong and Germany was still relatively weak, the French and British governments thought much more of what Hitler could do to them than of what they could do to Hitler. An effective Franco-British diplomacy would have entailed the threat of offensive action, and the attitude of both governments at all relevant stages of the crisis was radically and incurably defensive. The outcome, at once ludicrous and tragic, was that Hitler, in spite of repeated warnings from his military advisers that the German Army was in no state to fight a major war, was able to impose his will on a Europe which was fully capable of standing up to him in every respect except that its leaders lacked the resolution to assert themselves in the right way.

The Defence Requirements Committee which sat in London in the early winter of 1933–34 was one of the strongest bodies ever called upon to advise a British government on defense questions in time of peace. Besides the three Chiefs of Staff, the members included the permanent heads of the Foreign Office and the Treasury. The chairman, Sir Maurice Hankey, had an intimate knowledge of his subject, going back to the First World War and earlier. The committee were bound by terms of reference which required them to take account only of the *worst* deficiencies in the national and imperial defenses, but the program which they presented in 1934 was nevertheless a well-balanced one, which had the merit of being based on the sound assumption that, in spite of the obvious danger of war in the Far East, the real enemy was Germany. The War Office believed that Germany might be ready for war by 1938 or 1939. The general opinion was that Hitler would find it difficult to build up a strong army or navy within that time, but that he might be able to provide himself with a strong air force. The committee therefore recommended that the fifty-two squadron scheme of air expansion should be completed without delay, and that the security ban which had hitherto surrounded preparations for passive air defense should be lifted. They also proposed that something should be done to strengthen the notoriously inadequate seaward defenses of ports and harbors. But their most important recommendation was that an expeditionary force comparable with that which had crossed the Channel in August 1914 should be made ready for despatch to the Continent within a month of the outbreak of war, and that it should include both armored and air components. This was a vital element in the committee's program, not only because preparations to send troops across the Channel were more likely than anything else to convince Continental powers that Britain meant business, but also because bases and observation posts on the Continent were needed for the air defense of London.

From the strategic point of view, the government had little fault to find with the committee's recommendations. They agreed that completion of the fifty-two squadron scheme should have high priority, and indeed the only criticism of this part of the committee's proposals which seems to have been voiced in governmental and official circles was that additions to the scheme might be even more urgently needed than the committee thought. They also agreed that the proposal to send troops across the Channel to safeguard the Low Countries in the event of German aggression was eminently sound. Unfortunately they did not act promptly on these sensible conclusions. Succumbing to the perennial temptation of democratic governments to postpone the agonizing moment of decision at all costs, they remitted the proposals for detailed examination to the most convenient body, which happened paradoxically to be the Ministerial Committee on Disarmament. There the scheme came under searching fire from the Chancellor of the Exchequer, Neville Chamberlain. Chamberlain believed that a second world war would be a disaster for the British Empire, and that war was not likely to be avoided unless Britain were able to negotiate with the dictators from a position of strength. He therefore deplored the MacDonald-Baldwin policy of drift, and was all for energetic measures of rearmament. At the same time he was acutely conscious of the danger of doing anything that might hamper Britain's recovery from the aftereffects of the Wall Street slump. After devoting a great deal of thought to the Defence Requirements Committee's scheme, he decided that it was too expensive and that, in spite of his inexperience as a strategist, he was capable of drawing up a better one which would have the supreme advantage of being cheaper.

This was an astonishing conclusion, even for a man whose outlook on financial questions may well have been permanently colored by his having lost fifty thousand pounds of the family fortunes in a vain attempt to grow sisal in the Bahamas in his early years. The estimated cost of the Defence Requirements Committee's scheme was seventy-one million pounds, spread over five years. This was roughly half the average annual expenditure on the armed forces between the wars, and little more than the country had spent in a week at the height of the First World War. It is hard to believe that the scheme was really beyond the nation's means, as Chamberlain alleged, and that a government with an overwhelming majority in the House of Commons could not have carried through a program involving an annual expenditure of little more than fourteen million pounds, divided between three departments which were already spending well over a hundred million pounds a year.

Nevertheless, the financial argument was decisive. On Chamberlain's advice the government disemboweled the Defence Requirements Committee's scheme by slicing a third from the committee's estimate. At the same time they cut the army's share by about a half, so that no more was heard for several years of realistic preparations to fight on land. Rejecting a balanced strategy, they staked the country's future on an enlarged scheme of air expansion which promised an outwardly impressive array of bombers and fighters, backed by reserves so scanty that they would not be able to stand the strain of active operations for more than a brief period. The pretext for this admittedly unsound proceeding was that it was essential for diplomatic reasons to make a show of strength, and that reserves could be built up later if the threat of war were not averted. Yet even statesmen far less shrewd than Chamberlain and Baldwin might have been expected to foresee that the effect on Hitler and his circle would be the opposite of that intended. Observing that the cheapness of the air expansion program ruled out proper provision for reserves, what conclusion could the Germans draw but that the scheme was a mere façade and that their plans would not be seriously opposed? At the same time, the government's obvious eagerness to show the public that something was being done to make the country less vulnerable to air attack was a direct invitation to Hitler to play on British fears, and thus encourage the tendency of the European democracies to put their money into purely defensive precautions which need cause the Germans no anxiety.

At the end of June, when the British government were shaping their emasculated version of the Defence Requirements Committee's plan, Hitler improved his standing in the eyes of his admirers by liquidating a number of his more troublesome henchmen, among them his old associate Captain Ernst Röhm. When Hindenburg died in August 1934, his power became almost limitless. The only check he suffered throughout the entire year was inflicted not by the democracies but by the undemocratic Benito Mussolini, who moved troops to the Brenner when Hitler engineered the murder of the Austrian Chancellor, Dr. Engelbert Dollfuss, and showed signs of subjugating Austria by infiltration.

Dissatisfaction with British rearmament plans was one consequence of these alarms. Criticism of the new air expansion scheme did not throw much light on its real shortcomings, but showed that others besides members of the government shared their tendency to lose their sense of proportion in face of the threat of German air rearmament. In the course of a famous debate in the House of Commons in November, Winston Churchill asserted that Germany already possessed an air force which was not far off equality with the Royal Air Force. He was right in thinking that Hitler must be taken seriously, but badly misled about the relative air strengths of the two countries. The Royal Air Force was a well-established service with bases in many parts of the world and a first-line strength of nearly nine hundred aircraft. The German air force did not yet exist as a fighting force. Five weeks later, at the end of 1934, the number of first-line aircraft taken up by German first-line units was less than a sixth of British first-line strength. It was true that the number of aircraft of first-line type in Germany happened to be about equal to the first-line strength of the Royal Air Force in the United Kingdom, but the two figures meant quite different things. Moreover, the German total included many aircraft without engines or otherwise unfit to fly.

Attempts to peer into the future led to even worse misunderstandings. Mr. Churchill claimed that the German air force would be at least as strong as the Royal Air Force in November 1935, nearly half as strong again by November 1936, and almost twice the size of the Royal Air Force by 1937. As spokesman for the National government Stanley Baldwin did his best to rebut these charges, but failed, apparently through an honest error, to tell the House that the German air force was in fact expected to catch up with the Royal Air Force within the next two years. Yet discussions of parity based on figures which did not distinguish between aircraft of different types and categories would in any case have been misleading. Even where bombers and fighters were not lumped together, as they nearly always were, it was not necessarily true that one country was better or worse off than another because it had more or fewer bombers or fighters. There was no direct correspondence, for example, between the number of defensive fighters needed by the British, with their small, densely populated country and highly vulnerable capital, and the number needed by the Germans, whose capital was out of reach of British bombers in the middle '30s unless they flew from Continental bases, and whose industrial centers in Westphalia could be reached by some bombers from bases in the United Kingdom, but not by others.

One result of these confusions was that criticisms intended to galvanize the government into a more realistic attitude to defense problems had almost the opposite effect. Finding that such a redoubtable critic as Winston Churchill was at least as anxious about German air rearmament as they were, ministers were encouraged to devote themselves more one-sidely than ever to the struggle for a meaningless numerical parity with the German air force, often at the expense of other aspects of readiness for war which were at least equally important. At the same time their confidence in the account of German progress given by the Air Ministry was shaken, with the result that evidence of what the Germans were doing tended to be obscured by forecasts of what they might be able to do on the questionable assumption that every first-line aircraft turned out by a German factory could be counted as a direct addition to first-line strength.

This trend soon received added impetus from no less an authority than the Führer himself. In January 1935 a plebiscite was held in accordance with the provisions of the Versailles Treaty to determine the future of the Saar. Delighted with the results, which went overwhelmingly in favor of Germany, Hitler declared that he had no further territorial claims to make on France, and invited the British government to send a representative to Berlin to discuss a general European settlement. With the consent of the French government, a visit was arranged for early March. Displeased by British comments on German rearmament, Hitler postponed it at the last moment on the pretext that he had a cold, and announced the formal revival of the German air force and the introduction of conscription, both of which were forbidden by the Versailles Treaty although it was no secret that Germany had begun to rearm at least as early as 1934. The British government protested, but nonetheless sent Sir John Simon and Mr. Anthony Eden to Berlin on March 24. In the course of conversations which extended over several days and covered a variety of subjects, Hitler astonished his guests by asserting that the German air force was already as strong as the Royal Air Force.

Both the British and German Air Staffs knew that the claim could not be substantiated, and both said so, although the Germans were afterward obliged to make a partial retraction in order to save the Führer's face. The only possible explanation was that Hitler, either from propagandist motives or because he misinterpreted his own figures, drew a false comparison between the first-line strength of the Royal Air Force and the whole number of first-line aircraft in Germany, including in the latter total immediate and stored reserves and other aircraft not reckoned by airmen in either country as part of first-line strength. After the return of the two ministers to London, the British government came to the conclusion that probably the Germans were aiming at a true first-line strength of fifteen hundred aircraft by the spring of 1937. The sequel was a new and accelerated scheme of air expansion which purported to bring the growth of the Royal Air Force into line with the German program. But again the British scheme provided little depth, and the Germans were not deceived.

The introduction of the new scheme in the summer of 1935 coincided with a change of government which put Stanley Baldwin at the head of affairs in place of Ramsay MacDonald, but there was no detectable change in British military policy. The first air expansion scheme which made fairly good provision for reserves was not introduced until 1936, when the attainment of theoretical parity with the German air force in 1937 had begun to seem a less important aim than the creation of an air force fit to fight in 1939. Meanwhile the German air force continued to expand with reasonable steadiness until a moment came when its leaders, in their turn, were led by the desire for quick results to build up a bigger first-line than they could support, with the result that the effective strength of their squadrons tended to fall away during periods of heavy fighting such as occurred in 1940. Conversely the British, shelving their paper schemes and making a supreme last-minute effort, were able to find replacements for their losses in the Battle of Britain, and thus survived to win that crucial battle.

Apart from the perennial question of German rearmament and Hitler's intentions, the first big problem that confronted the new government in 1935 was that of relations with Italy. For months past trouble had been building up in the triangle of Northeast Africa between the Indian Ocean and the Red Sea. The focus of discontent was Abyssinia, known also to historians and geographers as Ethiopia. A backward, barbarous, and highly mountainous region, surrounded by British, French, and Italian protectorates and colonies, it owed its escape from annexation in the nineteenth century not only to the poverty of its communications and the ferocity of its inhabitants, but also to the reluctance of British governments to see the headwaters of the Blue Nile fall into the wrong hands. The decline in British influence after the First World War, and the lack of a well-defined frontier with Italian Eritrea and still more with Italian Somaliland, made Abyssinia an obvious target for Italian ambitions at a time when the flow of Italy's surplus population to the United States was checked by American immigration laws. Moreover, Mussolini was determined to make his influence widely felt, and was well aware that his popularity in his own country was likely to rise sharply if he succeeded in wiping out the memory of a defeat suffered by Italian arms at Adowa in 1896.

Haile Selassie, the Negus or Emperor of Abyssinia, was credited by his well-wishers with far-reaching plans to modernize his country and develop its resources, but his hold on his feudal chieftains was uncertain, and he was in no position to reject out of hand any honest bargain which promised his country secure access to the sea in return for economic or perhaps even political concessions. Lacking modern weapons, he looked to Britain to provide them, but soon found that a powerful section of the British Cabinet was reluctant to give him any for fear of precipitating the clash between him and Mussolini which the whole Cabinet wanted to avert. He decided, therefore, to stake his hopes on the ability of the League of Nations to persuade Mussolini not to go to war or, if he did go to war, to call off his attack at an early stage rather than see the whole world ranged against him.

As things turned out, recourse to the League of Nations proved the worst possible method of trying to settle the Abyssinian problem. Hitherto determined to show himself a good European and by no means reluctant to fall in with France and Britain against Hitler, Mussolini was equally determined not to accept dictation from the League in any circumstances. Endless appeals in Rome, Paris, and London failed utterly to shake him where adroit diplomacy unshadowed by the ever-present threat to appeal to Geneva might conceivably have been successful. On September 28, 1935, almost exactly a year after a mysterious frontier incident at Walwal sounded the first danger signal, Haile Selassie mobilized his forces while continuing to assert his hopes of a peaceful settlement. Five days later Mussolini opened hostilities with air attacks on Adowa and Addis Ababa.

As a result of precautionary moves ordered recently by the British government, the Royal Navy had about three times as many capital ships on the spot at the crucial moment as the Italian Navy, but they were partly dependent on the French for port facilities, and war material was so scarce in Britain that the effect of the moves was to leave the home country almost entirely defenseless. As usual at moments of crisis, Britain lacked the all-round strength required for independent action, and in any case her support was pledged to the League. Some fifty nations, most of them with no immediate interest in the dispute and no intention of risking a man, a gun, or a penny in support of either party, were in favor of imposing economic sanctions on Italy as indisputably the aggressor. The British and French governments, certainly not at one in their assessment of the situation but both eager to stay out of trouble, agreed to ban the sale to Italy of arms and certain raw materials, but were unwilling for two reasons that oil should be included in the list. Their first reason was that the French, especially, were keenly alive to the danger of driving Mussolini irretrievably into Hitler's camp. Their second was that Mussolini himself, who is said to have admitted later that an embargo on oil would have forced him to withdraw from Abyssinia within a week, declared at the time that such a step would be an act of war. In all probability it would not, in fact, have led him to make war on France and Britain, but would merely have caused him to redouble attempts to increase his supplies from the United States, where President Roosevelt was doing his best to reverse the usual order of events by putting pressure on the oil lobby, and perhaps from Russia. At the same time, it might have created an embarrassing situation in the Middle East, where an Italian-controlled company held the concession for a large tract of Iraqi territory crossed by the Iraq Petroleum Company's pipe-line from Kirkuk to the Levantine coast.

Nor did the British and French governments believe that Italy could defeat France and Britain in the long run if she did go to war with them. But they shrank from the risk of a "mad-dog act" which might do untold damage and might even precipitate a world-wide disaster. The British, in particular, feared that Mussolini might become so enraged as to order air attacks on their naval bases at Alexandria and in Malta.

In both countries, critics of the men in power demanded more drastic measures. The closing of the Suez Canal to Italian shipping was suggested, but the Suez Canal Convention of 1888 laid down the principle that the canal should be open to ships of every nation. Signatories to that convention could not logically have countered Mussolini's move by defying the international law which they claimed to be defending.

In the absence of a ban on oil or armed intervention, conciliation seemed the only way of escaping abject acquiescence in Mussolini's policy of seizing Abyssinia lock, stock, and barrel. With notable exceptions, British ministers were not unwilling to appease Mussolini if the alternative was what they feared it might be, while the French were undisguisedly eager to come to terms with him in order to buy his continued opposition to Hitler's designs in Europe. Even so, the British Cabinet were not prepared for the plan with which their Foreign Secretary, Sir Samuel Hoare, presented them. A sick man when he stopped in Paris in December on his way to Switzerland for a much-needed holiday, Hoare concocted with Pierre Laval, who was doubling the posts of Prime Minister and Foreign Minister, a scheme which promised Mussolini substantial benefits at Haile Selassie's expense in return for the calling-off of his campaign. The scheme was not entirely without advantages from the Abyssinian point of view, but the British public was not ready for a bargain which looked like a surrender to fascist methods, and which would in fact have been a surrender to expediency. The Cabinet, who had expected only tentative proposals and thought that Hoare had gone too far, bowed to a storm of protest by ostentatiously cold-shouldering the Hoare-Laval pact and thus giving its English co-author no choice but to resign.

This outcome was a source of satisfaction to the government's critics, but it did not prevent the Italians from going on to swallow

Abyssinia. At the same time it greatly injured British and French chances of keeping Mussolini out of Hitler's arms, and gave a sharp jolt to Anglo-French relations, already shaken by a naval agreement with Germany which the British had concluded in the summer. An earlier naval agreement between the great powers, the London Naval Treaty of 1930, had done nothing to blow the battle fleets of the nations opposed to Hitler out of the doldrums in which the Treaty of Washington had left them, and had limited the British to fifty cruisers in place of the seventy which their naval experts considered necessary to protect trade-routes.

Within the next months clear indications were received in London and Paris that Hitler was contemplating a breach of Articles 42 and 43 of the Versailles Treaty, which forbade Germany to build fortifications or maintain or assemble troops on the left bank of the Rhine or within fifty kilometers of the right bank. The Nazi authorities did not deny that Germany had freely agreed at Locarno to respect these provisions, but argued that France and Britain had introduced a new factor by drawing closer to Communist Russia. In February 1936 the French government sounded the British as to their attitude if German troops should enter the forbidden zone. Fears for the safety of Alexandria and Malta during the Abyssinian crisis had led the British government to strip the home country of most of its antiaircraft ammunition, as well as much other material normally available for home defense; they therefore replied cautiously that the question would have to be decided when the time came, but that meanwhile the French ought to make up their own minds as to what their attitude would be. They might have been less cautious if they had fully accepted the implication of reports from the British Embassy in Berlin that Hitler's service chiefs, who knew only too well that the German Army was in no state to withstand even the smallest countermove, were deeply disturbed by his proposal to march into the Rhineland. The Führer himself was well aware that he risked a humiliating setback, but he counted on British and French indecision, reassured his reluctant generals, and promised that the troops should be withdrawn at the first sign of trouble, adding characteristically that his definition of trouble did not include mere diplomatic protests.

Early on March 7 a token force of infantry and cavalry, without armor, entered the demilitarized zone. Three battalions crossed the Rhine with orders to push on toward Aachen, Trier, and Saarbrücken, but to be ready to fall back swiftly if the French advanced; the rest remained on the right bank so that they could be whisked away at once in case of opposition. These moves were regarded in German military circles as so dangerous that some service chiefs remembered the next few days as the most anxious they ever spent.

However, they need not have worried. The French Council of Ministers met within a few hours of the arrival of the first German soldier in the Rhineland, but learned that the General Staff had no plan to deal with the situation, although it came as no surprise to them. All their plans for war with Germany were purely defensive, and they could not even contemplate a military occupation of Saarbrücken or Kehl without elaborate preliminary moves and an extensive call-up. On March 11 General Maurice Gamelin, the Chief of Staff, announced that, in order to occupy a small part of the Saar between Saarbrücken and Merzig, he would have to occupy neutral Luxembourg as well, and would need an army of 1,200,000 men without counting the forces of the interior. In addition he would need a week's notice, the approval of the League of Nations, and the cooperation of Poland, Czechoslovakia, and Belgium. Yet no more information than any competent intelligence service might have been expected to provide was needed to tell him that a single mechanized column would have sufficed to push the Germans back.

There was no enthusiasm in England for far-reaching reprisals against the Germans. Many people argued that the Rhineland was as German as Sussex was English, that the Versailles Treaty was as dead as mutton, and that Hilter was morally entitled to send his troops where he pleased in his own country. On the other hand, there was no such clash of British and French interests as had existed at the time of the occupation of the Ruhr. The British government could not have objected to a prompt assertion of French rights, nor would the British public have been likely to do so if the nature of the Nazi menace had been as thoroughly explained to them as it was a few years later. The stumbling block was not British caution so much as the fantastic cumbrousness of the French military machine. The consequence was a fatal strengthening of Hitler's reputation in the eyes of the German military hierarchy, who saw that there was something, after all, in his claim to know better than they how much the democracies would stand.

9

APPEASEMENT

A FEW MONTHS BEFORE HE WAS FORCED TO RESIGN BECAUSE OF THE
concessions he proposed to make to Italy, Sir Samuel Hoare had
told the League of Nations that Britain was determined to take
the lead in resisting unprovoked aggression. His successor, Mr.
Anthony Eden, seemed to many people just the man to practice
what Hoare had preached. He had an excellent record as a brigade
major in the first World War and, more recently, as a progressive
Tory. A great advocate of collective security within the League
of Nations, he was known to believe in standing up to the
dictators.

But the League could provide no security not provided by its
members, and standing up to the dictators was difficult for a
country so unready for war that it could safeguard its naval bases
in Egypt and Malta only by reducing the home defenses to an
impotence hardly paralleled since the Dutch fleet sailed up the
Thames in 1667. If the British response to Hitler's remilitarization
of the Rhineland in the spring was cautious, the government had
at least the excuse that they could hardly urge the French to take
a strong line when they knew that they were not in a position
to give France much practical support. Shackled by the reluctance
of most of the Cabinet to risk a setback to trade by asking
industry to divert more than a fraction of its effort to war production, ministers and officials who feared the worst could only watch
the dictators arming with apparent indifference to warnings that
the democracies might really bestir themselves one day if they

were tried too far. Nor were the government helped by an Opposition which insisted that the rise of fascism must be checked, yet condemned even the mildest of rearmament programs as a senseless piling-up of armaments which could only lead to war.

Excitement about the Rhineland had scarcely died away when trouble began in Spain. Even at the best of times the Spanish provinces had never taken very kindly to dictation from Madrid. Since the abdication of King Alfonso XIII in 1931 a left-wing government had struggled to maintain itself in face of opposition from the Church, the army, and the landed classes, the intransigence of its own extremists, and conflicts of interest between town and country as well as between one region and another. Encouraged by promises of German and Italian support, an army officer, General Francisco Franco, launched a right-wing revolution in Morocco on July 17, 1936, and next day flew to Spain. Within a few weeks he was at the head of powerful forces which included most of the regular army and at least 10,000 Moroccan troops flown to Spain by a shuttle service of German transport aircraft.

Eyed askance by most professional soldiers in their own country, the Republican government relied chiefly on popular levies, a strong but uncooperative Soviet contingent, and a mixed bag of British, French, Dutch, American, and Czech idealists, adventurers and fellow travelers. Between July and September three Soviet merchant ships sailed from Odessa to Alicante and Cartagena carrying a first installment of Russian aircraft and aircrew, the latter all hand-picked by the Soviet authorities. As the war went on, both the Russians and the Germans powerfully reinforced their air contingents, the Russians openly sending members of the Soviet air force of whom the most successful were decorated for services to the Soviet government, while the Germans sent their airmen in the guise of volunteers or tourists. From the point of view of major tactics the most important lesson of the war, which ended only with Franco's triumphant capture of Madrid in the spring of 1939, was the value of ground-attack aircraft in close support of troops. In the light of experience in Spain the German Air Staff, who had hitherto thought chiefly in terms of strategic bombing, changed the whole basis of their doctrine and developed methods which brought startling successes in France and the Low Countries in 1940.

As a trial of strength between Communism and the dictatorships the war was inconclusive. Whether Franco or the Republicans won was of little interest to the Soviet government, whose attitude was based on the well-known Communist maxim that nothing furthers the ultimate interests of the proletariat so much as a long, costly, and disastrous war. The declared aim of the British and French governments, on the other hand, was to take the sting out of the Civil War by withholding help from both sides. But non-intervention did not save the European democracies from ideological conflicts which cut across national interests, concealed the true nature of the struggle in Spain, and diverted attention from the need to rearm quickly in order to avert the much worse war that was in the offing. Moderate Liberals and Socialists as well as left-wing extremists in both countries tended to interpret the attitude of their rulers as a tacit invitation to Franco to conquer Spain with German and Italian help, but that did not prevent millions of German and Italians from believing that the British and French governments were inflexibly hostile to German and Italian aspirations.

Nor was the policy applied with the undeviating strictness which would have made it at least worthy of respect. The principle of non-intervention was only intermittently honored by French statesmen, and even in Britain it was never very rigidly enforced. Neither the Republicans nor Franco's junta were recognized as belligerents, but at the same time they were not prevented from conducting recruiting offices and propagandist organizations on British and French soil. On the whole Franco's propaganda made little headway in Britain, while in France it appealed only to a small but powerful minority. On the other hand, sympathizers in both countries flocked to join the Republicans in the belief that to do so was to strike a blow for democracy against fascism. The British government knew, and the French government ought also to have known, that in reality the Soviet leaders were anything but well-wishers to the democracies; but case-hardened statesmen aware of the trend toward the left throughout the democratic countries shrank from the unpopularity which would have followed a resolute attempt to tell the public so. Convinced that the Spanish Popular Front was a respectable left-wing coalition on the lines of its French counterpart, the great mass of Englishmen and Frenchmen, to say nothing of the great mass of Americans, remained blissfully unaware that the Civil War had ceased, at any rate by its closing stages, to be a struggle between fascism and democracy and had become a struggle between fascism and Communism, with Communism holding most of the cards since a victory for either side would still enable it to profit from the confusion sown by moral and ideological conflicts in a divided world.

Fascist propaganda in the troubled '30s was more blatant than Russian, but its absurdities did not prevent it from scoring startling triumphs. The Nazi rulers, especially, worked hard to divide and confuse opinion in France and Britain, stress the effeteness of the democracies and glorify the relentless might of reborn Germany. At the same time they took immense pains to gain the ascendancy for Germany in international contests by a ruthless specialization and an expenditure of effort, time and money which seemed to democratic leaders utterly out of keeping with any benefits likely to accrue from even the most glittering success. To Hitler and his circle the winning by German competitors of more medals than were won by athletes of any other nation at the Olympic Games held in Berlin in 1936 was much more than a demonstration of the thoroughness of Nazi training; it was one more proof of Germany's fitness to rule the world. In some ways German successes in international motor racing were even more rewarding. As a move in the war of nerves, the supreme effort which gave two heavily subsidized German concerns thirty-seven victories in the fifty Grand Prix events held in the last six years of peace was well worth while, for it carried the implication that supremacy in the field of internal combustion engineering might make German military aircraft as invincible as German racing cars. The Italians, with ten victories, were put in their proper place at the tail of the Axis, while the French had three.

Perhaps fortunately, the effect was largely lost on the British, since British manufacturers had ceased many years earlier to compete in international Grand Prix events.

Shocked by the Rhineland fiasco, the French made a big effort between 1936 and the outbreak of war to overhaul and modernize their army. General Gamelin presented a four-year plan, and substantial funds were voted. Allocations to the army from the introduction of the four-year plan up to the early part of 1939 totaled nearly forty thousand million francs—a sum equivalent in purchasing power to at least four or five hundred million pounds, and probably more. Yet French military thinking remained so firmly wedded to the idea of linear defense that a wonderful opportunity of providing the army with a highly mobile offensive element was thrown away. Because neither side had ever made a a real breakthrough on the Western Front in the First World War, it was argued that the only sound strategy was to stand on the defensive, wait for the enemy to attack, and avoid taking the offensive until he had worn himself out by doing so, perhaps after several years of static warfare. Hence everything was subordinated to belief in an impregnable defensive front, and anyone who suggested that the development of armored fighting vehicles and aircraft had changed the relative positions of attacker and defender was branded as a heretic. This preoccupation with the defensive was reflected in the design of French tanks, which were heavily armored and well armed, but had a short radius of action and were very slow.

While the French were setting to work to modernize their army but not their strategy or tactics, the Air Ministry in London reported in the last quarter of 1936 that the German air force had reached a first-line strength of more than a thousand aircraft, as compared with a British first-line strength in the United Kingdom of roughly seven hundred. In many ways the loss of numerical parity was a blessing in disguise, for it finally disposed of the illusion that Hitler could be checked by paper schemes of air expansion, and encouraged the government to frame more realistic plans. Meanwhile the birth of a new weapons system had put a fresh face on the problem of air defense. The Hurricane and the Spitfire, all-metal monoplane fighters which combined high speed and a fast climb with tremendous hitting power, were coming into service. The defense layout first planned in the 1920s was being remodeled to meet attacks over a wider arc, and a very experienced officer, Air Chief Marshal Sir Hugh Dowding, had been chosen to command the fighter force and control the guns and searchlights provided by the army. More important still, an expert on thunderstorms, Robert Watson Watt, had suggested a novel means by which approaching aircraft could be detected and tracked while they were still a long way off. The antiaircraft batteries still had only an improved version of the three-inch gun introduced during the First World War, but new and better guns were promised in 1938 or 1939. Barrage balloons which would protect factories and built-up areas against low-level bombing were also on the way.

But the public had been taught that "the bomber would always get through." Unless the government were to risk letting the Germans into their secrets, the man in the street could not be told that Watson Watt's invention had transformed the outlook, that a chain of early-warning stations using what was afterward called radar would soon cover the approaches to the United Kingdom from the east and southeast, and that even the best and fastest German bombers, flying from bases in Germany and therefore without fighter escort, would then be at the mercy of the air defenses if they came by day. Nor did the public know that most German bomber crews had little or no experience of night attacks, or that there was no authentic evidence of German plans or preparations to attack British cities either at night or by day. Consequently the vast majority of voters, egged on by prophets of woe whose motives were sometimes good and sometimes bad, continued throughout the remaining years of peace to torment themselves with exaggerated fears of a "knock-out blow" which, finding the country unprepared, might reduce London to a heap of ruins if British statesmen dared to thwart the Führer.

In the early summer of 1937 the veteran Stanley Baldwin at last relinquished power, and Neville Chamberlain stepped into his place. Determined to preserve peace by negotiating with the dictators while rearming as fast as he could without cutting the feet from under British industry by interfering with normal trade, the new leader faced formidable problems. Collective security was dead. Even if the alliance with France could be kept alive in face of the reluctance of the French to choose between national survival and a forty-hour week, the shelter of the Anglo-French umbrella had begun to seem less attractive than neutrality to small, weak nations alarmed by the failure of the League of Nations to adjust the Abyssinian dispute. A Franco-Soviet pact, concluded in 1935, had weakened the chain of French alliances in Eastern Europe by arousing distrust in Rumania and Yugoslavia without bringing France any acceptable promise of Russian help. In Spain, non-intervention was openly flouted not only by Russia, Germany, and Italy but also by Portugal and even France. Joint action by Britain and the United States, thought Chamberlain, would amply suffice to bring the dictators to their senses, but the new Neutrality Act held out no prospect of American cooperation. Many Americans blamed European governments for not standing up to the dictators, but Englishmen and Frenchmen noticed that American statesmen seemed no more capable of outfacing Japan without incontestable naval superiority in the Pacific than British and French statesmen seemed capable of outfacing Hitler and Mussolini without incontestable military superiority in Western Europe. They noticed, too, that American producers were supplying Franco with three-quarters of his oil and the Japanese with two-thirds of their oil and nine-tenths of their scrap metal.

A weakness less obvious to Chamberlain was that he was handicapped as Prime Minister by his past misdeeds as Chancellor of the Exchequer. In 1934 he had turned down as too expensive a rearmament plan which would have added seventy-one million pounds to the cost of the armed services during the next five years. Yet one of his last tasks before he succeeded Baldwin was to defend and explain a five-year program scheduled to cost more than twenty times as much. Even so, he continued to take a perverse pride in the transaction which, less than three years earlier, had wrecked the Defence Requirements Committee's proposals for the sake of a bad air expansion scheme and a small financial gain which proved, after all, to have been false economy. It was true that a much sounder air expansion scheme had been adopted since that day and that the air defenses were shaping infinitely better by the time he became Prime Minister than could have been foreseen in 1934. But only a blinkered view of Continental psychology could ever have led him to believe that air power was a substitute for troops, above all as a diplomatic weapon. It was not likely that anything but a definite undertaking to send an expeditionary force across the Channel would extract from the French a promise to declare war in circumstances which might fall short of a direct attack on France, or that the Germans would be deflected from their purposes in Central Europe by the knowledge that the British possessed a home defense air force which they would be very reluctant to use against Germany unless the Germans attacked them first.

It was thus a weakness of the policy with which Chamberlain came to office that negotiation from strength with the dictators would be possible only if they were content to measure strength, as he did, in terms of the resources which both sides could ultimately command rather than of the forces which they could count on deploying within the next few years or months. On the other hand it was true that German rearmament was only in the early stages, especially where the army was concerned, that the French Army was still by far the largest in Europe, and that the Italians, extended by their Abyssinian and Spanish adventures, were in no mood for war, although their inspired press succeeded in giving the impression that Mussolini was ready to take on all comers. By 1937 even the reluctant British had begun to think in terms not only of air power but also of a much-strengthened navy and an expeditionary force of at least four divisions. Unfortunately the delays in getting major measures of rearmament under way which had seemed so regrettable when Chamberlain was only Chancellor of the Exchequer appeared no more avoidable when he was Prime Minister, and meanwhile nearly three years had been lost. Traditionally the British were noted for their talent for improvisation and the Germans for their thoroughness, but there were many occasions between 1937 and 1940 when it seemed that the roles had been reversed.

From the start the new Prime Minister's attempts to come to terms with the dictators encountered obstacles so baffling that a man less sure that he was right might well have concluded much earlier that Hitler was not a man amenable to reason and would rather make trouble for himself and everyone by doing things in his own way than adopt a better way if it were shown to him. Sir Nevile Henderson, who went as Ambassador to Berlin with the intention of taming the Nazi leaders by kindness and convincing them that their aims could be achieved without war and without unpleasantness, was coolly received and would probably have found his position intolerable if he had not been sustained by a dogged conviction that nothing was ever as bad as it looked and that failure should never be admitted until it was an accomplished fact. The Italians showed what Chamberlain took to be signs of readiness to trade opposition to Hitler if he tried to seize Austria against recognition of the rights they had established by force in Abyssinia, but their newspapers and radio poured out a stream of anti-British propaganda. Negotiations lagged in face of Anthony Eden's insistence that the Italians should start withdrawing their volunteers from Spain before a settlement could be discussed, and Eden's resignation in favor of a Foreign Secretary more sympathetic to Chamberlain's policy did not prevent a breakdown which left Italy linked with Germany in a pact ostensibly directed against Russia. Meanwhile reports from Germany indicated that rearmament was being pushed on with great speed, especially in regard to armored units and the air force.

On November 7, 1937, Hitler lectured his Foreign Minister, Konstantin von Neurath, his Defence Minister, Field Marshal Werner von Blomberg, and his service chiefs on Germany's need of living space, and went on to tell them how he proposed to tackle the problem. The most pressing task, he said, was the incorporation of Austria and Czechoslovakia in a Greater Germany, and he expected to deal with it between 1943 and 1945, when the balance of armaments in Europe seemed likely to be most favorable. Neurath, Blomberg, and General Werner von Fritsch, Commander-in-Chief of the German Army, all stipulated that nothing in the Führer's program should be allowed to lead to a conflict with France and Britain.

In the same month the British government seized an opportunity of making contact with Hitler and his circle by advising Lord Halifax, then Lord President of the Council but afterward Eden's successor at the Foreign Office, to accept an invitation which he had received in his capacity as a Master of Foxhounds to attend a hunting exhibition in Berlin. A visit to Hitler at Berchtesgaden was hardly a success from Halifax's point of view. At half-past nine in the morning the Führer received his guests in black trousers and patent-leather shoes such as were worn in England in the evening. He was in a peevish mood, complained of criticisms of Germany in the British Parliament and press, and suggested that the British government in India should make short work of its problems by shooting Gandhi. Halifax did not speak German, but he found that, even if he had done so, he would not have spoken the same language as the Führer. Chamberlain wrote afterward that the visit had nevertheless been a great success from his point of view, since it had achieved its object by creating an atmosphere in which a European settlement could be discussed.

Some ten weeks after the Führer's conference with Neurath and Blomberg, official Berlin was startled by the news that Blomberg had married a Fräulein Eva Gruhn at a private ceremony attended by Hitler and Göring as witnesses. Almost immediately afterward Fritsch asked for an interview with the Führer, complained that Fräulein Gruhn was not a suitable wife for a highly placed officer, or indeed for any officer who valued his good name, and demanded Blomberg's resignation. Reacting characteristically to unpleasant tidings, Hitler was extremely angry, but he turned his anger to good account by visiting his displeasure not only on the principals but on everyone even remotely connected with the incident who might be supposed to share their lukewarm attitude to his Central European program. On February 4, 1938, he announced that Blomberg had resigned on grounds of ill-health, dismissed Fritsch and thirteen other senior officers, and himself assumed supreme control of the armed forces. Making a clean sweep of his critics, he also dismissed Neurath and summoned the complaisant Joachim von Ribbentrop from the Embassy in London to replace him.

The British and French governments had scarcely had time to weigh the significance of these changes when Hitler gave them something more to think about. On February 12 the Austrian Chancellor, Kurt von Schuschnigg, was summoned to Berchtesgaden and forced by threats of violence to grant an amnesty to his National Socialist opponents in Austria and install a prominent Nazi, Artur von Seyss-Inquart, in the key position of Minister of the Interior and Chief of Police. Hitler promised in return to respect Austrian independence, but said nothing of his promise when reporting the negotiations to the Reichstag. Schuschnigg then decided to hold a plebiscite on the question of independence or union with Germany, but he was not given time to do it. On March 11 he was forced by pressure from Germany to resign, and next day German troops entered Austria at the invitation of Seyss-Inquart and under cover of a demonstration by a substantial but not very formidable array of German aircraft. Except that a third of the German tanks broke down on the way and that General Ludwig Beck, the Chief of the German General Staff, was dismissed for drawing attention to some imperfections, the result was a triumph for Hitler and everything he stood for. Far from resisting the invaders, the populace pelted them with flowers, while the Austrian military authorities gave them every assistance in their power. Mussolini made no move, the French were temporarily without a government, and the British contented themselves with a sharp protest which helped to confirm Hitler's impression that nothing was to be expected from the democracies but sound and fury.

The rape of Austria was a characteristic example of Hitler's methods and the difficulties they created for democratic statesmen. By 1938, and indeed much earlier, the clauses in the peace treaties which forbade Austria to make so much as a customs union with Germany were generally felt to have been unwise, not because they did any particular injustice to Germany but because it seemed unfair that Austria, with her territory disrupted and her economy shattered by the war and its aftermath, should be further punished by being forcibly deprived of the advantages which fiscal partnership with Germany could give her. The moral case for removal of the ban was so strong that it could hardly have been resisted if anyone but Hitler had been its advocate. It was the measure of his capacity for evil that he was able to make of Austria's good case a means not only of turning out the government of a friendly country, annexing its territory, and so corrupting its inhabitants that they welcomed their enslavement, but also of spreading fear, resentment, and confusion throughout Europe and beyond.

With Austria in German hands, the turn of Czechoslovakia was obviously not far off. Again, the cause which Hitler made his own was not so worthless as to deserve so disreputable a backer. The Czechoslovakia of the peace treaties was admittedly a gross denial of the principle of self-determination by which the peacemakers claimed to have been guided. As a reward for their disloyalty to the Hapsburgs, and to gratify President Wilson's Czech supporters in the Middle West, the leaders of the Czechoslovak National Council were given dominion over seven and a half million Czechs, three and a quarter million Austrian Germans, and three and a half million Slovaks, Magyars, Ruthenians, and Poles. This arrangement was defended in 1919 on the ground that Czechoslovakia would not be a viable economic or strategic unit unless territories inhabited mainly by Germans, Magyars, and Ruthenians were included; that the Czech and Slovak leaders were good democrats who could be trusted not to quarrel or abuse their powers; and that the new state, freed from the corrupting influence of a hereditary ruling class, would become "a sort of Switzerland."

Long before Hitler raised his voice on behalf of the Sudeten Germans and turned them into Nazis, it was obvious that these hopes had been pitched too high. The Czechoslovakian Republic was no Switzerland. Inevitably the Czechs played a dominant role in the new state although they contributed only just over half the population. The Slovaks had looked forward to equality, but they had been so rigorously kept down by their Magyar overlords under the old dispensation that they had few men capable of holding high positions. The Ruthenians, or Little Russians, had been even more firmly pushed into the background, and a high proportion of them were illiterate. The Germans, the Magyars, and the Poles were regarded by the rest of the population as hereditary enemies whom it was right to tolerate but not to favor. The outcome was a system in which a high proportion of the best jobs in the public service were held by Czechs. Exactly the same evils as had been imputed to the internal organization of the old Austro-Hungary were imputed to that of the new Czechoslovakia, except that the alleged oppressors were no longer haughty German, Magyar, and Polish aristocrats but well-meaning middle-class Czechs with professional or academic backgrounds. Both Germans and Slovaks complained that they were at a disadvantage in the law courts, the Germans also that they were excluded from key positions in the armed forces and that, while unemployment was twice as heavy in German-speaking areas as elsewhere, unemployment benefit was much lower for Germans than for Czechs.

Hitler's championship of the Sudeten Germans made the situation infinitely worse. Facing wholesale infiltration by Nazi agents, the central government had no choice but to discriminate against the large proportion of the population which had become politically unreliable, thus departing further than ever from the principle of equal treatment for all. Czech police were posted to German-speaking areas, freedom from arbitrary arrest was suspended in some districts, and suspects were closely watched by government agents. In spite of the ideals which had inspired its founders, Czechoslovakia assumed some of the characteristics of a police state. By 1938 the Sudeten Germans had made themselves so disagreeable under Hitler's tutelage that, whether the Czechs admitted it or not, the Sudetenland was lost unless the inhabitants could be bought off by large concessions which, in any case, were not likely to keep the Nazi wolf from the door for long. In April the Sudeten leader, Konrad Henlein, demanded either union with Germany or a form of autonomy which would give the Sudetens the right to profess German nationality and uphold Nazi aims.

After the German seizure of Austria there was talk in British political circles of building up Czechoslovakia as a bastion against any further advance, and even of a "grand alliance" to put Hitler in his place. These hopes came up against a barrier of logistics and and geography. Czechoslovakia had a well-equipped army of twenty to thirty divisions and a small air force, but her industries and centers of population were vulnerable to air attack, and she seemed unlikely to last long against a resolute offensive without outside help. She was entitled to rely for such help on her alliances with France and Russia, but her frontiers were two hundred miles from the Rhine and a hundred miles from the nearest Russian railhead. Her direct communications with France and Britain ran through German and Austrian territory and were at Hitler's mercy. Alternative routes through Yugoslavia and Hungary were not very practical, and in any case she was not on particularly good terms with either of those countries. Russian help, if she brought herself to ask for it and the Russians to give it, could reach her only through Poland, or else by a roundabout route through Rumania which was only of academic interest. The Poles, who despised the Czechs and had never forgiven them for claiming the disputed industrial area of Teschen at the end of the First World War, were not likely to help them by opening their roads and railways to Russian troops. In spite of the immense pains taken by the French to build a chain of buffer states in Eastern Europe since the war, Czechoslovakia was about as isolated by the spring of 1938 as it was possible for a country to be.

A few weeks after Hitler's triumphant journey to Vienna in the wake of his invading army, the French Radical Prime Minister, Edouard Daladier, and his Foreign Minister, Georges Bonnet, arrived in London for conversations with Chamberlain and Halifax. By that time Chamberlain had satisfied himself, after consultation with the Chiefs of Staff, that neither France nor Britain could send any direct help to Czechoslovakia which would prevent Hitler from overrunning the country if he saw fit to do so. The question was whether the British and French governments should discourage him from trying it by warning him that they would go to war with Germany if he did try it.

Chamberlain's attitude to this crucial issue was conditioned by a whole host of considerations, all of which added up to an entirely understandable but not entirely consistent point of view. On the one hand, he was convinced that the Germans understood no argument but force, that Hitler was "half mad," and that his intentions were serious and immediate. On the other, he told himself that Britain was not yet ready to fight (but was Hitler?), that he ought not to commit the country to war until there was a fair chance of beating Germany to her knees within a reasonable time, that Englishmen were not pledged to support the Czechs and that British governments since Lloyd George's time had consistently refused to give such a pledge when asked to do so. Neither the British public nor the Dominions, he felt sure, would approve of a war fought to prevent the Sudeten Germans from achieving self-government. Nor did he forget reports from secret sources which stressed Russia's interest in maneuvering Britain into war with Germany. Moreover, his belief that the Germans understood no argument but force did not prevent him from believing also that there must be some point at which they were amenable to reason. Rejecting his first impulse, which was to give the Czechs a guarantee and damn the consequences, he played for time by reminding the House of Commons long before the arrival of the French ministers that British and French interests were closely interwoven, and that Britain was very likely to find herself fighting beside France if the French did go to war.

The French must have found a decision even harder. Under a series of weak governments, political and ideological conflicts stirred up by the Spanish Civil War and kept alive by a stream of propaganda from all kinds of questionable sources had split the country from top to bottom. The last administration before Daladier's, a Popular Front government under Léon Blum, had held office barely a month and had devoted much of its attention to a desperate attempt to prop up its Communist-ridden counterpart in Spain by reopening the frontier to French munitions. In recent weeks a series of strikes had reduced aircraft production to zero at a time when Germany, with an output of four to five hundred machines a month, was exploring new sources of supply in Austria, yet was still so thin on the ground that convincing evidence from the French that they meant to honor their obligations in Central Europe at all costs might have had far-reaching effects on German policy, and conceivably on British policy. As it was, a press campaign which hinted that Czechoslovakia was not worth the sacrifice of French lives did not strengthen Daladier's position or foster confidence among the British that any undertakings he might give would be carried out by a successor. The London conversations were difficult and a breach was narrowly averted. In the end the statesmen agreed that nothing which could be construed as an ultimatum should be delivered to the Germans, but that the British government should sound them as to their intentions in the light of a promise which Hitler had given not to use force in Czechoslovakia. In the meantime both governments would press the Czechs to make concessions. The two governments also agreed to staff talks, on condition that these were confined to the level of the service attachés. The British were inclined to fight shy of anything more than an exchange of information about air matters, but finally conceded that other topics should be discussed on the understanding that there was to be no commitment at the Chiefs of Staff or governmental level. The upshot was a tentative plan, which held good until the spring of 1939, for the despatch of two British divisions and an advanced air striking force to the Continent if the French should find themselves at war with Germany.

Three weeks after the return of the French ministers to Paris, massive movements of German troops near the Czechoslovakian frontier were reported, and the Czechs ordered a partial mobilization. But a world war for the sake of the little-known inhabitants of the Sudetenland seemed no more attractive to most Germans than a world war for the sake of the Czechs did to most Englishmen and Frenchmen, and the crisis passed after the British government had warned Berlin in the mildest terms that Britain might not stand aside if Hitler went too far. On the other flank of the Chamberlain front, diplomatic pressure in Prague extracted from the Czechs a promise of concessions to the Sudeten Germans, though it also had the less desirable effect of encouraging the other minorities to stake out claims.

On the whole, the policy of "armed appeasement" seemed in

the summer of 1938 to be shaping fairly well. The fall of Austria had opened many eyes to the need to rearm thoroughly and quickly. The shackles of "business as usual" had been thrown off at last. The government had given the Air Ministry a free hand to order all the aircraft they could get, the Admiralty were working on substantial programs laid down in 1936, and even the War Office were beginning to sniff the air and awake from their long nightmare of cheeseparing and neglect. British and French naval strength were far greater than German in terms of firepower and tonnage, while the French Army was still numerically the strongest in Europe and was almost certainly capable of seeing the German Army off if its leaders would only grasp their opportunities and prepare a sound strategic plan. Paradoxically, weakness in the air and the shortage of antiaircraft weapons were the factors which caused the British government most anxiety, yet it was precisely because he wanted Britain to be strong in the air that Chamberlain had insisted in 1934 that the Defence Requirements Committee's program should be set aside and that the army, which provided all the antiaircraft guns and searchlights for air defense, should be left out in the cold. But four thousand new aircraft of all types and categories were promised from British factories by the spring of 1939, the new 3.7-inch and 4.5-inch antiaircraft guns were also expected to arrive in substantial numbers by that time, and in July the Prime Minister was told by a trusted subordinate, Sir Arthur Robinson of the Supply Board, that the country would be ready to fight "on more or less equal terms" in about a year. His problem, if he could not postpone war indefinitely, was therefore to postpone it for at least a year and keep the rearmament drive moving steadily in the meantime.

To devote himself to the rearmament side of his two-point plan and leave diplomatic negotiations to men already on the spot was not, however, a course which appealed to Chamberlain. The fear of a deadlock between the Czechs and the Sudeten Germans oppressed the British government with a sense that time was running out. At the same time, it was a symptom of the fascination exercised on the minds of British and French statesmen by legends of Nazi might that, while the unreadiness of the British Army for

war in 1938 was clearly understood, little weight was given
to the chance that the hastily improvised German Army might
also be unready, or to the possibility that Hitler, for all his bluster,
might be as reluctant to fight France and Britain without good
cause as France and Britain were reluctant to fight him. Determined to hasten a settlement in Czechoslovakia and thus buy off
the National Socialist bogy, the British government offered to
send an "investigator and mediator" to Prague, wrung a reluctant
assent from the hard-pressed Czechs, and early in August despatched Lord Runciman for the purpose. Like some members of
the British public, who felt instinctively that the Runciman mission was the most damaging admission of weakness made by any
British government for many years, the British Embassy in Berlin
showed no enthusiasm for a move which, in spite of Chamberlain's
insistence that an investigator and mediator was not an arbitrator,
seemed all too likely to confront Britain with the choice between
war and surrender if Runciman produced a plan which was not
accepted. Moreover, the mere fact that the British government
saw fit to go to such lengths was enough to give the impression
that they were eager to purchase a settlement at almost any cost.

Thus fortified, Hitler and Henlein were able to increase their
demands with the comfortable knowledge that nothing which the
British and French governments and Lord Runciman could do to
push the Czechs to the limits of concession would be left undone.
For Hitler there was also the satisfaction of knowing that, while
he could always avoid war and pass for a reasonable man by
accepting a compromise solution, it was also open to him to call
the Franco-British bluff at any moment by pitching his claims so
high that the other side would have no choice but to go to war or
confess that they were not prepared to do so.

German troop movements continued throughout August, and
Berlin responded so bleakly to British overtures that reports that
Hitler's service chiefs were against war were discounted in London.
By September 2, when Runciman sent word to Hitler that he
could have a plan ready by about the middle of the month if all
else failed, it seemed reasonably certain that Henlein would refuse
the offer of autonomy which the Czechs had been prevailed upon

to make, and that the Nazi Party Rally due to begin at Nuremberg on September 5 would be the signal for a show of violence. Both expectations were fulfilled. Even before Hitler announced on the last day of the rally that the Sudeten Germans could count on his support, German agents and SS men appeared mysteriously in Czechoslovakia, clashes between demonstrators and Czech officials brought rioting and bloodshed, and British and French statesmen began to ask themselves as a matter of urgency how they could avoid war without openly surrendering to Hitler's blackmail for the third time since he came to power.

An answer which had already occurred to many people, but which few Englishmen had hitherto cared to put into words, was sketched by an editorial writer in the London *Times* when he suggested on September 7 that, if the Sudeten Germans were not satisfied with autonomy, the frontiers of Czechoslovakia might have to be redrawn. A disavowal by the Foreign Office did not prevent some readers from concluding that the British government were feeling their way toward partition, and that they might not think it incumbent on the French to stick too closely to the letter of their engagement to the Czechs. As if to remove that impression, the British almost at once took the first step toward a partial mobilization by calling up vessels needed for minelaying and minesweeping. On the other hand, an announcement by the Prime Minister on September 11 that Britain would not stand aside if the integrity of France were threatened did not really change the situation very much, since it still left the onus on the French to decide between peace and war in the light of the best or the worst gloss they cared to put on British statements. On the same day Henlein fled to Germany; on the next the Führer wound up the proceedings at Nuremberg with a characteristically truculent and disagreeable speech in which he referred to the Sudeten Germans as "these tortured creatures," and added significantly that they were neither defenseless nor abandoned.

The French considered all these matters, and much else besides, at a meeting of ministers on September 13. They were not at all confident that the Russians, who were carrying out vast purges in the higher ranks of their armed forces, would do anything to help the Czechs, or that France or Czechoslovakia would gain anything from Russian assistance even if it were forthcoming. Like the Czechs themselves, they had their doubts about the advantages of having Russia on their side. Above all, they faced the knowledge that France was neither physically nor morally ready for war with Germany, that for years past their war plans had been framed for the sole purpose of protecting French soil from invasion, and that no purely defensive strategy could stop Hitler from marching into Czechoslovakia if he cared to take the kind of calculated risk he had already taken when he marched into Austria. In common with the British government they were haunted, too, by an almost obsessive fear that the German air force (whose thousand serviceable bombers and seven to eight hundred fully trained bomber crews would almost certainly have been devoted largely to army support work if Hitler had been forced to go to war) was keyed up to deal them a smashing blow which might knock them out before their strength could be deployed. Concluding that discretion was the better part of valor, they decided not to mobilize, and to warn Prague in even stronger terms than they had already used that they might have to reconsider their long-standing promise of support if the Czechs took too firm a line with the Sudeten Germans. And that evening Neville Chamberlain, who had been thinking for some days of trying a direct approach to Hitler if all else failed, sent off a telegram in which he offered to fly at once to Germany "with a view to trying to find a peaceful solution" of the Sudeten problem.

10

MUNICH

His first visit was made in the middle of the month on his own initiative, but after discussion with Lord Halifax. Holding firmly to his umbrella and his faith in human nature, he flew to Munich on Thursday, September 15, and traveled thence by train to Hitler's retreat at Berchtesgaden. He found the Führer bent on invading Czechoslovakia without delay, but willing to hold his hand if the British government would agree that the country should be partitioned on the lines of Woodrow Wilson's principle of self-determination. Chamberlain replied that he must consult his colleagues and the French, and would return in due course with an answer. Hitler's interpreter, Dr. Paul Schmidt, kept a record of the interview, but Chamberlain failed to establish his right to a copy and had to rely on his memory when he reported to the Cabinet. This seemed to British officials symptomatic of Hitler's attitude, and to bode ill for the success of the negotiations.

On the following Saturday, Daladier and Bonnet traveled to London for talks with Chamberlain and Halifax. The British and French ministers agreed that partition was better than war, and decided to propose that parts of Czechoslovakia in which more than half the population was German should be ceded under the supervision of an international commission. The Czechs at first refused to consider partition, but gave way when they learned that the alternative was to be left high and dry by the French.

On September 22 Chamberlain left for his second visit to Germany. Remarking that he was on his way to fight with a wild beast, he traveled to the Rhineland to impart the Franco-British proposals to Hitler at Godesberg, which the Führer had chosen as a more convenient rendezvous for the sixty-nine-year-old British statesman than far-off Berchtesgaden. He found his host in a particularly disagreeable mood, and the proceedings went badly from the start. It seemed that, just as the Austro-Hungarian government had been determined in 1914 to teach the Serbs a lesson even at the risk of a general war, so Hitler was determined to punish the Czechs at any cost. Rejecting the Franco-British proposals on the ground that they would involve intolerable delay and that Poland and Hungary, as well as Germany, had claims on Czechoslovakia which would not wait, he demanded immediate occupation of all German-speaking areas by German troops. That evening Chamberlain reported by telephone to the Cabinet that the outlook seemed unpromising, and next day the Czechs ordered general mobilization after ascertaining that neither the British nor the French were willing to take the responsibility of advising them not to do so. Rather than give a handle to his critics among German service leaders by breaking openly with the British, Hitler did, however, agree to wait until October 1 before staging his invasion.

The Czechs were not much reassured by this concession. They rejected the Godesberg ultimatum and showed that they meant to invoke the Franco-Czechoslovak alliance. The sequel was a token mobilization of half a million Frenchmen and another hurried visit to London by the French ministers, this time accompanied by General Gamelin. Within the next forty-eight hours the British government mobilized the fleet, ordered air squadrons to their war bases, and called up fifty thousand antiaircraft and coast defense gunners. They also distributed thirty-five million gas masks, and (without consulting the Russians) issued a communiqué to the effect that Britain and Russia would stand by France.

Meanwhile the Prime Minister, whose private opinion was that neither the French nor the Russians were to be relied upon, maintained contact with Hitler through the British Embassy in

Berlin and, more particularly, through his Chief Industrial Adviser and close confidant, Sir Horace Wilson. The gist of his communications to the Führer was that the British government regarded themselves as morally responsible for seeing that the Czechs carried out the Godesberg proposals, and that he was still willing to put pressure on Prague if Hitler would only abstain from seizing by force what the good offices of the British could easily secure for him without a fight. Hitler's reply, delivered at interviews with Sir Horace Wilson on September 26 and 27, was that he would negotiate with the Czechs only if they accepted his terms in advance, that the French and the British could do as they pleased, and that the whole of Germany was solidly behind him.

But Hitler was wrong. For once, at any rate, the whole of Germany was not solidly behind him. Toward midnight on September 27, only a few hours after he had told Chamberlain's messenger that he would "smash the Czechs," a long column of motorized and armored troops rumbled through Berlin from west to east. The marked lack of enthusiasm with which its passage was watched by the crowds in the streets was not lost on the Führer. He was used to opposition from his service chiefs, who were strongly against the Czechoslovakian adventure, but not even he could afford to disregard the masses. Furthermore, he was soon to find that his ally Mussolini was not as stanch a partner when a showdown was in view as when he was only called upon to bluff. Aware that Italy was almost wholly unprepared for a major war and had nothing to gain from a German triumph, the upholder of the southern end of the Rome-Berlin Axis showed himself during the next few days as wholehearted an appeaser as any British or French statesman could have wished.

September 28 was a busy day for Hitler. In the morning the French Ambassador, M. André François-Poncet, brought him detailed plans for the transfer of the Sudetenland to German rule. Sir Nevile Henderson followed with renewed offers of mediation and further promises to keep the Czechs up to the mark. Both interviews were interrupted by messages from Mussolini, the first counseling moderation and the second offering his services as conciliator at a four-power conference which he suggested that Hitler should summon. In the meantime President Roosevelt had issued an appeal to all concerned to settle their problems without war.

In face of such unanimity, Hitler seems to have concluded that not even he could order a reluctant army to fight for a tract of territory which the great powers were only too eager to hand him on a platter. Foregoing his punitive expedition with a reluctance which put him in a thoroughly bad temper for several days, he canceled a mass meeting at which mobilization was to have been announced, and invited Chamberlain and Daladier to meet him and Mussolini next day at Munich.

Accordingly the Prime Minister left London a few hours later on the third and last of his missions to Nazi Germany. The Munich Conference began soon after 1 P.M. on September 29 and ended almost exactly thirteen hours later, when the British, German, French, and Italian plenipotentiaries, recovering from the shock of finding that there was no ink in the inkstand provided for their use, put their signatures to a series of documents providing for the transfer of the Sudetenland to Germany in stages and under international supervision. As there was never any doubt about the outcome of the proceedings, the statesmen had little to do but agree on details of procedure and criticize the drafts prepared for them by experts. The hardest task for Chamberlain and his party was to assist afterward in breaking the news to the Czechs that the conference had signed away their rights without even going through the formality of inviting them to attend and state their case.

But most members of the public were far from regarding the agreement reached at Munich as a foregone conclusion. Convinced that an appalling calamity had been averted at the eleventh hour, ordinary men and women expressed their relief in an almost hysterical outburst of enthusiasm, such as Europe had not seen since the Armistice. On his return to London Chamberlain was greeted with such moving demonstrations of gratitude for his efforts that he, too, came to believe that something wonderful had happened at Munich and that the civilized world had been saved from disaster by consummate statesmanship. Even Daladier, who feared when he saw from his aircraft the crowds that had assembled to greet his return to Paris that they had come to lynch him for his betrayal of the Czechs, had the agreeable experience of finding himself a hero. In England about thirty members of the House of Commons who usually supported the government abstained from voting when the rights and wrongs of Munich were debated, and one minister, Alfred Duff Cooper, gave up his post as a protest against the Prime Minister's surrender. Yet even the abstainers did little to contradict the almost universal assumption that Munich had averted war.

But what war? For at least a fortnight before Munich the only war in prospect was a local war between the Germans and the Czechs. In spite of the alarm which accompanied and followed the Godesberg conversations, was there ever a time during those weeks when France and Britain ran any real risk of becoming involved in a general war unless they chose to start one? There could be no such war unless the French were willing to go to war with Germany, for the British had made it clear from the start that they would not fight unless the French did, and not even the bellicose Hitler was likely to go out of his way to involve himself in a two-front war by himself initiating hostilities in the West. Yet nothing was more certain than that the French were not willing to go to war with Germany, and that they were ready to snatch at any pretext to avoid doing so. According to his biographer, Chamberlain satisfied himself before he left Germany on his first visit in the middle of September that the French had no intention of fighting. Nothing that happened afterward gave him cause to depart from that opinion. The very fact that Daladier and his colleagues ordered a partial mobilization after Godesberg confirmed the rightness of his verdict, for they would not have contented themselves with a mere half million reservists if they had really meant to go to war. In 1936 Gamelin had asked for nearly a million and a quarter men, in addition to the forces of the interior, merely to occupy Luxembourg and a small part of the Saar. In 1939, with five million men at his disposal and the greater part of the German Army fighting on the Polish front, the best he could do was to advance five miles into German territory on a sixteen-mile front. What impression was he likely to make when he visited London after Godesberg, except that nothing was further from his thoughts than the tough and resolute offensive without which all talk of helping the Czechs was mere window dressing?

Nor were British military measures during the Munich crisis consistent with a genuine belief on the part of the government that a general war begun on British or French initiative was imminent. At most they indicated willingness to put up some sort of defense against a desperate act of revenge by a frustrated tyrant. The government mobilized the fleet, but general mobilization was not ordered, and the procedure laid down for the "precautionary period" which was supposed to precede hostilities was not put into force. In any case the armed forces were in no state to play even a supporting role in an Anglo-French offensive. Cruisers and destroyers were too few to protect trade, let alone provide a surplus for any form of offensive action. The naval harbors at Dover and Harwich were silted up, minesweepers could not have been made ready for war in less than three weeks, and reserves of naval ammunition had to be dispersed in sidings and on shipboard for lack of proper storage space. The army was in no position to send even a couple of divisions across the Channel at short notice. Fighter Command, which was not only responsible for air defense at home but was the sole source of battlefield fighters, had five squadrons of Hurricanes, no Spitfires, and no stored reserves. Apart from the Hurricanes, its mobilizable strength consisted of twenty-four squadrons of vintage machines, of which about a fifth still had some fighting value while the rest were almost useless against anything more formidable than slow-moving transport aircraft. Its only source of replacements, apart from new production, was an immediate reserve of fewer than two hundred aircraft of all types. With so few fighters, and with only about fifty modern and fewer than four hundred older antiaircraft guns toward an estimated requirement of more than twelve hundred, the country was in no position to invite attack, or to go to war at all unless the French could promise an offensive which offered a good chance of defeating the Germans while they were still preoccupied in Central Europe.

Since the French were notoriously unable or unwilling to make such a promise, and since the Prime Minister was well aware of the impossibility of fighting successfully without weapons, it is inconceivable that he would have committed his country to war unless he were forced to do so by an act of aggression against British or French territory. Even with Hitler in the saddle, the Germans were not likely to go out of their way to meet trouble by attacking France or Britain at a time when Czechoslovakia was still unconquered. While a sudden air attack on London or Paris was possible, and was indeed predicted in some quarters, it was not very probable, and nothing which came to light in later years suggested that the Nazi leaders ever nourished any such intention. Probably the worst that might have happened if Hitler had insisted, after all, on taking the Sudetenland by force was a series of Polish, Hungarian, and possibly Russian interventions which might have confronted France and Britain with problems similar to those raised by the war in Spain.

If the foregoing arguments are sound, it follows that the truth about the Munich crisis is that there was no crisis. The Munich Conference did not avert a general war, because there was never anything but a remote risk of a general war. At most it averted a local war in Central Europe, which might conceivably have led to an armed conflict between Germany and Russia. If that had happened, the Western democracies would have had the choice between non-intervention, and intervention on their own terms. If there was only a remote risk of a general war, it also follows that the millions of Englishmen and Frenchmen who hailed Chamberlain as their savior were victims of a misconception, although thanks were still due to him for helping to save Czech and German lives.

The fact remained that, for France and Britain, Munich was the culmination of a long series of surrenders. In 1936 it would have been comparatively easy to convince the Germans that, while there might be a case for remilitarization of the Rhineland, they were not entitled to take the law into their own hands by tearing up the Treaty of Versailles and the freely negotiated Locarno pacts. To teach them respect for international law when they seized Austria with the outward consent of the inhabitants, but in fact by fraud and treachery, would have been more difficult. At Munich the democracies were able to buy off Hitler only by sacrificing their self-respect and the future of the Czechs. When Chamberlain returned from Munich he waved a document pledging Britain and Germany not to go to war with each other and to adjust all differences by peaceful means; but he knew that such an agreement was not likely to be worth much except as evidence that he had done his best, at a last-minute interview with Hitler, to revive in him the spark of human feeling which he thought must smolder somewhere in the breast of even the most detestable of men.

Yet, even on the assumption that the Nazi rulers were still determined to make mischief even at the cost of their own ultimate destruction, there remained the hope that France and Britain might use the respite well, and perhaps even that British diplomacy, which had lost so many battles since the Armistice, might yet be able to prise Mussolini firmly from the Rome-Berlin Axis before Hitler made his next move. The policy which Chamberlain's critics called appeasement, but which he called armed appeasement, might yet succeed if the British and the French used their vast productive capacity to arm themselves at least as fast as the Germans were arming, and if they learned to pull together. But whether Mussolini was not also bent on his own destruction, and whether Chamberlain and Daladier were capable of inspiring such efforts as neither Englishmen nor Frenchmen had seen the need to make since the Germans were at the gates of Amiens in 1918, were among the awkward questions to which, as yet, there seemed to be no answer.

11

THE DESCENT TO WAR

THE CHAMBERLAIN GOVERNMENT LIVED, DIED, AND HAD ITS BEING IN a climate of paradox and contradiction. The Prime Minister took up office in 1937 with a firm resolve to bring the national defenses rapidly to a point at which the country could negotiate from strength with the dictators. Yet he found his guns already spiked by his interventions as Chancellor of the Exchequer. After Hitler's seizure of Austria in March 1938, Chamberlain announced his intention of abandoning conversations with Germany for the moment and making some gesture which would convince the Germans that Britain was not to be bullied. Yet the gesture he made was to give away his whole case by sending Lord Runciman to Prague. Rearmament was such a long haul after fifteen years of neglect and four of niggling economy that throughout the Czechoslovakian affair he was forced, if he negotiated at all, to negotiate from weakness, not from strength.

With Munich behind him, Chamberlain found himself a popular hero, yet bitterly criticized by the Opposition and even by some members of his own party. Among other misdeeds he was accused of forfeiting American good will by not quarreling openly with fascist Germany and Italy, and of missing chances of making friends with democratic Russia. These charges were hard for a Conservative Prime Minister to refute without aggravating his offense. Since he did genuinely value Anglo-Saxon unity, he could not very well point out that, as long as the United States government insisted on declaring its neutrality, American protests were likely to make even less impact in Berlin than British protests. Nor could he, without a breach of protocol, refer publicly to the secret service reports which convinced him that Russia did not care a straw for the democracies, and that her policy was to embroil them in a disastrous war with Germany for her own ends.

In some ways it was even harder for him to convince his critics that there was nothing new or sinister about appeasement. To seek peace had long been the aim of every British government except when the country was actually at war. Where Chamberlain differed from his immediate predecessors was that he saw more clearly than they the futility of talking about collective security as long as the countries whose rulers wanted peace were too weak to impose their will on those whose rulers wanted war. But to say so would have invited the charge that he had failed, nonetheless, to rearm quickly and radically enough to make his policy effective.

Thus the important part of Chamberlain's policy was the rearmament program which, after Munich, went faster but still not fast enough. The part which attracted most attention was his attempt to form a common front against German aggression without lending weight to Hitler's complaints of encirclement or mortgaging Europe's future to the Russians. Throughout the winter of 1938–39 he did his best to encourage French resistance to German menaces and draw France and Italy together, himself visiting Paris in November and Rome in January. So far as any visible change in Franco-Italian relations went, his efforts failed in face of Mussolini's propagandist claims to Nice, Corsica, and Tunis, objections from left-wing Frenchmen to any truck with the dictators, and a growing impression among right-wing Frenchmen that, if any dictator was worth cultivating, it was Hitler. To these obstacles was added the conviction of Frenchmen of all parties that in any case Italian friendship was worth very little. At first unwilling to agree that arms mattered more after Munich than negotiations, Chamberlain wrote in October that "the conciliatory part of the policy is just as important as the rearming"; but that opinion did not outlast the discovery that Hitler had no intention of honoring his engagements unless it suited him to do so.

Meanwhile the plight of the dissension-ridden Czechoslovakian state was going from bad to worse, and in March the crisis broke. Seizing the pretext of a quarrel between Czechs and Slovaks, Hitler declared a protectorate over Bohemia and Moravia, and his troops moved into the country under cover of a demonstration by about five hundred German aircraft. Simultaneously Slovakia declared its independence at his prompting, while Hungary seized Ruthenia. A week later Hitler helped himself to Memel, which the Allied and Associated Powers had taken from Germany at Versailles and afterward allotted to Lithuania.

Affronted and alarmed by the Führer's disregard of the promises he had made at Munich, Chamberlain reacted not only with startling energy but also with a startling contempt for consequences. Announcing on March 31 that Britain would support Poland in the event of "any action which clearly threatened Polish independence," he threw away the traditional caution of postwar British governments with respect to Central European commitments, thus voluntarily accepting the policy of eastern and western alliances which the far more adventurous Lloyd George had rejected as impossibly dangerous in 1921 and 1922. To emphasize his change of heart, he also doubled the establishment of the Territorial Army, introduced compulsory military service for men of twenty and twenty-one, sanctioned unrestricted staff talks with the French, and set up the Ministry of Supply against which he had set his face when it was previously urged on him. When Mussolini followed the German example by walking into Albania, already to all intents and purposes an Italian puppet state, the now-defiant Prime Minister added Greece and Rumania to the list of countries for which Britain was prepared to go to war, and threw in an agreement with Turkey for good measure.

Thus, by a crowning irony, the ultimate achievement of the profoundly and genuinely peaceloving Chamberlain-Halifax partnership was to saddle the British public with an unlimited liability to make war on behalf of a whole host of countries in which Britain had little or no direct interest, and for whose welfare the vast majority of Englishmen had either never felt, or had long ceased to feel, any particular concern. Nor was there the shadow of a hope that France and Britain could save Poland or Rumania from the consequences of German aggression except at the cost of the general war which it had long been the chief aim of British governments to avert. Yet so strong and widespread was the feeling on both sides of the Channel that Hitler's pretensions had become intolerable and that he must be told so, that the government was generally felt to have acted rightly. It was difficult for peaceable British and French citizens to understand that not even the threat of a major war would divert Hitler from his ends and that there was, in fact, no way of disabusing him of the belief that he would be allowed to do as he pleased as long as he did not directly threaten British or French territory.

Yet that was how matters stood in those last months of peace. Convinced that France and Britain would never take the offensive against Germany for the sake of Danzig or the Polish Corridor, Hitler prepared for his next venture on the assumption that, even if they did save their faces by declaring war when his armored columns thundered into Poland, they would hasten to make peace as soon as they were confronted with the reality of another German triumph. At the end of the third week in August, with thirteen infantry and five armored corps massed near the Polish frontier from Pomerania and East Prussia to the Carpathians, he summoned his generals to Berchtesgaden and treated them to a lecture on the Polish question. He told them of the impending Russo-German pact, claimed that it would make a British blockade of Germany ineffective, and assured them that the Fatherland had nothing to fear from the democracies. France and Britain, ruled by men of straw and notoriously deficient in air strength and antiaircraft weapons, would never, he felt sure, invite the heavy casualties they were bound to suffer if they attacked Germany. The generals, not at all confident that the British guarantee was meaningless but willing to believe that its outcome might be nothing but another Munich, returned to their headquarters, where on August 25 they received orders to attack Poland at dawn next day.

The British government remained equally unconvinced until the eleventh hour that a shooting war with Germany was imminent. Suppressing his distrust of the Russians, Chamberlain had agreed in the spring to negotiations with the Soviet government, but without much faith in their success. To buy an uneasy friendship with Russia at the expense of the Baltic States was not an attractive course, and in any case Britain was in no position to offer the Russians any bargain which the Germans could not cap, or to force the Poles to accept Russian help against their will. But, Russia or no Russia, the Prime Minister found it as hard to believe that the Führer would risk a major war for Danzig and the Polish Corridor as the Führer found it hard to believe that the Prime Minister would do so. Resisting demands for reassembly within three weeks when Parliament adjourned exactly a quarter of a century after the outbreak of the First World War, he encouraged members of his clan to take their holidays as usual. In the middle of August he himself left for the Highlands.

Meanwhile American complaints of British and French deference to the dictators did not prevent Congress from rejecting President Roosevelt's proposals to fortify Guam and amend the Neutrality Act so that arms and munitions of war could be sent to the democracies. More than seven years after Shanghai, so little had come of the expected Anglo-American cooperation in the Far East that nothing could be done to protect British subjects in China from humiliation at the hands of the Japanese for fear that any intervention might tempt the Germans to assume that Britain would soon have her hands full in the Pacific theater.

The Prime Minister had scarcely had time to sniff the Highland air of Scotland when he was summoned in haste to London by the news that Germany and Russia had reached an understanding. Even then, it seemed, the hope of peace was not quite gone. Warned that the British guarantee to Poland still held good, the Führer hesitated. Only a few hours after he had despatched his troops, but so late that one column was halted with difficulty only after a staff officer in an army cooperation aircraft had landed in front of it, he canceled the order, but directed that mobilization should continue. On the last day of the month, his faith in himself and his destiny restored, he ordered that, after all, the invasion of Poland should begin and that the troops should move next morning.

12

ALL QUIET ON THE WESTERN FRONT

AT DAYBREAK ON FRIDAY, SEPTEMBER 1, 1939, THE GERMAN ARMY launched its elaborately prepared attack on Poland with forty-two divisions of regular troops and one SS division, backed by sixteen second-line divisions newly formed or forming. That afternoon Sir Nevile Henderson informed Ribbentrop in Berlin that Great Britain would fulfill her obligations toward Poland unless Germany withdrew her troops from Polish soil. The French, after issuing mobilization orders in the morning, hung back for a few more hours in the hope that Italian mediation and secret negotiations might yet avert a clash, and also to gain time for at least some reservists to reach their units before the expected onslaught by the German air force was likely to be delivered. But at ten o'clock that evening the French Ambassador presented a communication on the same lines as the British.

These declarations, which amounted to a joint ultimatum in every respect except that no time-limit was specified and that they were separated by an interval of several hours, created something like consternation in Berlin. Up to the last moment the general expectation was that France and Britain would protest at the invasion of Poland but would stop a long way short of declaring war. When Hitler, addressing the Reichstag in the afternoon, spoke ominously of death or victory and went out of his way to refer to the capitulation of 1918, suspicion dawned that for once he had overreached himself and that the two-front war he had sworn to avoid was dangerously near. Experienced army officers who knew how hastily the units they commanded had been put together were appalled at the prospect of fighting France and Britain as well as Poland, and even some of the Führer's warmest admirers shared their fears. General Jodl, an intelligent man whom Hitler chose as Chief of the Operations Staff of the Supreme Command of the Armed Forces because, of all the German generals, he seemed to feel most faith in his master's strategic insight, took a poor view of the outlook, and even the usually confident Göring was shaken. "If we lose this war," he said, "may God have mercy on us!"

Where such were the views of men who had hitched their wagons to Hitler's star, no enthusiasm for total war could be expected from the myriads of Germans who, less than twelve months earlier, had troubled the Führer's sensibilities by hailing Chamberlain as the savior of peace. Nor was there the slightest eagerness for war in France and Britain. There, as in Germany, the older generation remembered the nightmare of the trenches. Throughout the democracies the young had been brought up on the theory, so eagerly propagated by armchair strategists and so valuable to German diplomacy after the revival of the German air force, that the next war would begin with massive air attacks on more or less defenseless cities. In 1914 crowds of suppliants to the god of battles had shouted for war in the streets of London, Paris, and Berlin, while their less sanguine rulers mourned the passing of an era and enquired anxiously whether there was no way of arresting the avalanche which their fears and jealousies had launched. A quarter of a century later, rulers and ruled were united in the conviction that a general war was a calamity. Not even Hitler actively wanted war with the democracies in 1939, if only because he knew that he was not yet ready to try conclusions with them. Prepared to gamble on the hope that, even if France and Britain declared war, they would not in fact make war unless they were attacked, he ruled on the day when he gave his final order for the invasion of Poland that the French frontier should not be crossed, that Belgian and Dutch neutrality should be scrupulously respected, and that the German armies in the West should use no more force than might be needed to repel minor attacks by local troops.

With a smoothness which seemed to belie reports that France was too disorganized to go to war, the French proceeded during the next three weeks to mobilize about five million men, the vast majority of them trained reservists who had done at least twelve months' service with the colors. In Germany, on the other hand, about half the three and three-quarter million men on the ration strength of the army in September were either raw recruits who had received no military training before reporting to their units, or veterans of the First World War who had not worn uniform or touched a weapon for twenty years. By limiting their forces of the interior to fewer than a million men, as compared with more than twice that number in France, the Germans were nevertheless able, like the French, to muster a field army of roughly two and three-quarter million men. With nearly a hundred and thirty thousand officers on the active list or the reserve, the French had an ample supply of subordinate commanders, many of them seasoned by service in the French colonial empire in Africa, the Far East, and Syria. The Germans, for many years restricted by the Versailles Treaty to a small voluntary army, were short of experienced regimental officers, but the very fact that their army was voluntary had helped them to use it as a forcing house for potential leaders. Yet, on balance, the creators of the new German Army were far from satisfied that they had been able to do a workmanlike job in the short time allowed. The consensus of opinion among them in 1939 was that they had succeeded, at Hitler's bidding and with Hitler's help, in improvising a force capable of defeating the Poles but far from ready to fight the army of a first-class power.

With field armies of approximately equal strength, the two sides mustered roughly the same number of divisions, but their forces were very differently disposed. Leaving ten of their ninety-nine divisions in Africa and nine opposite the Italian frontier, the French were able to concentrate the greater part of their troops between the Swiss frontier and the Channel. The Germans, with more than a hundred divisions, had fifty-nine on the Polish front or close behind it, leaving only eleven first-line and thirty-five inferior divisions to face eighty French and four British divisions on the Western Front. Hence it is not surprising that Hitler's instructions stressed the importance of doing nothing in the West to invite attack, or that his propaganda drew a flattering picture of the weakly held and hastily constructed Siegfried line. With the exception of the German General Staff, who dreaded an attack in the West while they were preoccupied in Poland, no one knew better than the Führer that his forces in the West were quite incapable of resisting such a blow as the French could easily deliver if they belied his hopes by taking the offensive.

Nor was the local superiority of the Franco-British alliance a mere matter of divisions. As long as most of the German armor and half the German air force remained on the Eastern Front, the French and the British shared an almost overwhelming superiority in tanks and a substantial superiority in aircraft. Notwithstanding the popular belief that the French had scarcely any armored fighting vehicles, they were well supplied with tanks which far exceeded any German tank in toughness and hitting-power, and whose low speed and limited radius of action need not have been serious handicaps if the French had fought a battle of their own choosing. As for aircraft, the British and the French had a first-line strength in the European theater alone of nearly a thousand bombers and more than twelve hundred fighters, as compared with a German establishment of roughly sixteen hundred bombers and twelve hundred and fifty fighters divided between two fronts. Moreover, their combined output of new machines exceeded that of the German aircraft industry, and they had more aircraft in reserve. In general, the relative ease with which tactical bombers on both sides could be shot down by fighters and antiaircraft gunners favored the Germans, who had more antiaircraft guns than their opponents and were more willing to gamble on the chances of swift success. On the other hand, the French were so well supplied with field guns and siege guns, most of which they never used, that they were not forced to depend to the same extent as the Germans on tactical bombers to tackle battlefield targets.

At sea the numerical superiority of the Franco-British alliance was absolute. On the outbreak of war the Germans had two battlecruisers, three pocket battleships and no aircraft carriers. Their opponents had seventeen capital ships and seven aircraft carriers. In cruisers and long-range submarines the British and the French outnumbered the Germans by ten to one and five to one respectively, while at Dover and Portsmouth alone there were almost as many destroyers as the Germans mustered at all their bases from the Baltic to the Ems.

In spite of the reluctance of the British and the French to go to war, and notwithstanding the slow pace of British preparations before Munich, there was thus no firm foundation for the legend that they were hopelessly outmatched at every point when they did go to war. Even without dive bombers, fast tanks and airborne troops, they did not lack the resources needed to break through the Siegfried line, roll up the weak formations holding it, and meet units returning from the Eastern Front on terms which might have brought an outcome very different from that of 1940. "We had the means," wrote General Gamelin, "of breaking open the Siegfried line." That this was not mere wishful thinking was shown by the verdict of German commanders and staff officers who testified that their hair stood on end when they contemplated the possibility of a French offensive in September, that the French could easily have reached the Rhine and even crossed it, that they were astonished that Gamelin did not seize his opportunity. Field Marshal Wilhelm Keitel, Chief of Staff of the Supreme Command of the Armed Forces, confessed at Nuremberg that his troops in the West could have put up "only a show of defense" if the French had attacked. "Why," asked General Fritz von Lossberg, "did not the French take advantage of their crushing superiority and send the weak troops occupying the West Wall flying?"

The answer which the German generals gave each other at the time was that evidently France and Britain had no real intention of making war, that once again the Führer had backed a winning hunch, that the next few weeks would bring a triumphant victory in Poland, followed by a negotiated peace with the democracies. But they were proved wrong when their victory in Poland brought no peace. There were many people in France and Britain who did argue that anything was better than a war which could bring nothing but harm to civilized Europe, irrespective of whether the Germans or the French and British won. (In three days, at the beginning of October, Neville Chamberlain received 1860 letters urging him to stop the war.) But there were millions more who believed that, no matter how disagreeable the consequences of a European war might be, there could be no peace with Hitler. "I pray the struggle may be short," wrote Chamberlain when the war was only two days old. But he added: "It can't end as long as Hitler remains in power."

Yet the perplexity of the German generals was understandable. If the British and French governments had really wished to reach an understanding with Hitler, their neglect of a chance of toppling him from power by overrunning the Rhineland while the best part of his army was in Poland would have been logical and states-manlike, though inglorious. Since they did not wish to reach an understanding with him, and were determined to unseat him, there was no logic in an inactivity which surrendered all initiative and strengthened his position. But the point which the German generals overlooked was that no appeal to logic could have shaken the conviction of the French High Command that only a de-fensive strategy was permissible. They had prepared for a long war of attrition, and a long war of attrition was the war they meant to have. Their textbooks told them that swift success was an illusion, and their textbooks must be right. "A continuous front," wrote the veteran Pétain in 1939, "is all-sufficient."

Thus it was not true that the French and the British did not mean to fight. On the contrary, they were so eager to engage the enemy that they were willing to wait until he was ready to turn his whole strength against them. The statesmen had their mis-givings about Gamelin, who seemed old beyond his years and whom Chamberlain described as sitting silent through a meeting and purring like a cat. But he had helped to draft the orders for the Battle of the Marne, and his reputation stood high in his own service. Content to leave the troublesome business of strategy to men who made it their life's work, the British and French govern-ments allowed their troops in northeast France to do practically nothing all the winter but consolidate positions which many of them were to exchange, as soon as fighting began, for an ill-prepared and almost unreconnoitered front on Belgian soil.

Meanwhile New York and Washington watched with mingled apprehension and disgust the latest round in the struggle between the haves and the have-nots in Europe. President Roosevelt had been deeply hurt by his failure in 1938 to persuade the British to turn their backs on Italy and pin their hopes on a proposal that he should lecture the nations on the benefits which might flow from a world-wide agreement to reduce armaments, observe the laws of war, and accept the principle of equal access to raw materials for all who could pay for them. Quite as firmly convinced as any Englishman could be that a victory for National Socialism would be an unparalleled disaster, many Americans found it as astonishing in 1939 that the democracies had not long ago solved their Central European problems by putting the dictators in their places as Hitler found it astonishing in 1937 that the British had not long ago solved their Indian problems by shooting Gandhi. From the robust standpoint of the New World the qualms of conscience which troubled Englishmen dissatisfied with the Versailles Treaty seemed mere hypocrisy, the British love of compromise a detestable heresy, the endless bickerings of left-wing and right-wing Frenchmen sinister and squalid. In a world where the rich were usually the strong it was hard, too, for most people to believe, although it was true, that such an outwardly prosperous nation as the British had failed for many years to provide themselves with the physical means of backing any foreign policy except one of acquiescence.

By the beginning of the war there was not much doubt left in the United States that sooner or later Hitler would have to be stopped, presumably by Americans if Englishmen and Frenchmen could not do it. Did America believe that Englishmen and Frenchmen could do it? Were the European democracies worth saving? In November Congress returned a partial and ambiguous answer by passing an amended Neutrality Act permitting the sale of arms to countries which could pay for them and fetch them. By this means the Roosevelt administration ensured that the side which commanded the seas would receive the benefit of such arms as the United States could supply as long as their money lasted, but deferred for later consideration the question of what would happen when their foreign balances were exhausted, or if they were defeated in the meantime.

13

DEFEAT AND DELIVERANCE

THE POLISH CAMPAIGN, COMPLETED IN LESS THAN A MONTH EX-
cept for mopping-up, made a name for the leaders of the new
German Army as exponents of lightning war. The more sober-
minded of them knew, however, that success in Poland was no
proof of the army's fitness for war with a first-class power. Against
the unsupported Poles, who fought with desperate courage but had
assumed until the last moment that they would have active help
from the French, the better-led and better-organized Germans
were bound to be successful. Nevertheless the campaign revealed
weaknesses which did not escape the German generals. Outside
picked units the general standard of training was poor. At the end
of the campaign the Chief of the General Staff reported "the
same signs of weariness as in 1917–18." On October 3 the Commander-in-Chief told Hitler that he needed the whole winter to
put things right. Reluctant though Generals Franz Halder and
Heinrich von Brauchitsch were to bolster the Führer's ambitions
by making success seem easy, they would hardly have drawn so
unflattering a picture of their own service without a background of
solid fact.

At any rate there was anything but jubilation in the higher
ranks of the military hierarchy when Hitler announced on September 27 that he had decided to take the offensive in the West
before the winter. Quite apart from the fact that many units
were only half trained and had never fired a live round, no preparations had been made for an offensive on the Western Front.

Essential aerodromes were without runways and hence usable only in good weather. Stocks of ammunition would have to be built up from new production before anything like a major attack could be delivered. Not for the first time, assassination of the Führer presented itself as an attractive solution of the problems of the High Command. As usual, nothing came of the proposal but vague plans accompanied by much soul-searching.

With the help of the weather, the generals were able to scotch Hitler's hopes of an autumn offensive, but his determination to settle accounts in the West when opportunity served remained inflexible. To make matters worse, the plan drawn up at his bidding seemed to combine the maximum of risk with the minimum of promise. The scheme reluctantly accepted by von Brauchitsch proposed that an Army Detachment and an Army Group under General Fedor von Bock, the whole comprising forty-three divisions and supported by a further twenty-two divisions advancing through Luxembourg and southern Belgium under General Karl von Rundstedt, should sweep through Holland and northern and central Belgium for the purpose of seizing as much territory as possible as a base for naval and air operations against Britain and a protective belt for the Ruhr. Since Germany had assured her neutral neighbors that their neutrality would be respected, the immorality of these proposals was apparent. A still more cogent objection to the plan was that it did not promise outright victory. Even if Bock's forces succeeded in biting off a sizeable chunk of territory, the British and French armies would merely be driven away from the North Sea coast and would probably be able to form a new defensive front. Given time to recruit their strength from overseas and exploit their well-known capacity for winning the last battle, the effete democracies might even end by turning the Germans out. In that case there would be few to praise either the military skill of the German leaders or their moral judgment.

General Erich von Manstein, von Rundstedt's Chief of Staff and afterward commander of an Army Group in Russia, was one of the ablest and most intelligent of Hitler's generals. Convinced of the uselessness of half-measures, he saw that what was wanted, if there had to be an offensive on the Western Front, was a move

which offered prospects of success so dazzling that all objections
would be silenced. He urged that the weight of the attack should
be shifted from Bock's front to Rundstedt's, and that the main
thrust should be made along a line from the Ardennes to the
mouth of the Somme with the object of driving a wedge through
the Franco-British armies and exposing the forces on both flanks
to defeat. Soon after making his proposals, which amounted to
a trenchant criticism of the plan approved by his superiors, Manstein was posted to command an Army Corps at Stettin, many
miles from any active front. But in February he was summoned,
with other corps commanders, to Berlin and was given a chance
of putting his ideas before the Führer. The plan approved by
Hitler a few days later reflected his so closely that it deserves to
be called the Manstein Plan.

Almost simultaneously General Gamelin was putting the finishing touches to his plan for the defense of France and the Low
Countries. He believed that the Germans, if they did attack,
would make their main thrust in the north. His chief preoccupation was to ensure that it was met before it gathered momentum
and before the industrial areas near the Franco-Belgian frontier
were overrun. If Holland as well as Belgium were invaded, nearly
a third of the hundred and four French and British divisions in
the Northeastern theater would be concentrated on or behind an
eighty-mile front from Breda to Namur. To these would be added
some twenty Belgian divisions which would fall back after fighting delaying actions farther forward. But Gamelin also made the
right wing very strong, allotting thirty-three field divisions as well
as the ten garrison divisions of the supposedly impregnable Magi-
not line to the sector from Longuyon southward, and earmarking
a further five divisions to guard against the improbable contingency
of an attack through Switzerland. These dispositions left the Commander-in-Chief of the Northeast front with so small a proportion
of his resources uncommitted that only ten divisions remained in
GHQ Reserve after twelve weak divisions had been allotted to the
ninety-five-mile stretch from Namur to Longuyon.

The weakness of Gamelin's center gave the impression that he
regarded an attack through the Ardennes as virtually impossible.

That was not so. He did believe, however, that the Germans would not attack in the Ardennes sector except after suffering a check elsewhere, and that in any case they would not try to cross the Meuse in that sector without first pausing to bring up masses of artillery. He concluded that local commanders would be able to give ample warning and that there would be plenty of time to reinforce them from the GHQ Reserve or by switching formations assigned to other sectors.

But the chain of command which Gamelin sponsored did not lend itself to rapid decisions. Until January he himself commanded the whole of the land forces in all theaters, with General Alphonse Georges as Deputy Commander for the Northeast front. In that month he persuaded the government to accept a new arrangement which made Georges Commander-in-Chief of the Northeast front, with his own GHQ and his own Command Post. One of the many evils which flowed from this reform was that the too-punctilious Gamelin's reluctance to give orders to a subordinate whom he had saddled with an independent command was matched by an equal reluctance on Georges' part to depart radically from dispositions sanctioned by his chief. Newly raised to independent status and in poor health, Georges was not, from the moral point of view, in a good position to rethink a crucial battle without a strong lead which Gamelin refused to give him for fear, as he put it, of "ruffling and humiliating" him at a time when he needed all his wits about him.

While ready to act as vigorously as they could if their own territory or that of their neighbors was invaded, the French and British governments had no intention in the early part of 1940 of themselves launching an offensive on the Western Front for at least another year or eighteen months. Their policy was to wear the Germans down by economic blockade, supplemented by such bombing as they felt they could safely undertake without precipitating an all-out struggle for air supremacy. Severance of the peacetime link between the ironmasters of Lorraine and the coalowners of the Ruhr made the Germans largely dependent on Swedish iron ore, which could reach them in sufficient quantities only as long as they were able to carry a good part of their supplies along shipping routes which passed close to the Norwegian coast. After taking careful diplomatic soundings, the two governments decided to risk a technical infringement of international law by laying mines in Scandinavian coastal waters. With the object of getting their blow in first if the Germans responded by landing in Norway, the British government arranged to embark troops at Rosyth and in the Clyde and rush them across the North Sea if the need arose.

Toward the end of March and early in April, reports that the Germans were preparing to descend on some or all of the Scandinavian countries were received in London, but they did not seem conclusive. Even when a substantial German naval force was seen at sea on April 7, naval experts in Whitehall were far more concerned with the threat to ocean trade than with any threat to Norway. By the evening practically the whole of the Home Fleet had left to intercept the German warships, but the Commander-in-Chief, Sir Charles Forbes, was so intent on catching up with them if they made for the Atlantic that he intentionally set a course which left the central part of the North Sea uncovered. Even the ships which were embarking troops at Rosyth and in the Clyde were ordered, after he had sailed, to reverse the process and put to sea. Thus the whole plan of the Scandinavian expedition was abandoned at the very moment when the time came to put it into practice with the wholehearted cooperation of the Norwegian government.

Commenting on these events in the House of Commons, Chamberlain expressed the opinion that Hitler had missed the bus. In fact, he had caught it with some hours to spare, and it was Chamberlain's own government which had neglected the timetable. By the morning of April 8 there was not much room for doubt that part, at any rate, of the German expedition was bound for Norway. Yet, in spite of Franco-British naval superiority, the German warships were able to reach their destinations next day without being intercepted on the outward route, while German paratroops were allowed to seize such obvious objectives as the aerodromes at Oslo and Stavanger without interference from

British troops and aircraft only a few hours' flying time away. Once on Danish and Norwegian soil and in possession of practically all the usable aerodromes in both countries, the comparatively small forces which the Germans devoted to the operation could not be turned out without an effort of which the French and British were not capable except at the cost of reducing their strength at home below the danger level.

Hitler's Scandinavian adventure crippled the German surface fleet, which lost half its destroyers and nearly a third of its cruisers, but it gave Germany valuable naval and air bases and made neutral statesmen more afraid than ever of incurring the Füher's wrath by accepting help from France and Britain. The most important consequence of the episode, from almost every point of view, was the fall of Neville Chamberlain and his replacement by Winston Churchill at the head of a coalition government. As First Lord of the Admiralty since the outbreak of war, Churchill was as much answerable as any minister for the Norwegian fiasco, but he had the advantage over Chamberlain that his denunciations of the Nazi ideology stamped him as an anti-fascist, under whom left-wing politicians were willing to serve in spite of the dislike of Communism which recommended him to right-wing Tories.

With the Manstein Plan accepted, the Germans were ready by the time the weather was suitable to launch their great offensive in the West without consideration for the right of Belgians and Dutchmen to opt for neutrality. On the assumption that twenty-four Belgian divisions were ready to defend their country, there was approximate numerical equality between the two sides so far as land forces were concerned. There was also approximate numerical equality in single-seater fighters, with roughly thirteen hundred aircraft on each side. Finally, the French Army had at least as many good tanks as the German Army. The Germans, on the other hand, had more bombers, many more antiaircraft guns, and more antitank guns. But numbers were never a decisive factor during the decisive phase. The French line at Sedan was effectively breached in five or six hours by about three hundred dive bombers and a small number of troops who crossed the Meuse in collapsible boats without tanks or artillery. During the forty-eight hours which saw the Germans punch a sixty-mile gap in the continuous front to which the Allies pinned their faith, only twelve battalions out of eighty-one in the French First Army were in action, and were enough to stem the enemy's advance although the French High Command continued to believe until too late that theirs was the crucial sector. The proportion of infantrymen who fired their rifles at the Germans in the Second and Ninth Armies, on whose front the main blow did fall, was probably still lower.

In spite of rumors and secret service reports, the launching of the German offensive on May 10 took the great mass of the French Army by surprise. Officers and men, among them a number of generals, were on leave as usual. On May 9 some units were far from their usual quarters on maneuvers, and had to be hastily recalled next day. For most of the troops the first warning that anything exceptional was happening was the roar of German bombers passing overhead to attack objectives in the rear. At General Gamelin's Command post at Vincennes, on the other hand, many reports of German troop movements toward the frontiers of Belgium and Luxembourg were received during the small hours of May 10, and were passed to General Georges. Nevertheless it was not until 5:30 A.M. that Georges gave the alert to General Gaston Billotte, commanding the First Army Group, and not until an hour later, after the Belgian government had asked for help, that the order was given to put Gamelin's plan into execution. By that time German columns were across the frontiers of Holland, Belgium and Luxembourg, parachutists had landed near The Hague, Rotterdam, and Maastricht, and Belgian forward positions were already threatened.

Gamelin's plan provided that the whole of the British Expeditionary Force and the French First Army, with the left wing of the Ninth Army, should swing forward into Belgium, pivoting on Givet. Between Givet and Longuyon the Second Army and the right wing of the Ninth Army were already in position. On the extreme left, the Seventh Army under General Henri Giraud was to race forward along the coast with the object of joining hands with the Dutch near Breda.

Unfortunately, no Dutch troops were to be found near Breda, and the Dutch soon decided to capitulate. Thus the sole effect of Giraud's move was to deprive the French, at a crucial stage, of seven of their best divisions and their only Reserve Army.

Through no fault of their own, the bulk of the formations which were to leap forward into Belgium were rather slow in getting under way. With the exception of a forward screen of mechanized troops, most of them had orders to move only in darkness in order to reduce the risk of bombing. As it was broad daylight by the time they received the green light, they could do nothing until dusk on May 10 but assemble their kit, take leave of positions on which they had been working all the winter, lock up their pillboxes, and hand the keys to custodians of whom a number were not to be found when the keys were needed again a few days later. Meanwhile the Germans continued to advance. By the morning of May 11 the Belgians were beginning to fall back from positions on the Albert Canal which they had been expected to hold for at least five days, and a German armored division was across the lower Meuse. Moreover, when the French did reach their forward positions they found that very little had been done to put them into shape.

Yet, despite these setbacks, the situation was soon in hand as far south as the Sambre. Moving in daylight as well as at night after the afternoon of the eleventh, the French did not find themselves much hampered by air attacks. Nor did the British. Within the allotted time the British Expeditionary Force, the French First Army, and the Belgian divisions which had fallen back were all well established between the perimeter of the Antwerp defenses and Namur. Both the British and the French beat off sharp attacks without exerting more than a small proportion of their strength, and were obviously capable of withstanding a much heavier assault than was made on them.

On the right of the French First Army, the Ninth Army under General André Corap did not fare so well. Corap's right-hand corps was already on the Meuse, holding organized positions with barbed wire, trenches, and pillboxes. His two left-hand corps had to cross about forty-five miles of Belgian territory to reach the river, and found on arrival that no positions had been prepared for them. Worse still, by the time the last of their troops came up, the cavalry covering their advance had been pushed back by German armor, and small parties of Germans had already crossed the river.

Even so, the situation was far from desperate. The Germans on the left bank of the Meuse had no tanks, antitank guns or field artillery, and could easily have been rounded up by local counterattacks. The doctrine of the continuous front was, however, so much part and parcel of French military thinking that even the boldest of regimental commanders tended to regard an attack launched from anything but a strong defensive line as heresy. Such local counterattacks as were delivered within twelve to sixteen hours of the arrival of the Germans, although successful, achieved little because they were on too small a scale to be decisive and were not followed up.

Early on May 14 German engineers succeeded in bridging the Meuse in Corap's sector, and General Erwin Rommel, commanding the 7th Panzer Division, was able to start assembling his tanks in the bridgehead seized by his forward troops. The well-equipped French 1st Armored Division, which had remained inactive all the previous day because the High Command could not convince themselves that it would not be needed farther north, was then sent forward to the bridgehead, a little more than twenty miles from its starting point, but arrived too late to attack that day.

Meanwhile Corap, who had been promised a powerful counterattack force but had received only one infantry division to which he allotted a purely defensive role, was growing desperate. At 2 A.M. on May 15 he announced his intention of withdrawing to his original positions on the Franco-Belgian frontier. Billotte raised no objection, but insisted on his forming an intermediate stop line. The outcome was chaos. Some of the troops went back to the frontier, some to the stop line. Others wandered away without knowing what their orders were, and ended by either deserting or reporting days later to units in the rear. Corap had scarcely

had time to arrange for the withdrawal when he was relieved of
his command and replaced by Giraud, who had returned from his
vain dash into Holland. But not even Giraud could make much
of an army of which two-thirds had disintegrated by the time he
took up his new post.

Like the right-hand corps of Corap's army, the Second Army
under General Charles Huntziger did not have to move to man
the front it was supposed to hold. At Sedan, in particular, the
French position was very strong. The troops occupied an entrenched line, with casemates and pillboxes, behind an unfordable
river sixty yards wide, and Huntziger's artillery commanded an
excellent field of fire extending to the edge of the forest about
six miles away on the far side of the Meuse. The left bank was
protected by barbed wire, there was a forward line of pillboxes
on the right bank, and tanks could not go down to the river except
by recognized roads and tracks. In any case the river itself was an
effective antitank ditch. The effect of the alert issued on May 10
was, however, to weaken rather than strengthen Huntziger's hand,
for it led him to order a redisposition which left part of his front
in a disorganized state at a crucial moment.

Moving much faster through the Ardennes than the French had
thought possible, forward elements of General Guderian's 19th
Panzer Corps reached the neighborhood of Sedan soon after midday on May 12. During the afternoon the French cavalry withdrew to the left bank, the bridges were blown, and the Germans
entered the town without firing a shot. The High Command responded to an anxious message from Huntziger by ordering two
divisions of the GHQ Reserve to positions in the rear of his left
flank, but almost everyone from the Commander-in-Chief down
continued to act on the assumption that the enemy was merely
"advancing to contact before engagement" and would make no
further move for several days. Artillery commanders, concluding
that they had better save their ammunition for the big occasion,
fired only sparingly at German tanks assembling in full view of
their observation posts.

Next morning the Germans began an air bombardment which
continued for about five hours and reached a climax between

three and four in the afternoon. If the French rank and file had been taught what to expect in the light of German methods in Poland and even in Spain, antiaircraft and machine-gun crews would have known that, while their own chances of survival were extremely good, the enemy's dive bombers were highly vulnerable to fire from the ground. Similarly, the troops in the front line would have understood that the bombardment was pretty sure to be followed by a direct assault on their positions, that it was bound to stop before the arrival of the assault troops, and that everything was likely to depend on their being ready to fire their weapons at the crucial moment, even if they did nothing in the meantime but keep their heads down. But the rank and file had not been taught what to expect. It was an article of faith in the higher ranks of the French Army that *Blitzkrieg* methods were not applicable to the Western Front and that the Germans would attack organized positions only after elaborate artillery preparations. With honorable exceptions the defenders, whose losses were afterward admitted to have been light, were so dazed by experiences for which they were unprepared that they allowed the vanguard of Guderian's riflemen, infantry, and dismounted motorcyclists to cross the river in pneumatic boats and advance over exposed ground with comparatively little opposition. "The assault proceeded," wrote Guderian, "as if it had been a training exercise."

To make matters worse, a rumor soon spread in the French rear to the effect that the German armor was already across the river and had advanced about four miles. The truth was that not a single German tank reached the left bank until next morning. Guderian's forward troops held only an insecure bridgehead from which, according to a German source, they could have been dislodged without much difficulty. A counterattack intended to dislodge them was, in fact, to have taken place at dawn, but was not carried out until about three hours later. By that time German tanks had been pouring for more than an hour across a hastily reconstructed bridge at Gaulier, below Sedan.

Before the war the British had agreed that, if the Germans invaded the Low Countries and a crisis arose on the Western Front, the Air Staff should waive their reluctance to send heavy bombers on any but "strategic" missions, and that collaboration with the French Army and air force in the land battle should then become the primary commitment of the entire British bomber force. Aware by the evening of May 13 that German engineers were working feverishly on the Gaulier bridge, General Billotte asked urgently that British and French bombers should attack it at dawn next day. Since the beginning of the war the inability of heavy bombers to attack defended targets in daylight without suffering prohibitive losses had become apparent; yet, even so, the outcome can hardly have given Billotte a favorable impression. Attacking in waves and supported by French fighters, about a hundred British Blenheims joined a smaller number of French bombers in heroic but unsuccessful attempts to destroy the bridge on May 14; but the eighteen squadrons of the heavy bomber force, which had hitherto made no contribution, were sent on the night of the fifteenth to bomb oil targets in the Ruhr, and did not appear in the battle area until two nights later. By that time the spearhead of Guderian's advance had reached the Oise, and the Meuse was spanned at many points.

Meanwhile the left wing of the Second Army was crumbling like the Ninth Army. By the evening of May 14 the two divisions which were supposed to be holding the Sedan front had ceased to exist as organized formations. Thereafter the rest of the Second Army took up new positions facing north from Longuyon toward the Aisne, with a new Sixth Army and a reconstituted Seventh Army on its left prolonging the southern front to the mouth of the Somme near Abbeville. In the north, the undefeated First Army swung southward to form a corresponding front along the Sambre. Between these two fronts stretched a corridor a hundred and fifty miles long and up to sixty miles wide, through which the German armor raced toward the sea. At dusk on May 20 the 2nd Panzer Division reached the Channel coast at the mouth of the Somme after taking Abbeville without much difficulty.

Nevertheless the situation of the German armored formations remained precarious for a good ten days after their breakthrough on the Meuse. Strung out over distances of up to sixty miles, and widely separated from the bulk of the infantry coming up behind them, the Panzer divisions risked being cut off by counterattacks from north and south. The problem for the French High Command, whose long schooling in defensive methods did not help them to act boldly, was to find and organize forces with enough mobility and hitting power to strike effectively before the opportunity was lost. The French had started the battle on May 10 with well over two thousand tanks, about half of them in independent battalions and the rest divided between three armored and three light mechanized divisions. The independent battalions were too widely scattered to be assembled as a coherent striking force. The light mechanized divisions, after covering the advance into Belgium, were in turn so thoroughly dispersed for purposes of linear defense that to knit them together again was a major task. As for the three armored divisions, not much was left of them after the fifth day of the battle. The 1st Armored Division suffered heavily as a result of its belated intervention in Corap's sector, losing many tanks which were burnt by their crews after running out of fuel. The 3rd Armored Division, which was to have hurled Guderian's Panzers back to the Meuse in the Sedan sector, lost its chance when the local corps commander, his resolution sapped by contradictory orders, played for safety by distributing its tanks over a twelve-mile front. And the 2nd Armored Division, caught by Guderian's advance from the Sedan bridgehead with its fighting vehicles separated from its supply column, fell apart when its components withdrew in opposite directions.

There remained the newly created 4th Armored Division under Colonel de Gaulle, with about a hundred and fifty tanks; the British 1st Armored Division, which the War Cabinet had ordered to France on May 11 although it was still incomplete; and a powerful body of French, British, and Belgian infantry which had suffered no defeat and was still capable of responding to realistic orders. But realistic orders were hard to frame where situation reports were sometimes wildly inaccurate. At 10:50 A.M. on May 14 Georges transmitted to Gamelin a report from the Second Army to the effect that the Second Army's troops in the Sedan bridgehead were in good shape and were holding positions only a mile or two behind the river. The facts were that most of the forward troops had bolted on the previous evening, leaving the divisional commander "almost alone with his reserve troops"; that German armor had been crossing the river for five hours; and that a belated counterattack by part of the divisional reserve had failed.

For five or six days after the breakthrough Georges continued to hope that the Panzer units racing toward the sea could be "contained" at one or other of a series of stop lines which they had always reached or passed by the time his orders reached anyone capable of acting on them. Until the Germans were at the mouth of the Somme the only serious attempts made to cut them off, as distinct from stopping them, were two counterattacks by the 4th Armored Division on May 17 and 19. Striking north and northeast from the southern flank of the Panzer Corridor, de Gaulle scored striking local successes on both days, but was unable to get far for lack of support. On the second occasion Georges did intend that de Gaulle's effort should link up with an attack from the north, but the southward thrust could not be made because the light mechanized divisions which were to have made it had not succeeded in reassembling their dispersed tanks.

On May 18 Gamelin saw on a visit to Georges' headquarters and command post that the Commander-in-Chief of the Northeast front was in bad shape physically, but still he hesitated to replace him. Early next day, however, he made his first important intervention since May 10 by issuing tactfully worded instructions for counterattacks from north and south against the rear of the German armor. Later in the day he himself was relieved of his command and replaced by General Maxime Weygand, still noted for his youthful energy at seventy-three, and still remembered for his part in helping the Poles to turn defeat into victory when the Bolshevists were at the gates of Warsaw in 1920. Taking effective command on the very day when the Germans reached the Channel, Weygand came to the conclusion that there was a good chance of cutting through the Panzer Corridor by launching simultaneous attacks from north and south near Arras, where the corridor was only about twenty-five miles wide.

Next day Weygand flew across the corridor to discuss his plans with Billotte, the King of the Belgians, and, above all, General Lord Gort, Commander-in-Chief of the British Expeditionary Force. Anxious not to miss a meeting in Paris on the following day, he nonetheless left without seeing Gort, who had been notified too late and was astonished to learn, on returning to his headquarters in the evening, that Weygand had not waited for him. To make matters worse, Billotte was seriously injured in a motorcar accident on his way back to his command post, and died two days later without regaining consciousness. So far as the northern armies were concerned, Weygand's intentions had to be pieced together from notes taken by a Belgian officer. Nor was there anyone north of the Somme to coordinate the actions of the British, French, and Belgian armies during the four days which elapsed before Billotte's successor was appointed.

In the meantime Gort had warned London that the loss of his southward communications might force him to re-embark his troops, the British government had responded by sending General Sir Edmund Ironside, the Chief of the Imperial General Staff, across the Channel with instructions to urge him to counterattack first, and Gort had made his own arrangements with Billotte and Ironside for a southward thrust. His attack, delivered on the day of Weygand's visit, was outstandingly successful, but its aims were limited and it was no substitute for the general offensive envisaged by the High Command. French troops which were to have taken part were not ready and did not attack until next day. Nor was there any simultaneous thrust from the south.

In the outcome the great offensive planned by Weygand was never launched. The date fixed by Billotte's successor, General François Blanchard, was May 23, but he had not yet been formally appointed, and lacked the power to goad all concerned into concerted action. Consulting the British on the twenty-second, he found that Gort intended to conform with a Belgian withdrawal on the left during the ensuing night, and could not be ready before the twenth-fourth. Meanwhile the Germans were building up their strength in the corridor, their infantry was arriving in force to support their armor, and the opportunity was passing. By the evening of the twenty-third the enemy had pushed so far to the northeast that the force which Gort had earmarked for next day's attack was in danger of being surrounded, and he saw nothing for it but to pull it back. The attack was then postponed until the twenty-seventh. Early on the twenty-fifth, however, the Germans broke through the Belgian front and threatened to drive a wedge between the British and the Belgians and cut Gort's communication with the sea. Some hours before receiving official notification of his new appointment, Blanchard signed the death warrant of Weygand's plan by decreeing that the First Army and the British and Belgian armies should fall back to form a bridgehead round Dunkirk. Next day the British began what seemed the impossible task of embarking their quarter of a million troops and ferrying them to England, with such men of the First Army as the French were willing to embark and as could be saved. The Belgians, unable to carry on the struggle, surrendered unconditionally on May 27.

For reasons afterward hotly debated, the Germans left interference with the embarkation largely to the overconfident Reichsmarschall Göring, Commander-in-Chief and political head of the Luftwaffe. On May 23, Rundstedt, commanding Army Group A, halted his armor "to allow the situation to clarify itself and to keep our forces concentrated." Next day Hitler arrived at Rundstedt's command post. He approved of the previous day's decision, agreed that Army Group B, under Bock, should assume responsibility for "defeating the enemy on the east," and "insisted on the absolute necessity of saving the Panzers for ensuing operations, and of not pressing too hard on the surrounded Allies, which would have the undesirable effect of restricting the Luftwaffe's field of action." Later the Panzers were allowed to push on to Gravelines, but they were afterward withdrawn.

In face of fighter cover provided by the Royal Air Force from bases in England, and hampered at times by unfavorable weather, Göring's bombers scored nothing like the triumph he expected. Weakened by their all-out effort during the past fortnight, they reduced their chances still further by devoting part of their attention to "strategic" targets far from the battle zone. As compared with the 40,000 or 50,000 men at most whom the British hoped to save, they succeeded in withdrawing 225,000 of their own troops, about 112,000 Frenchmen who were embarked on the same footing as the British from the day when the French High Command agreed to let them go, and some thousands of Belgians who chose exile rather than surrender. In addition about 50,000 Frenchmen were saved by French ships. But the retreating British Expeditionary Force left behind it nearly all its heavy equipment and huge quantities of supplies and ammunition. A deliverance but also a defeat, the disappearance of the northern armies from the battlefield left the French with fewer than sixty divisions to face the whole strength of the German Army on the Western Front. Among them were two British divisions which stayed behind with as many as were left of the tactical bombers, fighters, and reconnaissance aircraft of the British Advanced Air Striking Force.

14

THE SEA RETURNS

MANY OBSERVERS BELIEVED THAT AT DUNKIRK THEY WERE WITNESSING the last act of a drama whose inevitable end was the collapse of European civilization as they knew it. The French Army was already broken. The British had staked the greater part of their armed strength on the campaign just drawing to a close. It seemed that the curtain must soon fall to the accompaniment of a final roll of drums and clash of chords from the Nazi orchestra. With the tragedy accomplished, mankind would bid farewell to the spirit of liberal enquiry and unfettered commercial enterprise which had carried men of European stock to the farthest corners of the earth.

In war only results count. Germany's armed forces had achieved such spectacular results in the last few weeks that their success seemed foreordained. To assert that their reputation for invincible might was based on anything but hard facts would have seemed, in the summer of 1940, as perverse as it would have seemed otiose to point out that the strategic plan which had carried them to the Channel in ten days was not an infallible recipe for victory but an extremely bold and hazardous conception which might have led them to disaster if the French High Command had been prompt to seize their opportunities. From a practical standpoint, the soundness of the Manstein Plan seemed proved by the only test that mattered when the French surrendered less than three weeks after the last British soldier had left Dunkirk. "The English," said Hitler, "will not come back in this war."

Yet, viewed objectively, the German war machine was not so

mighty that the Anglo-French alliance could not have hoped to defeat it with better luck, more resolute leadership, and a more flexible organization at all levels. If Hitler's claim that he had provided the Fatherland with an army and an air force more up-to-date and more efficient than rival armies and air forces had an element of truth, it also had a large element of propaganda. In spite of his glib references to total war and guns before butter, German manpower and productive capacity had never been fully mobilized for war between 1933 and 1939, nor were they fully mobilized for war in 1940 or even later. Creating an army of more than a hundred divisions and an air force with a first-line strength of more than four thousand aircraft in six or seven years, he had done wonders but had come far short of achieving the impossible, or even of straining the national economy to an extent which might have injured his standing with industrial leaders on whose cooperation he depended. Speed, surprise, mobility were supposed to be the essence of his strategy, but to make the whole of the army as fast-moving as these words implied would have called for many more mechanically propelled vehicles than the National Socialist régime was ever able to provide, or at any rate saw fit to provide. Outside a relatively small number of armored, motorized, or airborne units, the German Army of 1940 depended, like that of 1914, on its own legs to carry it from its railheads into battle, and on horse-drawn transport for a great part of its supplies and services.

Nor did the output of the German aircraft industry between 1933 and 1940 suffice to give the air force depth as well as first-line strength. By the end of the campaign in France and the Low Countries many bomber, fighter, and tactical reconnaissance units had suffered losses which would have been difficult to make good if the next few weeks had not brought a respite. Even a month later, after some units had been back to Germany to rest and refit, many were still short of their nominal establishments, even with the inclusion of aircraft temporarily grounded for repair or overhaul.

Still less did the schemes of world conquest imputed to the Nazi leaders include adequate provision for war outside the European mainland. Even to disembark at undefended or weakly defended ports the relatively few troops used in Norway had strained the resources of the German Navy almost to the limit. The only specially constructed invasion craft which the Germans possessed in the summer of 1940 were thirty-eight tank-landing vessels which, as they were neither self-propelled nor suitable for the open sea, would have to be carried in transports and towed to the shore by specially modified motor lifeboats. With the exception of a few survivors of half-forgotten campaigns, German troops had little or no experience of desert or tropical warfare or of warfare in undeveloped countries.

At the end of the campaign in France and the Low Countries the Nazi leaders were, however, as far from seeing the need to engage in such adventures as they were from wishing to engage in them. "You take the sea and we'll take Europe," had been a recurrent theme in Hitler's pre-war conversations with British spokesmen. In *Mein Kampf* he had recorded in unmistakable terms his conviction that Germany's destiny lay in Europe. Although willing to claim the return of the German colonies in Africa as a means of putting pressure on France and Britain, he had never shown any intention of seizing them by conquest. By the summer of 1940 his patched-up friendship with Russia was wearing thin, and his oil supplies were threatened by Russian ambitions in Central and Southeastern Europe. With the French suing for an armistice and the British more or less disarmed, his obvious policy was to impose reasonable terms on France, make friends with Britain, and strike a short, sharp blow which would establish his predominance in the Balkans and give him as much of European Russia as he could hope to hold.

Such a policy seemed all the more reasonable to Hitler since Britain's military position was, in his opinion, "hopeless." He was unwilling to destroy the British Empire, which he regarded, according to the Italian Foreign Minister, Count Ciano, as "an important factor in world equilibrium." In any case, he lacked the means of doing so. On the other hand, he believed that Britain could be reduced to acquiescence by naval and air blockade if she proved stubborn. But Britain did prove stubborn, and blockade was slow. He soon saw that, if he wanted to defeat Russia in the autumn of 1940, or even in the spring of 1941, he must either face a two-front war or find a quicker means of settling with Britain than mere blockade.

It is possible that Hitler confided his intention of attacking Russia to his intimates before the fall of France, but the first date for which there is firm evidence is July 21, when he ordered the General Staff to make preliminary studies for a Russian campaign. Just over a week later he told his military adviser, General Jodl, that he had decided to carry out the undertaking. On July 31 he confirmed the decision at a conference of service chiefs, adding that he would have liked to smash the Russians in the coming autumn but that the attack could not be launched before the spring. Russia's defeat, he said, would not only end the risk of an Anglo-Russian combination against Germany, but would so transform the Far Eastern situation that the Americans would have no time to think of anything but the menace of Japan.

Meanwhile, on July 2, he directed the High Commands of the fighting services to draw up tentative plans for the invasion of Britain. A fortnight later, after approving an ambitious scheme submitted by Brauchitsch and Halder, he announced in formal terms that he had "decided to prepare, and if necessary to carry out, a landing operation against England."

Almost from the start, the naval and army planners were hampered by a fundamental disagreement as to the breadth of the front on which a landing could be made with any prospect of success. The army, earmarking eleven infantry and two mountain divisions as the first wave of the landing force, and contemplating a broad array of beachheads from Ramsgate to Lyme Bay, wished to put ashore in the assault phase of the operation some ninety thousand men and four to five thousand horses, accompanying them with hundreds of tanks and more than twenty-thousand bicycles; to follow swiftly with another hundred and sixty thousand men, the best part of another sixty thousand horses, more than thirty thousand vehicles and five hundred field-howitzers; and finally to add another seventeen infantry, six armored and three motorized divisions in three more waves. The navy, on the other hand, protested that they could protect the flanks of the crossing only if it were confined to a narrow front near the eastern end of the Channel, and that even then the landing of the first wave would have to be spread over about ten days and would absorb all the transports, barges, tugs, and motorboats they could muster without bringing important branches of German industry to a standstill. The consensus of opinion was, however, that, while a landing on a broad front was impractical for lack of shipping and escort vessels, and a landing on a narrow one likely to make the initial assault extremely hazardous, there could be no landing on any front at all unless the Luftwaffe first scored a resounding victory over the Royal Air Force.

Such a victory, Göring thought, could be won in about four weeks. On the assumption that naval preparations could be completed by the middle of September, the start of the air offensive was first fixed for early August, and afterward put back by successive postponements until just before the middle of the month.

Deprived by the swift collapse of France and the Low Countries of some of their usual sources of intelligence, the British government had no reliable indication of Hitler's plans until, at the beginning of September, air reconnaissance revealed significant concentrations of barges at the principal ports from Flushing to Le Havre. But they had no difficulty in guessing that invasion was probable, or in knowing that they stood a poor chance of defeating the German Army if it gained a foothold. The British Army had sent most of its best weapons to France with the Expeditionary Force, and the Expeditionary Force had returned without them, sacrificing six hundred tanks and well over two thousand field, antiaircraft, antitank, and heavy guns which could not be re-embarked. In addition to the twelve divisions which came back, there were already fifteen infantry divisions and one armored division in Home Forces, but these were not much more than nominally home defense divisions. The bulk of them were either newly formed divisions waiting to go abroad as soon as they could be equipped and brought up to strength, or holding divisions whose function was to provide drafts for units already overseas.

The average strength of these divisions at the time of Dunkirk was about half their nominal establishment, and their equipment was incomplete and generally inferior to that of the divisions which had gone to France. Until new tanks could be manufactured or combed from depots and training units, the 2nd Armored Division would remain, for practical purposes, an armored division without armor. In the whole of Home Forces there were only a hundred and sixty light tanks armed solely with machine guns, for all the heavier tanks considered fit for service, as well as a large number of light tanks, had gone to France with the 1st Armored Division, which returned in June with only nine tanks of all classes left. The state of the infantry divisions was no better, and in some cases worse. The ninety-mile stretch of coast from Sheerness to Rye, whose fixed defenses covered the seaward approaches to Dover and the Thames and Medway but not the beaches, and at whose southwestward end two German divisions would soon be planning to go ashore if Hitler gave the word, was guarded by the 1st London Division, whose commander reported on May 31 that he had no antitank guns, no armored fighting vehicles, no armored cars, and no medium machine guns. Toward the divisional quota of seventy-two 25-pounder field guns he had eleven, supplemented by four 18-pounders and eight howitzers. His allotment of antitank rifles was forty-seven, as compared with the three hundred and seven to which he was theoretically entitled, but not all of them had reached him. Of seven infantry divisions either allotted to Eastern Command or ready to move to its support in the event of a landing in Norfolk, Suffolk, Essex, Kent, or Sussex, only one had its full complement of antitank rifles, and even that highly favored formation had only eight antitank guns and two-thirds of the field guns it should have had.

On the first day of full-scale embarkation at Dunkirk, General Ironside left his table in Whitehall to take up the newly important job of Commander-in-Chief, Home Forces. A great bear of a man with astonishing powers of assimilation, a retentive memory and a poor opinion of many of his fellow soldiers and of most politicians, he claimed to have campaigned for years against defensive preoccupations which, in his view, had sapped the offensive spirit of the British Army, as of the French. But that did not save him from having to put his name to a scheme of defense in which the counteroffensive element seemed conspicuously lacking. Forced to think first of safeguarding London and the industrial Midlands, and with too few weapons and too little mechanized transport to garrison a strong defensive position and also provide powerful counterattack forces both in forward areas and in reserve, he put his main stop line a long way from the coast and relied on units in front of it to do little more than slow down the enemy's advance. The criticism that this meant allowing the enemy to overrun a great part of the country before any serious attempt was made to stop him would not have been a fair one if Ironside had been able to keep enough up his sleeve to be sure of delivering a knockout blow at his chosen moment. But in fact his GHQ Reserve was so deficient in armor that there seemed little prospect of halting the enemy at all unless the main stop line proved strong enough to hold him.

On July 20 General Sir Alan Brooke (afterward Lord Alanbrooke) succeeded General Ironside. With many more guns and vehicles in August and September than Ironside had commanded in June, he was able to give a new look to the defenses by strengthening local mobile reserves, stationing the GHQ Reserve farther forward, and treating the main stop line as a series of strong points and *ad hoc* rallying positions rather than a continuous front. Even so, only four of his twenty-seven infantry divisions were fully equipped, most of his troops had no firsthand experience of mobile warfare, and his five hundred antitank guns, three hundred and fifty medium and cruiser tanks, and five hundred light tanks were not likely to be a match for the armor the Germans could put ashore if they captured a port.

But it did not follow that the outlook for the British was as dark as Hitler claimed and as many neutrals thought. Britain's capacity to resist invasion had never been governed by her ability to defeat a foreign army on British soil, and it was not so governed now. Recent events had shaken the old belief that sea power was all-sufficient, but it was still as true as ever that no invader could land and supply an army unless his sea communications were secure. By the summer of 1940 all Germany's heavy ships had been put temporarily or permanently out of commission, and British warships in home waters alone outnumbered the effective strength of the German navy by eight to one.[1]

Even though the British overestimated Hitler's strength at sea, believing that he might be able to muster four capital ships, five or six cruisers, and perhaps ten destroyers, as compared with the four cruisers and eight destroyers which, in fact, were all he could hope to use before the winter, it seemed a fair assumption that he would rely largely on his air force to offset the weakness of his navy. Admiral Sir Charles Forbes, commanding the Home Fleet, was one of a number of British service chiefs who concluded that he would not attempt a landing without first doing all he could to defeat the Royal Air Force.

Immediately after the German breakthrough on the Meuse, Daladier's successor, Paul Reynaud, had asked the British government to send him ten fighter squadrons in addition to the equivalent of more than a dozen sent to France since the beginning of the war. Appearing before the War Cabinet on May 15, and following up his arguments with a strongly worded letter to the Air Council on May 16, Air Chief Marshal Dowding had succeeded in convincing Churchill and his colleagues that a point would soon be reached, if it had not been reached already, at which any further weakening of the fighter force at home might make it impossible to carry on the war, at any rate from bases on the European side of the Atlantic, if the Germans switched their air attacks to the United Kingdom. After sanctioning the despatch on May 16 and 17 of another eight half-squadrons as a final

[1] This comparison includes only capital ships (British 5 on July 1, German 0), aircraft carriers (British 1 on July 1, German 0), cruisers (British 11 on July 1 and more later, German 4), and destroyers (British 80 on July 1, German 8). It excludes submarines and light surface craft. At the beginning of July the British had 35 submarines, 34 sloops and corvettes (used chiefly for escort duties) and about 700 armed patrol vessels of various kinds, of which some two to three hundred were constantly at sea. The Germans had 26 submarines fit for active service, and some forty to fifty fast light surface craft of which a number were armed with torpedoes.

desperate measure, the Prime Minister had therefore ruled on May 19 that no more fighters should leave the country. The outcome was that, in spite of many thousands of sorties flown over the tactical area in May and June by British aircraft from bases on both sides of the Channel, the end of the campaign in France and the Low Countries found Dowding with his squadrons intact, although much weakened by the loss of more than four hundred aircraft since May 10. Altogether, the Battle of France had cost the Royal Air Force about as many aircraft as the entire first-line bomber and fighter strength of the French air force at the beginning of the war.

The Chiefs of Staff concluded, when things looked blackest, that the country's survival would depend primarily on the extent to which the government succeeded in making the public aware of the need for an all-out effort on the one hand, and on finding enough fighter aircraft to replace past and future losses on the other. "The crux of the whole problem," they wrote when the British Expeditionary Force was streaming back from Dunkirk, "is the air defence of this country."

The first requirement was met by Churchill's broadcasts, which caught the great mass of the British people in a mood to be reminded of their past greatness and their abiding dislike of being pushed about by foreigners. Always slow to recognize that a crisis was at hand, they could hardly fail to see after the first few days of June that the time had come for them to bestir themselves if they were not to be swamped as many of their Continental neighbors had been swamped. But the eloquence which galvanized the British public into unheard-of efforts had also the less happy effect of giving the impression in neutral countries, and especially in America, that Britain was in desperate straits at a time when she had almost overwhelming superiority at sea and incomparably the best system of air defense that the world had ever seen. Where even as stouthearted an Englishman as Churchill was inclined to underestimate the chances of success, it was not surprising that United States Ambassador Joseph P. Kennedy, who was not entirely in sympathy with English ways, should conclude that the

British had neither the means nor the resolution to defeat Germany.

To meet their second requirement, the Chiefs of Staff proposed that the United States government should be asked to provide as many aircraft as possible, even to the extent of combing through stocks of fighters held by their own armed forces. Lord Beaverbrook, who held the newly created post of Minister of Aircraft Production and was soon on excellent terms with Dowding although the two men could hardly have been more dissimilar, was nonetheless convinced that everything must be done to speed up production of the Hurricanes and Spitfires which Dowding wanted and to which his pilots and mechanics were accustomed. According to figures put before the Chiefs of Staff, British aircraft factories had delivered 747 fighters in the first six months of the war, and were expected to deliver 1983 in the six months beginning in May and ending in October. At Beaverbrook's prompting, and under the stress of the emergency depicted by Churchill in his broadcasts, they delivered 2679, thus exceeding the expectations of the Chiefs of Staff by more than a third and making it possible for Dowding's squadrons to weather the storm without using a single American fighter.

American war material which reached the United Kingdom during the next few months included about half a million rifles, large numbers of machine guns and field guns which had been stored for many years, and fifty old destroyers which arrived when the threat of invasion had been beaten off. In return for the destroyers, the British government granted the United States long leases of naval and air bases in Newfoundland, Bermuda, and the West Indies, some of which naval diehards opposed to the Washington agreement had proposed, twenty years earlier, to develop and fortify in the event of a serious dispute with the United States. Sympathetic Americans who wished to spare the feelings of the British pointed out that these terms, which seemed to some Englishmen similar in kind, though not in degree, to those which might have been imposed on them if they had already been defeated, were really a reflection of the President's need to purchase his freedom to help them by making a deal which could be represented to his isolationist opponents in Congress as a hard bargain. The fact remained that they were a stiff price to pay for fifty obsolete warships at a time when the Royal Navy had many more destroyers than the Germans, and were sinking Hitler's U-boats faster than he was building them.[2] The American ships were a useful addition to the navy's escort force when they did arrive; but Churchill, apparently relying on an unsound appreciation drawn up by the Chiefs of Staff in May, was doubly mistaken if he assumed not only that they would be needed to repel invasion, but also that they would be delivered in time to perform that role.

Göring began his great air offensive on August 13, after a month of preliminary skirmishing which gave him a limited degree of air control over the narrowest part of the Channel in daylight. The preliminary bout cost the British four or five of their eighty destroyers in home waters, about thirty thousand tons of merchant shipping out of a million tons which reached its destinations, and about a hundred and fifty fighters as compared with more than five hundred added to their strength from new production. The Germans lost the best part of three hundred aircraft, but had more bombers and fighters fit for use at the end of the preliminary phase than at the beginning of it.

On the eve of the main assault the three air fleets deployed for the assault on Britain at bases from Norway to Brittany mustered, between them, about fifteen hundred long-range bombers, of which about a thousand were serviceable on a given day, and about nine hundred single-seater fighters. The number of single-seater fighters serviceable at one time rarely, if ever, exceeded about seven hundred. The Germans also had about three hundred dive bombers and roughly the same number of multiseater fight-

[2] At the end of August 1939 the Germans had thirty-nine submarines at sea. At the end of August 1940 they had twenty-six fit for active service. In the meantime twenty-eight had been sunk. During the same period the German surface fleet had taken even heavier punishment. Warships sunk, scuttled, or put out of action for long periods since the beginning of the war included the battlecruisers *Scharnhorst* and *Gneisenau*, the pocket battleships *Graf Spee* and *Lützow* (formerly the *Deutschland*), the cruisers *Blucher*, *Karlsruhe*, *Königsberg*, and *Leipzig*, and ten destroyers.

ers, but aircraft of both these classes proved so vulnerable as to be, at best, of doubtful value. For all-out attacks on objectives vital to the British fighter force Göring soon found that he was limited to the area of southern England which his single-seater fighters could reach, and to the number of bombers which they could protect. Since at least two fighters were needed to protect one bomber, this meant that the biggest effort he could mount at one time was an attack by not more than three or four hundred bombers accompanied by six or seven hundred fighters.

Göring's principal objectives were to destroy Royal Air Force installations on the ground, and to bring on a major fighter battle in the air and win it. On the whole, the second was the more important, but his directives to commanders in the field did not always make that clear.

Air Chief Marshal Dowding began the battle with roughly eleven hundred fighters, about six-sevenths of which were Hurricanes or Spitfires and the remaining seventh multiseater Blenheims and Defiants. Just over seven hundred of these aircraft were serviceable after the first two days of heavy fighting, and the daily average, as calculated from week to week, never subsequently fell below that figure. Nor did the Aircraft Storage Units from which Dowding drew replacements for his losses ever hold fewer than a hundred Hurricanes and Spitfires ready for immediate issue to his squadrons. The number of pilots on his strength varied from a little under fourteen hundred in the middle of August to more than seventeen hundred at the end of October, but the returns included a growing proportion of unseasoned novices who needed nursing. In spite of his real anxieties about numbers of aircraft and pilots, one of his biggest problems before the battle began was to know how much of his strength he could afford to concentrate in the south, especially in view of the risk of crippling attacks by unescorted bombers on the fleet bases at Scapa Flow and Rosyth and on aircraft factories in the Midlands. Once heavy fighting began the problem more or less solved itself, since he could not in any case put more squadrons in the south than his sectors there could handle comfortably at a time of incessant strain when their communications were threatened with disruption.

If Göring's commanders in the field were sometimes left in doubt as to what was expected of them, the same was true, to some extent, of Dowding, except that his temperament and seniority put him in a better position than his opposite numbers to take an independent line. A fortnight after the outbreak of war he had been directed by the Air Ministry to review the disposition of his forces on the assumption that the aircraft industry was a likely objective for the German bomber force, but no one had ever disputed that London, to say nothing of Scapa Flow and Rosyth, was at least equally important and perhaps even more important. Whether it mattered more that the enemy should be kept away from vital objectives, or that his forces should be punished as heavily as possible irrespective of where they dropped their bombs, was a crucial question, yet it was never brought into the open until Dowding was about to be replaced, and was decided only after he had gone. Another important question which found no ready answer at the Air Staff level was whether it was better to think first of destroying German bombers, or of destroying German fighters.

In general, the policy adopted by Air Vice-Marshal Keith Park, commanding the vital No. 11 Group in the southeastern corner of Dowding's command, was to engage the enemy as far forward as he could, shoot down the largest possible number of his bombers, and engage his fighters only when he had no choice. His insistence on trying to meet the Germans before they reached their targets was criticized in some quarters on the ground that it led him to commit his squadrons singly or in pairs instead of waiting to assemble large formations. But there was no proof that large formations were particularly effective, and Park's methods did enable him to save some important objectives from serious damage and to wear the Germans down while conserving his own strength for the big occasion. The factor which limited Göring's effort after the first day or two was his lack of an overwhelmingly strong fighter force. Nevertheless it was the steady deterioration of his bomber force which frustrated his plans by forcing him to devote more of his fighters to close escort of his bombers, and thus to forfeit his chance of bringing on an all-out fighter-to-fighter battle on favorable terms.

At the start of the big offensive Göring believed that he could knock out the fighter defenses of southern England in a few days. He could hardly have been more wrong. In the first eleven days, which included four days of heavy fighting and seven days when activity was restricted by bad weather or the threat of it, he lost nearly three hundred aircraft without substantially reducing Dowding's capacity to carry on the battle. At the end of the first phase Dowding had more serviceable aircraft than at the beginning of it. The Aircraft Storage Units still held respectable stocks, the aircraft factories were turning out Hurricanes and Spitfires at a rate which more than covered average daily losses, and not one important fighter base had been put permanently out of action although several had been hit.

From the beginning the success gained by the British seemed almost too good to be true, especially as it was magnified by the incurable tendency of all air forces to overestimate the losses suffered by the other side in major actions. When the United States Ambassador suggested that British accounts of German casualties, which differed enormously from those published by the enemy, might be seriously overdrawn, Dowding suggested that the Air Ministry should ask the Foreign Office to point out that, while it was impossible to be sure that the British estimates were accurate, the American people would soon know whether the German figures were right or not. If they were, the battle would be over in a few days and the Germans would be in London in a week.

During the next phase, which began with the return of better weather on August 24 and ended on September 6, Göring did more damage on the ground, and also achieved a better ratio of losses inflicted to losses suffered, by ordering his bombers to concentrate on worth while targets and his fighters to stay closer to the bombers. In fifteen days of in-and-out fighting he lost 380 aircraft to Dowding's 286, as compared with 290 to 114 during the first eleven days. But the ability of his fighter force to seek out the enemy was correspondingly reduced, and the all-out fighter battle which he believed would bring him a favorable decision continued to elude him. Conversely, Park avoided premature commitment of his whole force on unfavorable terms, and was able, with Dowding's help, to keep up his strength in spite of severe losses and heavy damage to his bases. On August 29 General Kurt von Döring, who headed Göring's fighter organization, claimed that "unlimited fighter superiority" had been attained. On the very next day Dowding's squadrons proved him wrong by flying more than a thousand sorties in daylight for the first time in their history. They were soon flying not only more sorties than Göring's fighter force, but more sorties than his fighter and bomber forces put together.

On September 7 Göring switched his attack to London in an attempt to force a decision, and in deference to Hitler's demand for reprisals for a raid on Berlin which British bombers had delivered a few nights earlier in response to what is now known to have been the unintentional bombing of London by German crews unsure of their whereabouts on the night of August 24.

In the meantime air reconnaissance had shown that large numbers of barges were assembling in the Channel ports, the Germans were known to be concentrating dive bombers near the Straits of Dover, and four men caught landing in England had confessed that their mission was to report troop movements for the benefit of the German authorities. Toward 6 P.M. on September 7 the Chiefs of Staff concluded that invasion might be imminent and agreed with General Bernard Paget, General Brooke's Chief of Staff, that troops in Eastern and Southern Commands should be called to instant readiness. About two hours later Paget's deputy at GHQ, Brigadier John Swayne, decided to send out the appropriate signal without waiting for his chief, who had not yet returned from his interview with the Chiefs of Staff. The meeting of the Chiefs of Staff coincided with Göring's first daylight raid on London, but it was not connected with the sending of the signal except insofar as the raid probably delayed Paget's return to GHQ and thus led his deputy to take, on his own responsibility, the action which Paget himself would otherwise have taken, and which the Chiefs of Staff had authorized without Swayne's knowledge.

Not only was General Brooke fulfilling an engagement away from his headquarters that afternoon, but so too was Air Vice-Marshal Park. Park's subordinates could hardly be blamed for not guessing that London was the enemy's objective, nor was it his fault that he was not present to guide their judgment. The first daylight attack on London since 1917 was not very effectively opposed, did a fair amount of damage in crowded dockland areas, and was followed by an equally damaging attack at night. During the later raid the defenses, never very effective after dark, were hampered by unexpected troubles. A night-fighter base near London was so thickly covered with smoke that no aircraft could leave the ground, and some antiaircraft units were cut off for considerable periods by landline failures. A second daylight raid on September 9 was much more vigorously countered, but further raids on September 11 and 14 seemed successful enough, by the German reckoning, to lead the ever-confident Göring to hope that victory might not be far off.

Yet it was not the British for whom the sands were running out. The German service chiefs were aware that there could be no invasion of Britain in September unless Hitler gave the preliminary order on September 17, and that he would not give it unless he were assured of air superiority. The navy needed at least ten days to sweep Allied mines and lay their own, and the next date, after September 27, on which moon and tide would make a landing possible was October 8, too late to give the army more than a gambler's chance of consolidating a bridgehead before the winter. For practical purposes there was no escape, unless the British succumbed unexpectedly to naval and air blockade before the spring, from either a favorable decision on September 17, or a two-front war in 1941. At nightfall on September 14 Göring thus had barely more than forty-eight hours in which to gain the sweeping ascendancy he had promised, or confess that he had failed.

Had he been capable of weighing his chances objectively, he would have known from the mere numerical strength of Park's response to his recent attacks that they were slender. He had tried for nearly a month to destroy the Royal Air Force on the ground and tempt Park into a losing battle in the air, and he had not succeeded in doing either. Moreover, so far as his first and less important object was concerned, he had made the cardinal mistake of switching his attacks away from Park's fighter bases just when Dowding and Park were becoming seriously worried by them. At the end of ten weeks of ceaseless anxiety, Dowding had more aircraft in his operationally fit squadrons, more aircraft serviceable, and more pilots on his strength than at the beginning of the preliminary bout in July, and his average daily effort showed an upward trend. Stored reserves had fallen sharply since the middle of August, but were still a long way from exhaustion at current rates of loss and input. Conversely, the German air force in the West had fewer single-seater fighters, and fewer of them serviceable, than at the beginning of the battle, and its average daily effort against the United Kingdom by aircraft of all categories was declining.[3]

But much of the picture was hidden from Göring. The British, after reacting with surprising vigor on September 9, had failed on the eleventh and fourteenth to save valuable objectives from being bombed in daylight. Himself a fighter pilot who had done well in the First World War, Göring believed that, if his pilots had not succeeded hitherto in driving the enemy from the skies, it was because they had not tried hard enough or because their tactics were at fault. Nor did the British know how near they themselves were to success. As early as July 31 the Prime Minister had cabled to President Roosevelt that "the air was holding well" and that he hoped for a favorable outcome if Britain could get through the next three or four months. He did not foresee that, in much less than three or four months, "the air" would achieve so decisive a victory that Hitler's chances of invading Britain would be smashed.

What proved to be Göring's last serious bid for air superiority was made on Sunday, September 15. Field Marshal Albert Kessel-

[3] For the figures on which these comparisons are based, see Derek Wood and Derek Dempster, *The Narrow Margin* (1961), and the author's *The Defence of the United Kingdom* (1957) and *The Battle of Britain* (1962).

ring, commanding Luftflotte 2 in Holland, Belgium, and northeast France, had recently been given command or control of all but a handful of the single-seater fighters in the West to enable him to keep up the daylight offensive while his neighbor, Field Marshal Hugo Sperrle, commanding Luftflotte 3 in northwest France, attacked at night or with cloud-cover. Even so, the number of serviceable aircraft at Kesselring's disposal, already down to about four hundred and fifty long-range bombers and fewer than six hundred single-seater fighters on September 7, had dwindled so much by the crucial day that he was forced not only to restrict his bomber effort to the minimum that was likely to provoke a major response, but also to parcel it out between two attacks separated by an interval long enough to allow some of his aircraft to fly double sorties. The result was that, instead of bringing about his long-awaited fighter-to-fighter battle on terms favorable to himself, he presented his opponent with a double chance of catching his depleted force at a disadvantage.

Park seized his opportunity with both hands. In his youth he had gained a reputation as an amateur boxer. Perhaps unconsciously, he had long held himself in check, although he was not naturally a cautious man. With a boxer's instinct, he recognized that the time had come for a supreme effort. Throwing in everything he had in both the morning and the afternoon, and calling on his neighbors to reinforce him to the limit, he twice forced Kesselring's armada to run the gauntlet of upward of three hundred Hurricanes and Spitfires, took the measure of his fighters in an all-out contest with no holds barred, and harried his bombers relentlessly over London and its outskirts. The sixty German aircraft lost were only about a third of the number of the British believed they had destroyed when they reckoned up the score that evening, but the figure took no account of the many bombers which limped home badly holed and with one or more of the crew killed or wounded.

After twice seeing Dowding put more fighters over the southeastern counties in an hour and a half than the German intelligence service believed him to possess in the whole country, and with Kesselring's striking force so battered that, even after two days' rest, only about seventy bombers set out on his next daylight raid on London, not even the blustering Göring could claim that air superiority had been attained or was likely to be attained within a foreseeable time. The Royal Air Force, the German Naval Staff observed, "is still by no means defeated." Hitler agreed. On September 17 he decided not to give the order for a landing in Britain, and suspended the operation until further notice. Next day he countermanded the assembly of invasion craft and sanctioned the dispersal of transports and naval vessels to lessen the risk of bombing.

And that, for practical purposes, was the end of Hitler's hopes of doing what Philip II of Spain and Napoleon had failed to do. Whether the British, having won that crucial round, could go on to drive him out of the countries he had already conquered was another matter. "Give us the tools," said Churchill, "and we will finish the job." This was a saying whose inmost meaning afterward puzzled more than one enquirer. Did Churchill believe in his heart that Britain could finish the war alone? Or did he merely think it expedient to tell the world that she meant to try? Obviously, neither he nor any statesman could give a pledge that the scope of the war would not be widened. But some, at least, of his hearers took his words as a promise that, while the British government would be glad to buy all the American material they could pay for or to which their credit would stretch, they would make it one of the chief aims of their diplomacy to keep America out of the fighting and prevent the simmering quarrel between Japan and the United States from boiling over.

15

THE WIDENING WAR

AFTER THEIR DEFEAT IN THE BATTLE OF BRITAIN, THE GERMANS STILL had a chance of knocking their one remaining enemy out of the war by devoting their main effort at sea and in the air to a resolute blockade of the United Kingdom. By dispensing with luxuries, the British could manage with three-fifths of their normal imports, but they would not be able to go on fighting long if much less than that proportion reached them. At the same time, or alternatively, an eastward drive along the North African coast and thence into Palestine and Syria offered the glittering prospect of bringing Turkey into the war on the Axis side, cutting out Britain's vital sources of Middle Eastern oil, and ending Germany's dependence on supplies from Rumania and Russia.

The second of these proposals had only a limited appeal for Hitler. The argument that a successful advance to the gates of the Middle East might make his projected attack on Russia unnecessary was no recommendation to the Führer, determined as he was to settle his account with Stalin not only for the sake of the oil of Maikop and Grozny and the wheat of the Ukraine, but also in order to establish Germany's military supremacy in Eastern Europe. Then, too, the Mediterranean was an Italian lake insofar as it was not a British one, and the leaders of the German Army were understandably reluctant to stake the future of a North African expeditionary force on the ability of the Italian Navy to safeguard its communications. If only for that reason, success would be difficult without active support from Vichy France and

Franco's Spain. Both Pétain and Franco expressed their readiness to collaborate "in principle," but the former was unwilling to do more than defend French colonial possessions against direct attack, and the latter was encouraged by British and American diplomatic pressure to put his demands so high, and urge them so inflexibly, that for once the Führer met his match. "Rather than go through that again," he reported after his interview with Franco at Hendaye on October 23, 1940, "I should prefer to have three or four teeth out." In the end—although it proved to be not quite the end—the projected advance to Suez and beyond was whittled down to the despatch, in February 1941, of a small force whose commander, General Rommel, had orders to cooperate with the Italians in the defense of Libya and on no account to launch a major offensive without express authority.

If Hitler lost his chance of inflicting a spectacular defeat on the British Empire when he failed to take up the North African project wholeheartedly and push it through with his usual ruthlessness, blockade remained a weapon with which he might have done lethal damage if he had ordered both the German Navy and the Luftwaffe to devote their energies to attacks on British seaborne trade from the moment when he first saw that invasion had become impractical. As it was, a good many weeks were lost before the Battle of the Atlantic became a major preoccupation for the British government. In spite of his humiliating setback in the summer, Göring still believed that he could wear the British down by bombing. The greater part of his effort during the winter was devoted to night attacks on British cities. These were, at best, a devious contribution to blockade. They caused much suffering and much needless loss of life, but they never looked like giving the Germans a decision. On the contrary, they defeated the very purpose they were meant to serve by stiffening the determination of the British to go on fighting until Hitler was beaten, even if it cost them their last penny.

The so-called "area attacks" on German cities, on which the British government decided in October, were equally pointless, and still more illogical since Britain professed to have no quarrel with the German people except that they allowed themselves to be ruled by Hitler. Even if the indiscriminate slaughter of non-combatants seemed to Winston Churchill and his colleagues a rational way of persuading the Germans to repudiate their leader, it could hardly be expected to strike the Germans themselves in exactly the same light. No matter how skillfully one side or the other might seek to cloak their aims with specious definitions of the term "military objective," the obvious and inescapable consequence of the sanctioning by both of haphazard bombing of built-up areas was to deepen the conflict at a time when the long-term interests of Europe and the British Empire alike demanded that it should be ended before it became world-wide.

Meanwhile events were showing that Britain was still a power to be reckoned with. While Hitler and Roosevelt might both look forward, from their respective viewpoints, to the day when the British Empire could be administered as "a vast estate in bankruptcy," the fact remained that British refusal to accept defeat was still the most important single factor in world politics. Convinced by the late summer of 1940 that their ambassador had underestimated the fighting qualities of the British and that Britain was still worth backing as the one remaining obstacle to German hegemony in Europe, the United States government lent powerful support to British diplomacy by warning Franco in August that henceforth they would permit the export to Spain of no more oil than the British were content that he should have to meet domestic needs. As winter deepened over Europe, British ships and troops rubbed home the lesson by severely punishing the Italian fleet at Taranto and driving the Italian Army from Cyrenaica. Urged in the light of British success to make America "the great arsenal of democracy," the House of Representatives agreed in February to do so by passing the Lend-Lease Act.

Hailed by Churchill as "the most unsordid act in history," this farseeing move was welcomed by many of his compatriots as a sign that their plea to be given the tools and left to finish the job had not gone unheeded. But that interpretation was not altogether borne out, even if it was not altogether contradicted, by another transaction which took place that month. As the outcome of Anglo-American staff talks, held in considerable secrecy in London, the two governments agreed that if the United States became involved in war with both Germany and Japan, their joint effort should be directed first against Germany. To persuade the Japanese to attack British possessions in the Far East was meanwhile becoming an important aim for Hitler, who believed that the effect would be to lock up a strong British force at Singapore and shift "the center of gravity of American interest" to the Pacific. When the Japanese objected that another effect might be to expose Japan to a stab in the back from Russia, the German Foreign Minister replied that in that case Germany would at once attack the Russians, but did not add that she had already arranged to do so, although the date on which Hitler hoped to launch his Russian campaign was only about two months ahead.

While both sides were thus contemplating the extension of a war which both had every motive for limiting and shortening, a far-reaching clash of interests in the Balkans gave a new twist to the kaleidoscope. In August, Hitler, alarmed by Italian troop movements toward the frontiers of Greece and Yugoslavia, had warned Mussolini against doing anything to upset the "new order in Europe" which he claimed to be creating. Disregarding the injunction, Mussolini greeted the Führer at Florence on October 28 with the news that his troops had invaded Greece that morning. His three divisions were soon halted by the Greeks, but the situation remained explosive.

The British government, believing that it was important to gain a foothold in the Balkans as a base for future operations against the Axis and to rally as many as possible of the Balkan countries on their side, responded by landing a token force on Greek soil and promising more substantial help when it was needed. The Greeks were reluctant to acquiesce in a step which might lead Hitler to intervene against them, and doubted whether the three or four divisions offered by the British would restore the balance if he did, but allowed themselves to be talked into acceptance.

The moment to redeem the pledge came when, in April, Hitler sent powerful forces to Greece and Yugoslavia after telling his service chiefs that he was prepared to delay his attack on Russia for four weeks while he secured his Balkan flank. But British or Commonwealth troops for Greece could be found only by depleting General Archibald Wavell's forces in North Africa at the very moment when Rommel had decided to defy the prophets by taking the offensive within six weeks of his arrival in an unfamiliar theater. Overwhelmed by vastly superior forces on the Greek mainland and afterward thrown out of Crete, the British paid a third time for the dispersal of their effort when Rommel swept through Cyrenaica with an impetus which carried him to the Egyptian frontier. There he stopped to recruit his strength, unable to go further while an undefeated garrison remained at Tobruk to threaten his communications.

Physical preparations for the attack on Russia began at least as early as October 1940, when the development and construction of aerodromes in Poland was put in hand. In the spring the Germans redoubled their efforts. Elaborate security precautions did not prevent the British government from learning enough of what was in the wind to be able to give good warning to the Russians. Characteristically, Stalin gave no sign that he was either grateful for the information or willing to act on it. The general disposition of the Soviet Army when the Germans attacked was well suited to defense in depth, but units near the frontier were taken by surprise and seem to have received no special warning.

The Germans opened their assault at dawn on June 22, 1941, with three powerful groups of armies supported by two-thirds of the German air force. The whole of Kesselring's air fleet was withdrawn from the Western Front before the assault began, leaving only three hundred bombers to threaten the United Kingdom and its shipping. Measures intended to conceal the eastward movement of flying units included a considerable volume of bogus wireless traffic and a series of raids on London by crews who made two or three sorties a night to atone for their lack of numbers.

During the last big raid on London, Rudolf Hess, Hitler's nominal deputy, arrived in Scotland by baling out of a long-range fighter in which he had flown solo from an aerodrome near Munich. He astonished his captors by announcing that he had come on an important mission and demanding to see first the

Duke of Hamilton, a blameless Scottish landowner and officer in the Royal Auxiliary Air Force whom he had never met and who did not even know him by sight, and secondly a member of the government. The obvious inference was that he had come to enlist British support for the Führer's forthcoming crusade against international Communism, but he succeeded in convincing his interrogators that he was not aware of the impending attack on Russia and knew less of Hitler's intentions than they did. The gist of his message was that he had traveled from Germany entirely on his own initiative, that he had consulted no one except a German professor who had advised him to seek out the Duke of Hamilton on the ground that dukes notoriously had the last word in Britain, and that his object was to make peace between the British and German governments before Britain was consumed by the Führer's wrath. Failing to persuade his captors that he was anything but a tiresome and not particularly well-informed crank who might nevertheless become a source of embarrassment if the general public learned too much about his exploit, he fell into a state of profound dejection, made at least one attempt at suicide, and spent the rest of the war as an unwelcome but closely guarded guest of the British government.

In London, as in Berlin, Russian capacity to resist Hitler's bid for conquest was grossly underestimated. The wholesale liquidation of service chiefs before the war had given an unflattering impression of the state of the armed forces, and the Soviet Army had made slow progress in Finland in 1939 and 1940. The general opinion was that the Russians might hold out for six months or so, but were more likely to collapse in six weeks. Most people forgot that, even if Stalin could be sure of nothing else, he could count on huge reserves of manpower and an almost unlimited field of maneuver. Where the interests of individual citizens counted for nothing and where undertakings which represented years of patient effort could be sacrificed almost without a qualm as long as it was physically possible to duplicate their activities in safer quarters, the vastness of Russia offered virtual immunity from defeat to a defender willing to barter a thousand square miles of scorched earth for the escape of half an army corps.

As it happened, Stalin had many other assets. In spite of purges, or because of them, his armies were competently led by officers trained in a hard school where failure cost the lives of generals as well as privates. His output and reserves of war material were much greater than had been thought, but that did not prevent him from exploiting his deficiencies to the utmost in order to extract as much help as he could from his allies and supporters. Above all, he had the inestimable advantage of an adversary whose capacity for self-delusion was becoming almost boundless. If Hitler deceived himself when he supposed that the Russians could be beaten in a single campaign, he blundered still more grossly in thinking that he could, at one and the same time, defeat the major part of the Soviet Army on the road to Moscow and capture important political and economic objectives far away at Leningrad and in the Ukraine.

As soon as he was attacked, Stalin called urgently on the British to form a Second Front in Europe, and his parrot cry was loudly echoed by left-wing sympathizers in Britain and elsewhere. Already committed in North Africa, and without the means of forming and equipping an expeditionary force which would have stood the least chance of establishing itself in northern France, the British government had, in fact, anticipated the demand for a Second Front by ordering the Commanders-in-Chief of the Metropolitan Air Force, nearly a week before Hitler delivered his assault on Russia, to concert plans for a series of daylight attacks on objectives within reach of escort fighters as a means of checking or reversing the flow of German squadrons to the Eastern Front. The attacks cost the Royal Air Force many more fighters than the Germans lost in trying to repel them, and were a failure so far as any discoverable effect on the disposition of the German air force was concerned. But Stalin had no reason to complain that no sacrifices were being made to help him.

By December the southern group of German armies had reached the Don Basin and the Crimea and were about to attack Sebastopol, but the rest of the Führer's program was still far from completion. Leningrad was threatened but untaken, and the Soviet Army was undefeated although German troops were in the outskirts of Moscow. No provision had been made for a winter campaign in the over-all plan for the attack on Russia, but Hitler, apparently fearing a repetition of Napoleon's retreat from Moscow, refused to hear of disengagement. He considered his decision justified when a series of counterattacks nourished by British and American supplies failed to dislodge his troops from the most important of the positions they had won. But the intense cold which had to be endured by men without adequate clothing or accommodation led to heavy wastage in the northern and central groups of armies, and the Luftwaffe, in particular, was never fully to recover from an ordeal which followed without respite after months of all-out fighting and incessant strain. By mid-winter some commanders were down to less than a third of their nominal establishment of aircraft, and could see little hope of ever getting back to normal in face of competition from rivals at a vast array of bases from the North Cape to the Mediterranean and from the Atlantic to the Sea of Azov.

While Germany was still outwardly strong and the Führer still nominally devoted to the principle of decisive strength at the decisive point, by the end of 1941 the armed forces of the Third Reich thus reached a degree of dispersal bordering on nightmare. Besides holding down half a continent, the German Army was pursuing at least three distinct aims in Russia. In Africa, Rommel would soon be asking for reinforcements to enable him to press on to Suez and perhaps, if fortune favored him, complete a gigantic pincer movement by linking up with German forces advancing through the Caucasus. Still more widely scattered in proportion to its size, the German air force faced demands from army commanders in every active theater, and had only a handful of aircraft for its all-important task of hunting convoys in partnership with submarines. Even the navy's interests were divided between the rival attractions of underwater and surface power.

If no other factor had been present, this situation might have opened golden opportunities for the British Empire. Had their hands been free, the obvious policy for the British would have been to hold on in Africa until they were strong enough to lure the impetuous Rommel to his destruction, at the same time use their growing naval and air power to wrest command of the Mediterranean from the uncertain grasp of the Italian Navy and the German air force, and in due course strike hard at the "soft underbelly of the Axis."

But over these prospects lay the shadow of events in the Far East. Since the 1920s the British had followed a difficult and unattractive policy in that part of the world. Faced with the prospect of a naked struggle for command of the sea in which they feared that the advantage might lie with the Almighty Dollar, and also to calm Australian apprehensions and preserve the link with Canada, they had tacitly repudiated their long-standing alliance with Japan by accepting the Washington naval agreement after the First World War. Little more than ten years later, the Shanghai incident had shown how little reliance could be placed on the hope of Anglo-American cooperation where armed strength was lacking. Just as in Europe Neville Chamberlain had been forced by his parsimony as Chancellor of the Exchequer to adopt, as Prime Minister, a conciliatory attitude toward Germany and Italy in spite of protests from some of his supporters, so in the Far East the two Anglo-Saxon powers had found it necessary, for precisely similar reasons, to conciliate the Japanese and reject the alternative policy of imposing sanctions on them. For some months in 1940 the British government had even felt obliged to buy a respite from Japanese intervention by interrupting supplies to the Chinese Nationalist leader Chiang Kai-shek.

But Franklin Delano Roosevelt was not, by temperament, an appeaser. It was not by compromising with the powers of evil that he had triumphed over an appalling physical handicap, and had gone on to become the world's most powerful ruler and had saved the greatest nation on earth from bankruptcy. Firmly established in his third term as President, he had reason to feel a growing confidence in his ability to shape the affairs of a troubled world to his country's profit and the profit of democracy. At the same time, the Japanese also had some grounds for believing that the future might be molded to their advantage. Not merely the Russo-Japanese Neutrality Pact concluded in the previous April but, much more, the German attack on Russia had averted, at least temporarily, the risk of Soviet aggression. Industrial America seemed preoccupied with Lend-Lease contracts. The powerful United States Pacific Fleet at Pearl Harbor was America's Far Eastern shield, but a shield could be pierced. The time might not be far off when Japan could take her revenge on the powers which had begun by urging her to renounce her old ways and become a great producing and exporting nation, but had turned against her when she did so.

The position in the early winter of 1941 was that diplomatic exchanges between the Japanese and United States governments had been going on for many months, but had failed to reconcile conflicting views as to Japan's future role in China. On November 26 the United States government delivered a communication described by the Japanese Prime Minister, Hideki Tojo, as an ultimatum. The United States government contended that it was not an ultimatum, but a statement of proposals designed to settle relations between the two countries on an amicable basis.

The Japanese were an adaptable people. They observed that the elaborate code of honor by which they had regulated their affairs until the nineteenth century was outmoded in the twentieth. Even the rough and ready principle of fair play for all seemed to lack force at a time when access to markets and raw materials was a prime requisite of existence for an overcrowded island state. Perhaps the person who remarked that the time to give a man a kick was when you met him coming round a corner with a bag of salt on his back came closer to the spirit of the age.

The Japanese were also a realistic people. Two days after receiving the American proposals they despatched, in profound secrecy, a powerful task force with orders to deliver a surprise attack on the American Pacific Fleet.

Astonishingly, in view of the probable outcome of their diplomacy, the Americans were unprepared. While the Japanese armada was steaming eastward toward Hawaii, negotiations continued in Washington. At Pearl Harbor the fleet went about its usual business and awaited orders. The British had disclosed the secrets of radar to the American authorities, and American radar sets had been manufactured and delivered to service users. American military attachés and staff officers knew that only unceasing radar watch had enabled the British to win the Battle of Britain, and that Hitler's preparations to land troops in England might have gone unnoticed but for constant air reconnaissance. According to a report which reached the British government, the Japanese striking force was in fact detected by radar before it reached its objective, but the equipment was not officially in use and the warning went unheeded. The attack on Pearl Harbor, delivered by carrier-borne aircraft at 1:30 P.M. Washington time on December 7, achieved surprise and the American Pacific Fleet was crippled.

Almost simultaneously, although differences in local time made the synchronization of the Japanese attacks not immediately apparent, the British lost two capital ships which were proceeding without fighter cover to investigate a report that Japanese troops had landed in British-controlled territory. At one stroke the virtual loss of the American fleet as well as the two British warships exposed the whole of the British possessions in the Far East and as far west as the Arabian Sea to attack from seaward. The plan which envisaged the sending of the Home Fleet to Singapore in the event of war in the Far East had long since been discarded, and ultimately the security of Singapore depended on the always dubious assumption that no attack from landward was possible. With the loss of Anglo-American command of Far Eastern waters, and in view of the penetration of French Indochina by Japanese troops with the connivance of the Vichy government, that assumption became more untenable than ever.

On the other hand it was obvious that the Japanese had made a gambler's throw and that their action was bound to tell against the Axis powers in the long run. If Britain, the United States, and Russia combined against their enemies as they were henceforth bound to do, the ultimate success of the Allies could only be a matter of time unless they made some major blunder. Unless the outlook were again transformed by some new hazard, the ultimate defeat of Germany was certain. At the same time, the mere defeat of Germany, and even of Japan as well, was no longer enough to ensure a stable peace. The question yet to be answered was whether British, American, and Russian rivalries and aspirations would prove compatible with a secure future for Europe and the world.

16

ARCADIA TO TEHERAN

AS SOON AFTER PEARL HARBOR AS THE NECESSARY ARRANGEMENTS could be made, the President of the United States and the British Prime Minister, with their service advisers and other experts, met in Washington to discuss the future conduct of the war to which both countries had become committed. Agreeing to pool their resources and unite their efforts, they set up an Anglo-American staff committee, the Combined Chiefs of Staff, to direct a common strategy. At the same time the British learned, to their immense relief, that the United States government still adhered to the principle that Germany must be defeated first. Fiercely assailed, and at times eroded, by American commanders who regarded the Pacific as the only theater in which American interests were seriously engaged, the strategy of "Hitler first" remained, in spite of all assaults, the bastion of the Anglo-American alliance until the end of the war in Europe.

But the province of the Combined Chiefs of Staff was confined to military questions. No comparable body existed to formulate and review the political aims for which the war was fought. Nor was it probable that such a body could have accomplished much in face of the wide differences of outlook which divided the English-speaking peoples, even where their interests were not seriously in conflict. An important aim for the British was, if not to restore the balance of power which existed in 1914, at any rate to ensure that no militant and aggressive nation such as Germany or Russia gained sway over an inordinately large tract of Europe.

To Americans accustomed to take a remote view of European politics, the very thought of allowing Anglo-American strategy to be guided by such considerations seemed improper. Yet probably they would have agreed, in the last resort, that wars were fought for political ends, that they themselves were fighting to destroy German hegemony in Europe, and that the struggle would be fruitless if its outcome were merely to replace one ambitious despot by another. But whether Stalin was, in fact, an ambitious despot, and Russia a militant nation, were questions on which Americans and British did not always think alike.

At the time of the Arcadia Conference, as the first of the summit conferences at which the Americans were present as belligerents was called, the Russians had already astonished the world by the strength of their resistance to German aggression, but no one could yet be sure how long they would hold out. President Roosevelt was eager that American troops should be brought to bear against the Germans while the Soviet Army was still capable of pinning down a great part of the German Army on the Eastern Front. British warnings that no assault on German-occupied Europe could succeed without careful preparation seemed an understandable echo of past setbacks, but not necessarily valid for the future. Not convinced that a landing in France was out of the question in 1942, the President nevertheless accepted in principle the Prime Minister's proposal that Anglo-American forces should land in Tunisia as early in the year as possible. Thence they would press eastward against Rommel's rear while the British made a westward thrust. If the venture succeeded the Germans and Italians would be driven from North Africa, and control of the Mediterranean would be within the grasp of the Allies. The mass of shipping needed to make the long haul round the Cape would then be freed for other tasks.

That it would succeed seemed almost certain when, after a series of hard-fought actions near the Egyptian frontier in the last few weeks of 1941, the British forces in North Africa, now under General Sir Claude Auchinleck, drove Rommel out of Cyrenaica with the loss of more than half his troops, nearly all his tanks, and four-fifths of his aircraft. But the picture changed when events in the Far East showed that, unless the Japanese were to be allowed to push westward and southward without check, reinforcements intended for Auchinleck would have to be diverted farther east and shipping needed for American landings in Tunisia be retained in the Pacific theater. On May 27 Rommel, making a spectacular recovery from his setback at the beginning of the year, launched a powerful attack directed at Tobruk. By the end of June the British were back behind the Egyptian frontier with most of their armor gone, and Rommel's chances of reaching the Suez Canal were being seriously weighed in Cairo.

Meanwhile America's new status as a belligerent power had created fresh opportunities for German submarines, hitherto forbidden to operate in the Western Atlantic. Especially in the spring and early summer, U-boat commanders found rewarding targets in unarmed American merchant vessels not organized in convoy, without fighter cover, and clearly silhouetted at night against the bright lights of seaboard cities. In May alone nearly half a millon tons of Allied shipping were sunk in American waters. Thereafter American merchantmen sailed in convoy and lights ashore were dimmed, yet losses continued on a massive scale for another year.

Still bent on landing troops in France before the end of the year if it could be managed, President Roosevelt sent his personal representative, Harry Hopkins, to London in April with the proposal that the Allies should at once begin preparations for a large-scale invasion of Europe in the spring of 1943, and that meanwhile they should hold themselves ready to put a force ashore in 1942 as a sacrifice to save the Russians from imminent collapse. General George C. Marshall, who accompanied Hopkins to London, argued that such a force might hold a bridgehead in readiness for the landing in the spring.

The British had been studying the problem of an opposed landing in France since 1940. They pointed out that the troops and shipping needed to meet Marshall's minimum requirements would not be available before October. They doubted whether the nine divisions to which, at most, the force could be built up would be capable of holding out until the spring. Nor did they believe that the Russians would be saved from collapse by a force which the Germans could reasonably hope to contain or defeat without removing a single division from the Eastern Front. Displeased by what seemed to them the excessive caution of the British, the Americans nevertheless agreed that a landing in 1942 (Operation Sledgehammer) should be attempted only if the plight of the Russians called for desperate measures, and that the build-up of American forces in Britain (Operation Bolero) should continue in readiness for a landing in 1943.

Almost simultaneously, President Roosevelt invited the Russians to send their Foreign Minister, Vyacheslav Molotov, and a military adviser to Washington to discuss "a very important military proposal." Arriving at the end of May, Molotov was received at a conference attended by the President in person.

The sequel was a convincing demonstration of the dangers of diplomacy by conference. Molotov began by warning the President that the Soviet Army might not be able to hold out. He added that he had asked the British to contribute to a Second Front and received no satisfaction, but hoped for a straight answer from the President. A trained diplomatist might have seized the chance of letting the Russians see that Britain and the United States were determined to follow a common strategy, and were not to be diverted from their aims by crude appeals to national prejudice. President Roosevelt was not a trained diplomatist. He asked General Marshall whether it could fairly be said that a Second Front was in preparation. Marshall replied, correctly, that it could. The President then authorized Molotov to tell Stalin that the United States government expected the formation of a Second Front before the end of the year.

Marshall knew that, except as a last resort, there would be no Second Front *in Europe* in 1942. After the meeting he did his best to ensure that the Russians were not left with a wrong impression, but without success. From Washington, Molotov traveled to London with the draft of a communiqué, approved by the Americans, to the effect that the British, United States, and Russian governments were all of the opinion that the formation of a Second Front in Europe in 1942 was an urgent task. The

Prime Minister assented to the publication of Molotov's formula as a means of confusing the enemy, but added that the British government could not, in fact, promise a landing on the Continent in 1942. Molotov was handed a written warning in that sense. When the Russians pointed out later that the end of the year had come without a landing in Europe, the British could at least point to their warning, but the Americans had not even that defense.

In spite of this chastening experience, President Roosevelt retained full confidence in his ability to deal with the Russians. He had already told Churchill that he was satisfied that he could handle Stalin better than either his own State Department or the British Foreign Office could, and he remained of that opinion.

At a further Anglo-American conference in Washington in June, the British pressed for the landing in Tunisia to which the Americans had agreed in principle, but the meeting was interrupted by news of Rommel's advance. Rommel reached the Egyptian frontier with only twelve tanks, and seemed in no position to launch a further attack for at least some weeks. General Auchinleck was confident that he could hold the position at El Alamein to which he had retreated, and expected to be able to counterattack about the middle of September, by which time he would have received more armor and fresh troops. Disturbed by reports of alarm and despondency in Cairo, and in the light of other factors, the British government decided, however, that the time had come for a new deal. On August 15 General Harold Alexander assumed command of the theater and General Bernard Montgomery of the Eighth Army in the Western Desert.

These changes were not the only consequences of the government's evaluation of the situation in Egypt. British fears that the Germans might break through in the Middle East and join hands with the Japanese led American critics of the "Hitler first" strategy to claim that the British were receding from their undertaking to prepare for a landing in France, and brought demands that the United States should turn its back on Europe and concentrate on the war with Japan. Refusing to reverse the Arcadia decision, the President sent Marshall, Hopkins, and Admiral Ernest King to

London with orders to press for a landing in France in 1942, but accept a landing in North Africa as the next best thing if they failed to shake the British.

By the time the Americans reached London, half the summer had gone. The British were convinced that to attempt a landing in the Pas de Calais or Normandy in the autumn with the resources available would be to invite disaster. To the intense disappointment of Marshall and King, and also of Major General Dwight D. Eisenhower, commanding the United States Army in the European theater, they firmly rejected Sledgehammer and pressed for the North African landing (Operation Torch). The belief of the American service chiefs that Sledgehammer could have succeeded was, however, shaken by the heavy casualties suffered by a Canadian force which raided Dieppe in August, and Eisenhower afterward conceded that objections to the plan were sound. Meanwhile the President, accepting the British decision, had ruled on July 25 that Torch should take place "not later than October 30."

In contrast to their hopeful estimate of the chances of a landing in France, the American experts took a view of the prospects in North Africa which seemed to the British unduly gloomy. The original intention was to land troops as far apart as Casablanca in the west and a point as near as possible to the naval base at Bizerta in the east, although the British were willing to forego a landing at Casablanca if the front were thought too wide. Influenced by heavy losses suffered by a Malta-bound convoy in August, the Americans refused to countenance initial landings farther east than Algiers, and in consequence a chance of forestalling the Germans in Tunisia was lost. But the American attitude was not due merely to excessive caution. The Americans were willing to run risks in order to land troops in France and save the Russians from collapse, but it did not follow that they were ready to make sacrifices in order to pull the chestnuts out of the fire for the British in Egypt. The Joint Chiefs of Staff could understand the strategic importance of the Suez Canal and Middle Eastern oil as an intellectual proposition, but they would not have been one hundred per cent Americans if their instincts had not led them to ask themselves at times what business the British had to be in Egypt anyway. Moreover, they did not believe that the Eighth Army could beat Rommel.

There they were wrong. Auchinleck had predicted that Rommel would attack before the end of August, but would hardly be strong enough to attempt the conquest of the Nile Delta except as a gamble. On the last day of the month Rommel did attack. His intention was to cut off and encircle the Eighth Army by breaking through in the south and swinging north toward the sea. General Montgomery saw when he took up his command that the key to the El Alamein position was a ridge at Alam-el-Halfa which his predecessor had begun to prepare for defense. He decided to refuse his left and lead Rommel's armor toward the ridge, where it would come up against a whole division in entrenched positions and supported by artillery and tanks. Montgomery's maneuver succeeded brilliantly, and Rommel withdrew on September 3 with heavy losses. Seven weeks later Montgomery attacked with a big superiority in numbers and equipment, and in fifteen days the Eighth Army advanced seven hundred miles from El Alamein to Benghazi.

The Allied First Army which began to go ashore in French North Africa on November 8, on the other hand, seemed doomed from the start to disappointment and frustration. Anglo-American disagreements had so delayed the landings, and so reduced their scope, that the force had little chance of achieving anything worth while before the winter rains unless it could push eastward without further loss of time. Attempts to persuade the incorruptible but unsympathetic Admiral Jean Darlan to receive the Allies as liberators failed to shake his loyalty to Vichy, and some opposition from local garrisons had to be overcome before the build-up could be completed. Most of the troops were raw. Commanders were unused to the handling of an inter-allied force. While the First Army was advancing with painful slowness through the Little Atlas toward the Plain of Tunis and the Eighth Army taking Tripoli, the German High Command was hastening to put at Rommel's disposal in Tunisia the reinforcements it had refused him for his advance to Suez.

Expecting by February that the First Army would fall on his rear as soon as he was next engaged with the Eighth Army, Rommel decided to get his blow in first. On February 14 he attacked the inexperienced U. S. 1st Armored Division between Fondouk and Gafsa with about a hundred tanks supported by dive bombers. In a few days he was through the weak defenses of the Kasserine Pass, with the prospect of a brilliant tactical success before him. His advance was stopped on February 22, after General Alexander had correctly predicted that he would turn north in the hope of rolling up the Allied line from Gafsa to the sea.

The end came in May, when Alexander accepted the surrender of a quarter of a million German and Italian troops. By their victory in Africa the Allies gained control of the Mediterranean and Atlantic seaboard from Casablanca to Port Said, freed a million tons of shipping for fresh tasks, and exposed thousands of miles of enemy-held coastline to the threat of invasion or seaborne raids. But success had been too long delayed for a landing in northern France to be possible before the spring or early summer of 1944. Meanwhile the tide was turning in favor of the Russians on the Eastern Front, where Hitler's refusal to give ground in order to gain a tactical advantage had already cost the Germans nearly a third of a million men at Stalingrad alone. Before British and American troops were ready to go ashore in France, twelve months or more would elapse during which the Soviet Army could be expected to draw nearer to the heart of Germany, its masters to the realization of the age-old Russian dream of a Pan-Slav empire stretching from the Pacific Ocean to the Danubian states and from the Arctic Circle to the Adriatic. Although the fact was not fully apparent at the time, Anglo-American grand strategy would be judged in the future largely by the use that was made of those twelve months.

Russian victories did not worry President Roosevelt, who had, he told an American diplomatist, a hunch that Stalin wanted nothing but "security for his country" and would "work for a world of democracy and peace" if treated generously. But presidential hunches were no substitute for reasoned statecraft. Stalin's conquests, won by a ruthless expenditure of Russian lives and physical assets and with the help of equipment and supplies for which American and British taxpayers would ultimately foot the bill, might not directly threaten American or British interests, but they made it more than ever incumbent on the statesmen of both countries to ensure, to the best of their ability, that Soviet ambitions did not prejudice the postwar security of Europe and the world.

As early as December 1942, Roosevelt and Churchill had proposed a three-power conference, from which Stalin excused himself on the ground that he could not leave Russia even for a day. Meeting without him at Casablanca in January 1943, the President and the Prime Minister recognized that the conquest of Tunisia was not likely to be completed for some months, and that it would then be too late for the resources needed for a landing in northern France to be assembled in time for the operation to be launched with any prospect of success in 1943. The question was what should be done with their forces in the meantime. The obvious answer might have seemed to be to abandon the cross-Channel invasion in favor of an operation which *could* be begun in 1943, but that solution was not seriously considered. The Allies were not prepared to go back on their decision to land in northern France as soon as they could, nor were they willing, in the absence of a Russian representative, to do anything which might be construed as a breach of faith with Stalin.

The British proposed, as an interim measure and not as a substitute for the cross-Channel invasion, a landing in Sicily as a steppingstone to the Italian mainland. An assault on Italy, they claimed, would hasten Mussolini's fall, draw off German forces from Northern Europe, and give the Allies bases from which they could strike at the Rumanian oilfields and other objectives out of reach of bombers based in Britain. American service chiefs opposed the plan as likely to dissipate resources needed for the invasion of France, and urged that the main effort in 1943 should be directed against Japan. Such a course seemed to the British even more likely than an attack on Italy to lead to dissipation of the resources needed to conquer Germany. They promised that, if the Americans held fast to their declared intention of putting Europe first, they would throw in everything they had against the Japanese as soon as Hitler was defeated. Furthermore, it seemed beyond dispute that the Allies could not afford to remain on the defensive in Europe in 1943 if by doing so they risked allowing Hitler to concentrate his forces first against the Soviet Army and afterward against themselves. The Russians were doing well, but they might make peace, or be defeated, if they were left to carry too big a share of the burden for many months.

In the light of these arguments the statesmen agreed that the "Hitler first" strategy was still valid and that preoccupation with the Pacific theater must not be allowed to jeopardize their chances in the West. They embodied their agreement in a formula which virtually empowered the United States Joint Chiefs of Staff to decide how far the war in the Far East could be pressed in 1943 without detriment to the European theater. At the subsequent Trident Conference at Washington in May, the Combined Chiefs of Staff upheld a recommendation from the Joint Chiefs that the Far East should take precedence over the Mediterranean during the latter part of the year. At the same time it was, at least ostensibly, common ground between the British and the Americans that pressure must be maintained on Italy. Accordingly, General Eisenhower was given authority to invade Sicily as soon as he was ready. But the American Chiefs of Staff were not convinced that a major effort would be necessary to conquer Italy once Sicily was in Allied hands, and they laid their plans on the assumption that Eisenhower would be able to do without the large number of landing craft needed to put a substantial force ashore on the mainland in face of serious opposition. Their attitude was all the more understandable since the Americans suspected the British of pursuing ends of their own in southeast Europe. Yet, if Churchill did have in mind the importance of forestalling Stalin in the Balkans, to do so would have served the long-term interests of the United States just as much as those of Britain.

If the Allies failed to hold firmly to their intention of putting

Europe first until Hitler was defeated, that was not the only respect in which the Casablanca Conference did not show British and American statesmen at their best. A week before the conference opened, the American Chiefs of Staff approved of a proposal from the President that the war aims of the Allies should include the "unconditional surrender" of their enemies. The Prime Minister accepted the formula in the course of an informal conversation with Roosevelt and Hopkins at Casablanca, but suggested that Italy should be excluded. On referring to his colleagues in London he found, however, that they were in favor of including Italy. No reference to unconditional surrender was made in the communiqué issued at the end of the conference, but the President repaired the omission by letting journalists know that that was what he and Churchill had in mind.

The disclosure was afterward seen to have been a blunder. It was natural that Anglo-American views at the height of the war should be colored by awareness of the handicap which the Allies were thought to have inflicted on themselves in 1918 and later years through their failure to carry the First World War into the heart of Germany. But the British and American governments did not advance their interests by letting it appear in 1943 that their enemies would gain nothing by repudiating their leaders and renouncing their errors. Even the most abject of surrenders implied some kind of contact between the two sides before hostilities could cease. Since the Allies were determined not to treat with Hitler, it followed that there could be no end to the war with Germany until Hitler was replaced by someone with whom they were prepared to treat. By publicly and prematurely proclaiming that unconditional surrender was their aim they went a long way to ensure that no such person would be found until Germany was in turmoil and the whole of Central Europe in Russian hands and ripe for Communist penetration. In Japan the declaration similarly strengthened the hands of extremists determined to fight to the last ditch, by presenting them with the argument that the Allies meant to beat the country to its knees and that death was better than dishonor.

The invasion of Sicily on July 10 was so successful that Eisenhower decided within a week that the Italian mainland, too, must be invaded. Mussolini's fall a few days later made it no less desirable to get the assault over before the German troops already in Italy were strongly reinforced. He soon found, however, that the reduction of his resources for the benefit of other theaters, already begun on orders from Washington and due to continue during the succeeding months, would make his proposed landing at Salerno impossible before September, and that even then its scope would be severely limited by lack of shipping. The British urged that the opportunity created by Mussolini's fall should be promptly exploited, but were powerless to reverse the Trident decision to give precedence to the Far East until the end of 1943, which they had already tried to circumvent at the cost of attracting a brisk rejoinder from Washington. In the outcome, the troops which went ashore at Salerno narrowly escaped disaster. Handicapped by bad weather as well as by meager resources and lost time, the Allies made slow progress in their subsequent advance through the length of Italy. Marshal Pietro Badoglio, Mussolini's successor, believed that, since Italy was Italy and emphatically not Germany, the "unconditional surrender" formula would not prevent him from making reasonable terms with the invaders. Even so, he could not prevent the Germans from pouring troops into his country and putting up a stout resistance.

Meanwhile detailed planning had begun in London for the cross-Channel invasion to be launched in 1944 (Operation Overlord). The Overlord planners found themselves handicapped, just as Eisenhower's staff in the Mediterranean theater were handicapped when they planned the Salerno venture, by the small number of landing craft allotted to them. In consequence they were unable to contemplate putting ashore more than three seaborne divisions in the assault phase and two more in the immediate follow-up. In addition two airborne brigades would take part in the initial assault. Thereafter the troops ashore in France would grow to eighteen divisions at the end of the first fortnight, and ultimately to about a hundred divisions. In view of the smallness of the initial assault the planners felt bound to point out that the undertaking could succeed only if the German armies in France had no more than twelve mobile divisions in reserve in France at the crucial stage.

At the Quadrant Conference at Quebec in August 1943, the Overlord plan was accepted with misgivings on the part of the British, and May 1, 1944, was chosen as the target date. The British urged that the weight of the initial assault should be increased by a quarter, but the Americans were unable to agree since the additional shipping could be found only at the expense of their operations in the Far East. As an alternative to the British proposal they suggested that a diversionary landing in the South of France (Operation Anvil) should be staged with resources already available in the Mediterranean theater.

The misgivings of the British were increased when they learned at Cairo in November that the Americans were proposing to avert the collapse of Chiang Kai-shek's forces in China by invading Burma in 1944 with amphibious forces which could, the British thought, be far more usefully employed for Overlord. Determined not to risk disaster by landing in France with insufficient forces, they proposed that, if the American Chiefs of Staff were unwilling to provide the additional landing craft which they believed to be essential, then the venture should be postponed until subsidiary attacks had so weakened the Germans as to give a reasonable prospect of success. The Prime Minister, who thought little of Anvil, had in mind landings in northern Italy, increased help for Marshal Tito's partisans in Yugoslavia, and possibly operations farther east in partnership with the Turks if they could be persuaded to enter the war on the Allied side. The American service chiefs had no faith in these proposals. The President, on the other hand, was inclined to accept the argument that further offensives in the Mediterranean were needed before Overlord could be begun, but agreed with Churchill that a decision should be postponed until after a conference with Stalin which the Western Allies had arranged to hold at Teheran later in the month.

According to Robert E. Sherwood, a member of the President's personal staff, the United States Chiefs of Staff went to Teheran prepared for battles "in which the Americans and the Russians would form a united front." The President himself arrived full of confidence in his ability to handle the Soviet leaders and in their good intentions. At a preliminary meeting with Stalin before the conference he made it clear that he and Churchill did not see eye to eye on all matters and that he did not mean to be unduly influenced by British views.

The hint was not lost on Stalin, a shrewd judge of character and presumably well briefed in the light of Molotov's exchanges with the President in 1942. He proposed that Roosevelt should take the chair at all sessions of the conference, warned him of a supposed German plot to assassinate him, and invited him to move from the American Legation to his own quarters at the Soviet Embassy while he himself moved to a small cottage in the grounds. Notwithstanding these attentions and his own determination to establish cordial relations, the President at first found difficulty in breaking down Stalin's reserve. Eventually he did so by teasing Churchill at the conference table "about his Britishness, about John Bull, about his cigars, about his habits." As farfetched an examplar of British phlegm as the Georgian Stalin was of Russian waywardness and charm, the embullient, impulsive, half-American and wholly articulate Prime Minister was at any rate British enough to feel embarrassed and grow red, although he had been warned by Roosevelt to prepare himself for the experience. Stalin, according to the account afterward given by the President to his Secretary of Labor, "broke out into a deep, hearty guffaw," the President called him Uncle Joe, and the ice was broken.

In his more serious moments Stalin pressed for Overlord, supported the American case for Anvil, and opposed the British case for diversionary operations in southeast Europe. He also made a profound impression on the Americans by promising that, if the Western Allies agreed to strike resolutely at Germany through France, Russia would throw her weight against Japan as soon as possible after Hitler was defeated.

The effects of Stalin's diplomacy at Teheran were thus to give Russia virtually a free hand in the Balkans, and at the same time ensure that the main effort of the Western Allies in the European theater was devoted to a venture which, even if it failed, promised to keep substantial German forces far from Russian spheres of interest at least until its failure was manifest. Rooscvelt's advocacy of Anvil, in preference to British plans for a diversion farther east, was bound to seem to the Russians like an invitation to gobble up southeastern Europe. To make the picture still gloomier for the British, the U. S. Chiefs of Staff agreed to postpone their projected invasion of Burma only after the Prime Minister had made a personal appeal to the President. From the resources thus released, they agreed to allot to Overlord enough landing craft to enable the strength of the initial assault to be increased by one division.

17

THE ROAD TO BERLIN

AT THE CASABLANCA CONFERENCE, IN JANUARY 1943, THE COMBINED Chiefs of Staff defined the objects of Anglo-American air attacks on Germany as "the progressive destruction and dislocation of the German military, industrial and economic system, and the undermining of the morale of the German people to a point where their capacity for armed resistance is fatally weakened." During the next fifteen months Allied heavy bombers dropped an immense weight of bombs on Germany in pursuance of these aims.

Many attempts were made by both Allies and Germans to assess the military value of these attacks. Spectacular damage was done to buildings and plants, but the Germans had a big reserve of domestic and imported labor and showed great skill and ingenuity in stopping gaps and improvising new production programs. The German Ministry of Armaments and War Production reported that loss of output in 1943 was "held within tolerable limits." In February 1944 the Allies went all-out to smash German fighter factories, but in April the aircraft industry produced more fighters than in any previous month since the beginning of the war. Germany was severely hampered during the last year of the war by lack of oil, but the shortage had wider causes than bombing.

If there was doubt as to whether the Allies achieved their first aim, there was none where the second was concerned. In spite of incredible hardships, the German people were not so cowed by bombing that they became incapable of fighting or encouraging their troops to fight. Even after ruthless attacks in the closing months of the war had reduced some Westphalian towns to heaps of rubble where only a few damaged houses were left standing, elderly survivors had enough spirit left to brush the pulverized mortar from their doorsteps and shake their fists at the invaders.

In face of keen opposition from the commanders of the British and American heavy bomber forces, who argued that no respite ought to be given to Germany until the Allies were about to go ashore in France, a great part of the Anglo-American effort was devoted in the spring of 1944 to targets suggested by the Overlord planners. At the same time the build-up of British and American fighter and tactical bomber forces, as well as the striking power of their heavy bombers, gave the Allies advantages without which Overlord would not have been a practical operation of war. "The operation in its present form and with our present strength," said General Eisenhower before the assault, "is possible only because of our very great air superiority."

Toward the end of 1943 General Eisenhower was appointed Supreme Allied Commander for Overlord, and General Montgomery to command the British land forces and exercise operational control over all land forces during the assault phase. More than six months had elapsed since the Combined Chiefs of Staff decided in Washington that the target date for the invasion should be May 1, 1944, and more than three months since they considered, at Quebec, the plan submitted to them by the Chiefs of Staff to the Supreme Allied Commander (Cossac). Five months before the target date, the plan was at last formally presented to the man who would have to take the responsibility of rejecting it or putting it into practice.

Eisenhower had been shown, unofficially, a copy of the Cossac plan in October, when he did not know that he was to be Supreme Commander, and had remarked that the weight of the assault and the breadth of the front proposed were both inadequate. On receiving his official copy, on January 1, 1944, he repeated his criticism, with which Montgomery agreed. But the fault did not lie with the Cossac planners. The Combined Chiefs of Staff had meant to allot to Overlord enough landing craft for a five-division front. Through an almost incredible oversight, they had not only allowed themselves to be led astray by a miscalculation which caused them to allot only enough for a three-division front, but had failed to put matters right when the inadequacy of the Cossac plan in the form thus imposed on it attracted comment from Churchill and others at Quebec.

The outlook when Eisenhower took up his command was thus unpromising in the extreme. The Combined Chiefs of Staff had just reaffirmed an earlier decision that two-thirds of the landing craft for Overlord, as well as all the warships needed for bombardment, escort, and cover, should be found from British, British Dominion, and European Allied sources, leaving only one-third of the landing craft to be found by the United States Navy. When the mistake was discovered the United States Joint Chiefs of Staff had nominally at their disposal enough landing craft to meet the deficiency many times over; in practice, the allocation of these craft was in the hands of the United States Chief of Naval Operations, Admiral King.

Admiral King was credited with the remark that he had had enough of British tutelage when part of the Atlantic Fleet, in which he was then serving, was put at the disposal of the Royal Navy during the First World War, and was determined that no part of his resources should be placed under a British commander if he could help it. Even if that was a true expression of his sentiments it would, however, be wrong to suppose that his attitude to Overlord was founded on nothing more than prejudice. A keen advocate of an Anglo-American landing in Europe in 1942, he had been deeply disappointed by the lukewarmness of the British, which he attributed to their reluctance to take a calculated risk rather than their sincere conviction that a premature invasion stood no chance of success. When even a landing in 1943 was ruled out, again he was perhaps more inclined to blame British caution than to recognize that the decisive factor was the slowness of the Allied advance in Northwest Africa. If his conviction that the operation must be carried out remained in the early part of 1944 as strong as ever, that did not necessarily prevent him from feeling that nothing would ever be done unless the

British were forced by a display of American toughness to pull their weight. At the same time, his own interests had come to be increasingly focused on the Pacific theater, which was pre-eminently an American concern. To most of the United States Navy, if not to King himself, the Far Eastern war was the real war and Overlord a sideshow.

In consequence of what were at any rate thought by British and American officers in London to be the admiral's views, the Overlord staff concluded that they stood little chance of receiving enough landing craft from his resources within the next few months to allow of an assault on a five-division front in early May. Admiral Sir Bertram Ramsay, Commander-in-Chief of the Allied Naval Forces, was not sure that even the Cossac requirements would be met. Yet Overlord was the operation for which the American Chiefs of Staff, Admiral King included, had been pressing since 1942, and of which the Combined Chiefs of Staff had declared, on the day of Eisenhower's appointment, that "nothing undertaken in any part of the world" must jeopardize its success or that of its sister operation Anvil!

In this desperate predicament Eisenhower decided, with reluctance, to forego the benefits of a long campaigning season and postpone the landings until June in order to give himself a chance of collecting more material. His decision was certainly right, but the consequences of the delay were serious. Had the Allies gone ashore at the beginning of May, a month of fine weather would have stretched ahead of them. In June, rough seas delayed unloading to an extent which threatened to put the whole enterprise in jeopardy. The effect on the minds of commanders and staff officers did not improve Allied chances of winning the war with Germany before the Russians overran Poland and were in Berlin.

The immediate effects of the postponement, however, were favorable. There was more time to train and assemble crews for airborne landings. The size of the airborne assault was increased from two brigades to three divisions, two of them American. By taking advantage of another months' output, persuading the U. S. Chiefs of Staff to agree that Anvil must be put off until July, and squeezing everything he could from the Mediterranean, Eisenhower was able to lay his hands on 6047 landing craft, as compared with the 3323 allotted by the Combined Chiefs of Staff, and thereby double the weight of the seaborne assault and the breadth of front. With seven weeks to go to the postponed target date, he succeeded in extracting from Admiral King a task force of three battleships, three cruisers, and forty destroyers. Four battleships, twenty-one cruisers, two monitors, and a hundred and sixteen destroyers were provided by the Royal Navy and the Royal Canadian Navy, three cruisers and eight destroyers by various Allied navies. Of more than five hundred frigates, corvettes, and miscellaneous light naval craft which completed the bombardment, escort, and covering forces, the Royal Navy and the Royal Canadian Navy found three-quarters and the United States the remaining quarter.

But naval and air superiority alone were not enough to ensure success. The Germans had sixty divisions in France and the Low Countries, eleven of them armored. A resolute attempt to smash the Anglo-American forces before they could establish themselves on shore was expected of Rommel, who had been appointed to command the German troops in the crucial area under the Commander-in-Chief in the West, General von Rundstedt. Should Rommel fail to halt the Allies on the beaches, the build-up would still be hazardous. Even with almost overwhelming naval and air strength at his disposal, and in spite of elaborate measures devised by the British General Hobart to give the assault troops support from submersible tanks and other special vehicles as they were landing, Eisenhower could not count on succeeding without a stratagem.

The essence of the Overlord strategy was that the enemy must be made to think before D-day that the Allies meant to land in the Pas de Calais, and after D-day that the landings in Normandy were a diversion and that the main assault would still come in that quarter. A far-reaching deception plan, which included heavy bombing of objectives between Le Havre and Dunkirk, the concentration in Kent of divisions not needed for the initial assault or immediate follow-up, and the sowing of a fertile crop of false reports, was worked out by Eisenhower's Anglo-American staff and put into effect. The supremacy won by the British air defenses made it possible to ensure that few German reconnaissance aircraft photographed anything which it was not good for the German High Command to know about. Even so, enough was seen by May to make Hitler suspect that the Allies might land in western Normandy. Believing that the Führer had allowed the Allies to pull wool over his eyes, Rundstedt remained convinced that the blow would fall in the Pas de Calais, while Rommel expected a diversion west of the Seine but not that the main assault would be delivered there.

The Overlord strategy was designed to give the Allies an all-American bridgehead on the Cotentin peninsula, and an Anglo-American bridgehead between the Orne and the Vire. As soon as possible the two would fuse to form one bridgehead. Montgomery's tactical plan was framed accordingly, and was based on two assumptions. The first, which rested on the known disposition of the German armor, was that Rommel would counterattack strongly from the east and southeast if he failed to throw the Allies back into the sea in the first two days. The second, implicit in Eisenhower's logistic plan, was that the early capture of Cherbourg was essential to the American build-up. Montgomery planned, therefore, to use the British Second Army, on the left of the bridgehead, to protect the left flank of the United States First Army, on the right, and thus enable the Americans to take Cherbourg and afterward push southward with the object of enlarging the bridgehead to form a substantial lodgment area from which the Allies could advance. His intention was that the Second Army should seize Caen and the open ground immediately beyond it, and there engage Rommel's armor.

After anxious consultations with his weather experts, the Supreme Commander chose June 6 as the crucial day. Airborne troops landed in darkness on both flanks of the assault area, and soon after dawn the seaborne troops began to go ashore on two American and three British beach-heads. By nightfall the Allies held four bridgeheads separated not only by the expected gap between the American troops on the Cotentin peninsula and those on their left, but also by a gap of seven miles between the American and British armies and one of three miles between the British 3rd Division, at the mouth of the Orne, and the Canadian 3rd Division on its right. The situation at midnight was that no final D-day objectives had been reached at any point on the American or British fronts, and that unloading was from eight to twelve hours behind schedule, mainly because of rough weather. Meanwhile German armor had counterattacked from the direction of Caen, and the British advance had been held up by congestion on the beaches and consequent delay in the arrival of follow-up formations.

All these factors, and especially the fear that, because of delays in unloading, the build-up might be prejudiced if troops which were able to advance pushed on too fast, played their part in impeding progress on the second day. By nightfall on June 7 the Second Army was well established in a continuous bridgehead twenty-two miles wide and from five to ten miles deep, had entered Bayeux, held a long stretch of the Caen-Bayeux road, and had made contact with the First Army in the main American bridgehead. But Caen and the open ground beyond it were still untaken. The Germans were thus able to set up a defensive screen in the difficult *bocage* country west and southwest of Caen.

Within a few days Montgomery saw that, even if the battle of maneuver in which he had hoped to grapple with Rommel's armor had eluded him, he could still carry out his intention of protecting the First Army's left as long as he was able to keep Rommel busy on the Second Army's front. "My general policy," he told Sir Alan Brooke, the Chief of the Imperial General Staff, on June 11, "is to pull the enemy on to Second Army so as to make it easier for First Army to expand and extend the quicker."

In point of fact, the Germans were already fighting a losing battle, in which the odds were heavily weighted against them by Allied air superiority, Hitler's tactical interventions, and their conviction that the main thrust had still to come and that it would therefore be madness for them to weaken their grip on the Pas de Calais and the Somme. Rommel's chance of scoring a decisive success had gone when, with his armor halted for half a day by a standstill order from the Führer, he failed to drive the Allies into the sea while they were still groping to consolidate their bridge-heads. On June 12, Keitel and Jodl, of the Supreme Head-quarters Staff, agreed with Admiral Doenitz that "all France was lost" if the Allies succeeded in breaking out. At a conference with the Führer five days later, Rommel and Rundstedt hinted at peace overtures, but Hitler refused to listen.

The Führer's solution was to open an attack on London with flying bombs in the hope that Eisenhower, under pressure from the British government, might fling his supposed reserve of un-committed assault divisions against the powerful defenses of the Pas de Calais with the object of capturing the launching sites. Since 1943 air power had enabled the Allies to hamper German preparations to bombard Britain with long-range weapons, but the Germans were not prevented from building inconspicuous sites from which a stream of missiles was despatched in the next few months. From September Hitler was also able to mount a minor offensive with long-range rockets. Antiaircraft guns and defensive fighters soon defeated the flying bomb, but no answer was found to the long-range rocket in the absence of a scale of attack which would have justified the Allies in diverting a big share of their bomber effort to countermeasures. British airmen believed, how-ever, that the Germans could not substantially have increased their rate of fire without accumulating stocks which would have been vulnerable to bombing, even if stored in caves and tunnels.

By the middle of June, General Omar N. Bradley, commanding the First Army, had united the two American bridgeheads and was tightening his grip on the Cotentin. On June 19 his troops began their thrust to Cherbourg. Pounded by the American ham-mer on the anvil of Hitler's refusal to sanction tactical withdraw-als, the German forces in the peninsula collapsed after a week of dogged fighting. Organized resistance in Cherbourg ceased on June 26, to the profound dismay of the Supreme Command. "What shall we do?" asked Keitel despairingly on July 1. "Make peace, you fools!" was Rundstedt's answer.

From Cherbourg to the Seine the way was clearly charted by Hitler's refusal either to make peace or to make war according to the rules. When the city fell Montgomery directed that General

Sir Hugh Dempsey, commanding the Second Army, should continue to hold on to the enemy on the eastern flank while General Bradley, pivoting on his own left, came forward to a line from the base of the Cotentin to the Normandy Hills before swinging westward into Brittany and southeastward toward the Sarthe. The Second Army's role grew daily more difficult, more expensive, and more misunderstood as the enemy became increasingly aware that an American breakout was imminent. Dempsey's gains in ground won and objectives taken seemed inconsiderable and disappointing. The true measure of his achievement was that, on the eve of the American advance, his fourteen divisions were holding down a like number of German divisions, with six hundred tanks, and that only nine divisions, with about a hundred tanks, were left to oppose the nineteen divisions of the American First and Third Armies.

Advancing with great skill on a narrow front on July 25 after an abortive start earlier in the month, Bradley made such rapid progress that a week later Rundstedt's successor, Field Marshal Gunther von Kluge, reported that his left flank had collapsed and that "the whole western front" had been ripped open. By the middle of August the Allies held practically the whole area west of the Orne and north of the Loire, with the exception of a pocket between Falaise and Argentan in which a hundred thousand German troops were threatened with encirclement. About two-fifths escaped before, and even after, the closing of the pocket on August 19, but the loss of up to five hundred tanks and enormous quantities of artillery and transport was a major disaster for the Germans.

On August 1, General Bradley assumed command of the newly formed 12th Army Group, consisting of the American First Army (General Courtney H. Hodges) and the American Third Army (General George S. Patton, Jr.). In the British sector the Second Army (General Sir Hugh Dempsey) and the First Canadian Army (General Henry Crerar) made up the 21st Army Group under General Montgomery, who continued until the end of the month to direct the operations of both Army Groups.

Meanwhile dissension between Hitler and his service chiefs had reached a climax with his attempted assassination on July 20. As if determined to make their task as difficult as possible, the Allies responded to the news by announcing that Hitler's removal would not cause them to abate their demand for unconditional surrender. In the middle of August Hitler dismissed von Kluge on suspicion of wishing to treat with the Allies, and replaced him by Field Marshal Walther von Model.

By that time the German armies in northern France were already crumbling. On August 20 the American Third Army established a bridgehead across the Seine at Mantes. On August 25 and 26 American and Free French troops entered Paris at the invitation of French leaders who had organized an insurrection in the city on the night of August 19. On August 29 the last of Model's forces withdrew across the river after losing much of the scanty equipment which they had succeeded in extricating from the Falaise pocket. Since D-day the German armies on Eisenhower's front had suffered half a million casualties and had lost up to nine-tenths of their heavy artillery and armor, in addition to vast quantities of transport and substantial stocks of much-needed fuel.

Meanwhile Anvil had been put into effect after a further postponement, and the American Seventh Army (General Alexander M. Patch) was ashore in the South of France. Not convinced by reports that the German Army in the West was breaking up, the Supreme Commander intended to continue his advance on a broad front, link up with the Seventh Army, and attempt no deep penetration into Germany until he could deploy at least sixty divisions and maintain them in the field. "We wanted," he wrote later, "to bring all our strength against the enemy, all of it mobile and all of it contributing directly to the complete annihilation of his field forces."

To Montgomery this policy seemed likely to lead to nothing but stagnation. In the middle of August he had suggested to Bradley that, after crossing the Seine, the 12th and 21st Army Groups should be kept together as "a solid mass of forty divisions" and should push northeastward with their right flank on the Ardennes. A week later he urged Eisenhower not to split his forces by sending part of them north of the Ardennes into Belgium and Holland and the other half south of the Ardennes toward Alsace and the Saar, but to concentrate on one decisive thrust. Either, he said, Eisenhower should halt his right and strike with his left, or he should halt his left and strike with his right. He also proposed that he himself should continue to direct the operations of both Army Groups after they crossed the Seine, or alternatively that Bradley should do so if a British coordinator was not acceptable.

Anxious to secure the Channel ports and Antwerp, Eisenhower agreed that two of the First Army's three corps should support the British advance into Belgium, but made it clear that he still meant to move on a broad front as soon as Antwerp was in his hands. He added that he intended to take direct control of the land battle at the beginning of September.

In effect this meant that henceforward there would be no tactical coordination of the land battle. With the incorporation of the Seventh Army into the Allied Expeditionary Force and the consequent addition of a third Army Group, there would be, as Eisenhower himself admitted, three Commanders-in-Chief, each responsible for his own front. A successful and indispensable Supreme Commander, Eisenhower was in no position to exercise direct control in the field, even if his lack of experience as a field commander had been no handicap. On the day after D-day, Montgomery had set up his Tactical Headquarters in Normandy, less than ten miles from the front. Eisenhower's headquarters at the beginning of September were at Granville, two hundred miles from Paris and four hundred miles from the German frontier. He had no means of receiving prompt information from forward areas, and could communicate with his Army Group commanders only by letter or wireless telegraphy. On a day when his decision on a matter of urgent operational importance was awaited at Montgomery's headquarters, he was in bed at Granville with a leg in plaster, and the garbled text of his reply took thirty-six hours to reach its destination from the time of its despatch.

Montgomery began his advance across the Seine on August 29. On August 31 his troops reached Amiens. On September 2 they crossed the Belgian frontier. Next day they were in Brussels. On September 4 they entered Antwerp, two hundred and fifty miles by road from their base in Calvados. Often reproached as over-cautious, Montgomery had proved that no commander could act more swiftly to exploit an opportunity.

The British were now barely ninety miles from the Ruhr, still the source of half Germany's hard coal and half her steel. Before them lay a fifty-mile gap in the German front, plugged only by the equivalent of two or three weak divisions at the most. As Montgomery had already pointed out, his case for a swift advance at the decisive point was reinforced by powerful logistic arguments. The communications of all Eisenhower's armies were now so stretched that the factor governing further progress was the rate at which supplies of fuel could reach them. The flow was insufficient to support a simultaneous advance on a broad front, but not insufficient to support a powerful offensive on the left if other considerations were subordinated to it. The troops on that flank had the most valuable objectives in front of them, their communications were less extended than those of Patton's Third Army in Lorraine, and they could be supported by aircraft based in England.

From his headquarters in Belgium, Montgomery pleaded with Eisenhower to give priority to a "powerful and full-blooded" thrust toward Berlin by the First and Second Armies at the cost of halting Patton. Eisenhower agreed, in theory, that the left should have priority. In practice, his allocation of fuel to the First Army was too grudging to enable Hodges to give Montgomery the full support he asked, nor did he restrain Bradley from counseling and encouraging Hodges to consume a generous share of his resources in supporting Patton.

With his cherished plan thus frustrated, Montgomery decided, with Eisenhower's approval, to stake his remaining hopes on an attempt by the Allied Airborne Army to seize the crossings of the Dutch rivers and canals and thus open a way for his armor to cut through Holland at one bound and establish a bridgehead beyond the Rhine on the western fringe of the North German Plain. But the operation could not be launched until September 17, and by that time the worst gaps in the German defenses had been filled by new formations hurriedly improvised from Luftwaffe paratroops and ground crews. With a caution which its commander afterward regretted, the British 1st Airborne Division was put down too far from its objective at Arnhem in the interests of an accurate landing and a safe drop. Although taken by surprise, the Germans were lucky enough to have an armored division close at hand, and bad weather on the second day delayed the arrival of British and American reinforcements.

With the failure of this imaginative but ill-starred plan, the Allies lost their last chance of ending the war before the winter. In consequence, their prospects of entering Berlin before the Russians were reduced. Worse still, the enemy was presented with an opportunity of staging a comeback which further delayed the Allied advance by many weeks. In the middle of December the Germans launched an offensive in the Ardennes which they hoped would take them to Antwerp almost at one bound, and which did punch a dent some forty miles deep and up to forty miles wide in an extraordinarily weak part of Eisenhower's line between Elsenborn and Diekirch. Taken by surprise and with practically nothing in reserve, the Supreme Commander took the bold step of bringing Montgomery back to coordinate Allied operations in the threatened area while the crisis lasted. Thus the tried and proven principle of a single commander on the ground was restored for a time and to a limited extent when the Allies were in trouble, but only to be dropped again as soon as the mercury in the Supreme Headquarters barometer surged back to its old level of blissful optimism.

18

ANVIL TO NAGASAKI

WHEN THE ALLIED ARMIES OF LIBERATION LANDED IN NORMANDY ON June 6, 1944, the United States Fifth Army and the British Eighth Army had entered Rome, and were standing on a line across the breadth of Italy from the Tiber to the Sangro after fighting their way northward from Salerno in face of bitter opposition. Just over a week later, on the day when American troops in the Cotentin began to drive westward across the peninsula with the object of isolating Cherbourg, the Combined Chiefs of Staff ordered the Allied Supreme Commander in the Mediterranean Theater, General Sir Henry Maitland Wilson, to continue his offensive to the Pisa-Rimini line and prepare for a subsequent landing in the South of France, on the French Atlantic coast, or at the head of the Adriatic.

Of these three courses, the last seemed to General Wilson the most promising. At a conference on June 17 with General Marshall, Chief of Staff of the United States Army, and General Arnold, Chief of Staff of the United States Army Air Corps, he proposed that General Alexander, commanding the Allied forces in Italy, should support a landing in Istria by continuing his offensive beyond the Pisa-Rimini line into the Po Valley. The Allies would then strike through the Ljubljana gap into the Hungarian Plain with the object of threatening the Danube Basin, thus forcing Hitler to divert troops from the West by presenting him with a challenge which no German government could ignore. Wilson's views were wholeheartedly endorsed by Allied commanders in Italy and notably by General Mark Clark, commanding the United States Fifth Army. Meeting Marshall while he was in Rome, Clark argued strongly in favor of an advance in the direction pointed out by Wilson.

Unanimity among the men on the spot was not, however, matched by a corresponding harmony at a higher level. The U. S. Chiefs of Staff were bent on the landing in the South of France (Operation Anvil) which they had always advocated. They were willing to consider, although not necessarily to endorse, an alternative plan for a landing in Western France, which was finally scotched when Eisenhower insisted that the capture of Marseille was essential to his logistic plan and that Brest was not an acceptable substitute. But they did not look kindly on a thrust into southeast Europe which threatened, according to Marshall, to leave Alexander "beating the air."

American opposition was equally firm on the political plane. The President was not willing that American lives should be risked to further "real or fancied British interests in the Balkans," and he did not agree that British interests were also American and European interests. By 1944, and indeed by 1943, Americans of the highest standing in governmental and official circles were reconciled to the prospect that Russia would "dominate Europe" at the end of the war with Germany. Anxious to secure Russian help against Japan when the war was over, Roosevelt was determined to take the hint which Stalin had given him at Teheran and stay out of southeast Europe. He was the readier to do so since he believed that he and Stalin understood each other and that Americans and Russians had much in common. "We find the Russians as individuals," his intimate adviser Harry Hopkins wrote in 1945, "easy to deal with . . . They are a tenacious, determined people who think and act just like you and I do."[1]

The British shared neither Marshall's opinion of the strategic outlook nor the President's equanimity in face of the danger of Russian ascendancy in Europe. Since the mere threat of a landing in the South of France was already pinning down ten German

[1] Robert E. Sherwood, *Roosevelt and Hopkins: an Intimate History* (New York, 1948)

divisions there, they did not believe that an actual landing, accompanied by a drastic weakening of Allied forces in Italy, would do much to persuade Hitler to shift troops from Eisenhower's front in Normandy. As for the political aspect, Churchill and his colleagues faced the knowledge that the President, although no isolationist, looked forward to the withdrawal of the United States Army from Europe within two years of the end of the war with Germany. Hence it seemed likely that the burden of reconstructing Europe and enforcing respect for international law would fall largely on themselves or their successors. They were quite willing that Russia should have a voice in the future of the Balkans, but their task would become immensely difficult if the whole of the Danube Basin, to say nothing of Poland, were allowed to become a Russian sphere of influence. President Roosevelt might believe that Stalin had no territorial ambitions which sympathetic treatment would not lead him to renounce, and General Eisenhower that the Russians were "free from the stigma of colonial empire-building by force." The British Foreign Office, less sanguine than the President and better versed in Russian history than the general, could hardly be expected to share such views. They saw no reason to suppose that the Soviet leaders were any less eager to extend their power than the ferociously acquisitive Romanoffs whose mantle they had inherited, and whose last and least disreputable representative they had murdered just twenty-six years before the President courted Stalin's friendship and called him Uncle Joe.

But the British Chiefs of Staff proved no match for their American colleagues. Fifteen days after the American Joint Chiefs had agreed with their British counterparts that the ultimate choice between Anvil and a landing elsewhere should await "the general development of the strategic situation," Marshall persuaded Roosevelt to intervene decisively in favor of Anvil by informing Churchill that he would regard any alternative as a breach of the Teheran agreement. After a final attempt by the British to find an agreed solution, the United States Seventh Army, with seven divisions reluctantly surrendered by General Clark, and supported by the French First Army, went ashore on the Côte d'Azur. Electing to fight a delaying action in the Rhone Valley, Hitler promptly withdrew all but his garrison troops from the neighborhood and transferred two armored divisions from Italy to Eisenhower's front and one to Poland.

Thus the effect of Anvil on the disposition of the German Army was the opposite of that intended by Marshall and his friends. Instead of compelling Hitler to disperse his forces, it allowed him to concentrate still more of his strength on the Western and Eastern fronts at the expense of a theater in which he no longer feared surprise or the profitable exploitation by the Allies of the favorable situation they had won.

But the long-term consequences of the failure of the Allies to follow up their success in Italy were far more serious. Five days after the landings in the South of France, the Russians launched an offensive between the Transylvanian Alps and the Black Sea which carried them almost at one bound to the Ploesti oilfields and Bucharest. By prearrangement with the Allies, and on the strength of an assurance from the Russians that they had no intention of "altering the social structure" of Rumania or claiming any Rumanian territory except Bessarabia, King Michael arrested the pro-German Marshal Ion Antonescu and accepted an armistice. By the beginning of September Russian troops were on the Bulgarian frontier; by the middle of the month they were in Sofia. At the end of the third week in October they entered Belgrade. With the Danubian states within their grasp, the Soviet leaders enjoyed the comfortable knowledge that the Western Allies had no troops in the Balkans except Tito's partisans and a small British force in Greece, and no means of holding Russia to her promises even if they had an undivided will to do so.

There was thus an ominous parallel between the situation which faced the British in 1944 and that which had faced them and their European Allies in 1918. On both occasions developments at the heart of Europe threatened to defeat their ends at the very moment when they seemed about to attain them after years of painful striving. On both occasions those developments were accelerated by policies which their statesmen knew to be perilous but in which they were more or less bound to acquiesce. The

British no more intended, when they went to war in 1939, to give their lives and consume their substance in order to make half-Asiatic Russia supreme in Europe, than they intended in 1914 to unsettle the Continental balance of power by destroying Austro-Hungary. Yet that, it seemed, was the direction in which they were being led as surely as Europe had been led to cripple herself in the first round of the struggle.

In the West, the failure of the Allies to seize their opportunity at the beginning of September had allowed the initiative to pass temporarily to the Germans. By Christmas the recovery which enabled Hitler to stage his drive through the Ardennes put the Germans almost on the Meuse at Dinant. In the end it was the Nazi leaders who were astonished by the toughness and resilience of American armies which they had thought deficient in staying power, but the early weeks of 1945 found the Allies no nearer to the heart of Germany than in the autumn. Meanwhile the Russians, after suffering a check which led Stalin to suggest in October that, after all, a drive by the Western Allies into Austria might not be unacceptable, faced diminishing resistance from German armies weakened by withdrawals to the Western Front. Soon they were sweeping onward through Poland and into Germany. By early February the Soviet Army was less than fifty miles from Berlin, only eighty miles from Vienna, and in the suburbs of Budapest.

Against this background of Russian triumphs and Anglo-American setbacks the statesmen of the three great powers met, on Russian soil and on a date fixed by Stalin, to discuss at Yalta the postwar reconstruction of Europe and the division of the spoils. Meeting the Americans for preliminary conversations, the British found that Roosevelt's confidence in Russian good faith was unshaken, and that American distrust of British colonialism was as strong as ever. To purge Europe of fascism and to "free people all over the world from a backward colonial policy" stood high among the President's war aims. The liquidation of the British Empire was the return for Lend-Lease aid which he intended to claim under the clause in the Atlantic Charter which bound Britain to assist in restoring sovereign rights and self-government to peoples who had been forcibly deprived of them.

In making this claim, the President was not conscious of following a policy which the British would regard as hostile. It seemed to him that "Empire ideas" must appear to twentieth-century Englishmen as "archaic" and as "medieval" as they appeared to him. Hence it was no more possible for Englishmen to convince him that they did not regard their colonial policy as backward than it was for them to tell him to his face that the British Empire had nothing at all to do with the Middle Ages. Nor did it make any difference that Britain had already granted self-government to Canada, Australia, New Zealand, and South Africa, and that their only reason for not yet extending the full benefits of Dominion status to India was that they knew that no power on earth except the British Raj was capable of keeping Hindus and Moslems from each others throats. With one part of his mind, the President accepted all this as just and true. With another part, he continued to think of the modestly paid civil servants who ruled Britain's Far Eastern Empire as bloated despots engaged in taking the wealth out of their domains and giving nothing in return. In precisely the same fashion, he was capable at one and the same time of knowing that Stalin had far-reaching designs on Europe, yet believing that he would not give effect to them as long as the United States government took pains to keep on the right side of him.

In the light of their experience at the end of the First World War and after it, by the time they reached Yalta the British were not inclined to see Germany so impoverished by the coming peace settlements that the Western powers would have to bolster her economy indefinitely in order to save the whole European system from collapse. They had thought better of their earlier endorsement of the Morgenthau Plan, in which United States Secretary of the Treasury Henry J. Morgenthau, Jr. had proposed that the Ruhr should be stripped of its industrial equipment and that Germany should be transformed into a predominantly agricultural and pastoral country. In view of their guarantee to the Poles before the war, they were also bound to ensure, so far as it was in their power, that Polish sovereignty and independence were restored.

Russian aims were very different. Stalin proposed at Yalta that Germany should be partitioned into a number of separate states, that she should be deprived of four-fifths of her heavy industry, and that she should pay reparations in kind to the value of twenty billion dollars, of which half would go to Russia. In regard to Poland, he asked that her eastern frontier should be pushed back to the so-called Curzon line which the Allies had suggested in 1919, and that she should be compensated at Germany's expense by the redrawing of her western frontier along the line of the Oder from the sea to the junction of that river with the Neisse, and thence along the Neisse to the Czechoslovak frontier. Above all, he was determined that the Western Allies should turn their backs on the exiled Polish government in London, and should recognize as the provisional government of Poland the "National Committee of Liberation" which had been set up under Communist auspices at Lublin.

Roosevelt was said to be not unsympathetic to British views on these questions, but his attitude was strikingly similar in some respects to that of Woodrow Wilson. Like Wilson, he was emphatically, almost ostentatiously, non-European. Wilson had wished to see Germany defeated and the Kaiser overthrown. Roosevelt wished to see Germany defeated and Hitler overthrown. Beyond that he hardly went. He showed little of the concern for Germany's future, and by implication Europe's future, which was shown by Lloyd George in 1919 and by Churchill in 1945. Like the British, he had repented of his flirtation with the Morgenthau Plan, especially as well-documented references to the plan had appeared in the American press with embarrassing consequences. But he did not unequivocally reject Stalin's proposals for the partition of Germany, and was willing that Stalin's figure for reparation should serve as a basis for discussion.

Again, Woodrow Wilson attached immense importance to the adherence of the great powers to the League of Nations, which he hoped would replace the old system of alliances as a better means of preserving peace. Rather than that the Japanese should drop out, he was willing to give them Shantung at the expense of China. Roosevelt attached equal importance to the adherence of the great powers to the United Nations, and for precisely the same reason. Rather than that the Russians should drop out, and also to clinch Stalin's promise of help against Japan, he was willing to give them much more than Shantung. In return for an undertaking to join the United Nations on agreed terms and a few minor concessions, Stalin received at Yalta almost everything he asked in Poland, and soon took the rest. As the price of his promise to enter the war against Japan within three months of Germany's defeat, he received not only Port Arthur, Dairen, and everything else which Russia had lost to Japan in 1904, but also the Kurile Islands and a sphere of influence in Manchuria. To this bargain, struck at conversations between Roosevelt and Stalin from which the British were excluded, the Prime Minister felt bound to assent, although the Foreign Secretary, Anthony Eden, is said to have begged him not to do so.

These concessions to Stalin seemed to Roosevelt justified since he had been told that, without Russian help, the conquest of the Japanese homeland might cost the United States a million casualties. Yet it was still true that Russia had only a shadowy claim to the Kurile Islands, that the promise of a sphere of influence in Manchuria without the prior consent of the Chinese was just the kind of transaction which many Americans conceived themselves to be fighting to prevent, and, worst of all, that the general effect of the Yalta conversations was to strengthen Stalin's belief that he need fear no interference from the Western Allies in the countries he had conquered. The conference was barely over when the Soviet government forced King Michael of Rumania to install a Communist government by threatening to resume hostilities if he refused. Soon it was clear that Poland was to be no more than a Russian puppet state. And Yalta was not two months old when Stalin, as if to test his power, accused the British and American governments of seeking to make peace with Germany behind Russia's back.

Meanwhile the Allied armies in the West resumed their methodical advance toward the heart of Germany. Eisenhower had received no special instructions to race the Russians to Berlin, and the United States government were reluctant to tie his hands by agreeing that he should be given any, although they recognized that the case for a show of strength in face of Soviet intransigence was becoming stronger every day. On reaching the Elbe on April 21, he halted his center, informed the Russian High Command that he did not propose to advance further but would bring his left to Lübeck, and sent his right to smoke out the powerful remnants of the German Army which were wrongly thought to be preparing for a last stand in the largely mythical National Redoubt near Berchtesgaden. Next day Russian troops entered the northern suburbs of Berlin, and on May 2 they completed the capture of the city. When the war in Europe ended six days later, Bucharest, Sofia, Belgrade, Budapest, Warsaw, Berlin, Vienna, and even Prague had fallen within the Russian orbit. Of the great European capitals, only Paris, Rome, and Brussels were in Allied hands.

Thus the downfall of Nazi Germany found the armies of the Western Allies and the Soviet Colossus facing each other across the breadth of Europe, with only the slender barrier of their prior agreement to occupy specified zones of Germany to prevent a clash between them. Too late the Western Allies regretted the doubts, the hesitations, the divided councils, the petty national and personal jealousies which had restrained them from staking their fortunes on a bold thrust toward the heart of Germany in the autumn and thus gaining, if they succeeded, the immense accretion of bargaining power which would have resulted from their reaching Berlin while the Russians were still wondering whether the Soviet Army had the strength to cross the Vistula. In January the Russians had stood on a line from Memel to Lake Balaton, three hundred miles from Berlin, two hundred and eighty miles from Prague. By the time of the Yalta Conference in February the picture was very different. Yet, even in April, the Western Allies could have entered Berlin before the Russians if they had had the will to do so. As late as May they could easily have liberated Prague if Eisenhower had not been bound by a gratuitous promise not to advance in that direction without prior reference to the Soviet High Command.

As it was, they soon saw that all the efforts they had made since 1939 to save Europe for the civilized world had resulted only in replacing the threat of Nazi domination by the threat of Communist domination. At the cost of immense sacrifices, the tide of dictatorship had been pushed back about two hundred miles.

But Harry S. Truman, unexpectedly becoming, with Joseph Stalin, one of the two most powerful men in the world on the sudden death of President Roosevelt in April 1945, inherited more than the unsolved problems of relations with Russia. He also inherited the atom bomb.

The atom bomb was not an American invention, although American resources and technical skill made its production possible. The calculations and researches which led to its development were largely the work of Central European mathematicians and physicists, many of whom emigrated to Britain or the United States before the war, either because they were persecuted or because they disapproved of persecution. In 1939 a number of them offered their services to the British government, others to the United States government. Since America was not at war, those living in the United States were not under the same moral obligation to impart their knowledge to the authorities as was felt by those in Britain. Some of them would have preferred that, if agreement had been possible, nuclear physicists throughout the world should bind themselves not to reveal their secrets to any government. They believed, however, that their colleagues in Germany were much nearer to success than in fact they were, and that it was essential to forestall Hitler by warning their peace-loving hosts that a weapon of unprecedented destructive power had become a practical possiblility. Albert Einstein, who helped to put refugee physicists in touch with the White House, said afterward that he would never have lifted a finger if he had known that the Germans would not succeed in making an atom bomb by the end of the war.

In 1942 the British and United States governments agreed that development of the atom bomb should be carried on as a joint project in Canada and the United States. A Military Policy Committee, consisting of three American service chiefs and two American scientists, was set up to direct the American share in the enterprise. Its leading spirit, Major General Leslie R. Groves, confessed in 1954 that he had always regarded cooperation with the British as a mistake and added, "I did my best to hold back on it."

At the end of the war in Europe many of the scientists concerned with the project concluded, with mingled relief and disappointment, that the weapon would never be used. But the atom bomb had passed out of the realm of pure science into that of high politics and strategy. In the spring of 1945 a team of experts drew up a short list of four Japanese cities on which it might be dropped with the object of shortening the Far Eastern war and saving many lives. Since the British were expected to play only a subordinate part in the Pacific theater, there seemed no reason to consult British service chiefs, although the British government would have to be consulted before the weapon was actually brought into play.

Truman knew nothing of the atom bomb when he became President. He had not been let into the secret, did not belong to the intimate circle of Roosevelt's advisers, and he had seen his predecessor only twice on official business during the past eleven weeks. A strong case for the use of the bomb against Japan was put before him by men who argued that it would cost far fewer casualties than invasion. This was countered by the argument that the Japanese were already about to surrender or, if they were not, could soon be brought to do so by orthodox bombing and without invasion.

Powerful arguments against the dropping of the bomb, at any rate before a specific warning was given to the Japanese government, were advanced, too, by some of the scientists working on the project. A committee comprising seven of the most eminent of these men, and headed by the Nobel Prize winner James Franck, pointed out that nations other than the United States were likely to possess the bomb within three or four years, and that the United States would be in a stronger position to press for international control if she did not use it. Their report was remitted to a panel of their fellow scientists who "didn't know beans about the military situation in Japan," and who could not agree as to whether the bomb should be used or not.

When that attempt failed Leo Szilard, one of the signatories of the Franck Report and a pioneer of nuclear fission whose association with the research project had gone far to convince President Roosevelt that it was worth backing, made an independent bid to persuade Roosevelt's successor not to use the weapon at the cost of provoking competition with Russia. Failing to reach the President, he was interviewed by James F. Byrnes, who had been specially detailed to handle such matters and was appointed Secretary of State a few weeks later. Byrnes made light of Szilard's fears, arguing that the Russians could not make the bomb without uranium and that, so far as he knew, there was no uranium in Russia. Yet a man charged with such responsibilities might have been expected to brief himself well enough before the interview to know that the only important source of uranium in Europe, at Joachimsthal in Czechoslovakia, had recently fallen into Russian hands. Had Byrnes gone a little deeper, he might even have concluded that American troops could have reached the area first if the government had had the forethought to warn General Eisenhower not to comply with Stalin's request that he should refrain from pushing his advance in that direction.[2]

Besides their reluctance to incur the heavy losses which invasion of the Japanese homeland might bring, the Western Allies had another reason, if not for using the bomb against Japan, at any rate for hoping that the war in the Far East might be cut

[2] The pitchblende deposits at Joachimsthal, a rich source of uranium, became famous in 1898 as a result of Professor and Madame Curie's discovery that they also contained radium. Other important sources known in 1945 included Katanga, in the Belgian Congo, and those in Canada on which the Western Allies were drawing. Ten years later the world's most fruitful sources of uranium, besides Joachimsthal and Katanga, were Port Radium and Beaver Lodge in Canada, Colorado Plateau in the United States, Witwatersrand in the Transvaal, Rum Jungle and Radium Hill in Australia, and (according to published accounts) a group of sites in Soviet territory between the Aral Sea and the Tien Shan. The chief sources of thorium, also a fissionable material, were in the United States, Brazil, South Africa, Southern India, Ceylon, Australia, Malaya, and Indonesia.

short. By the summer of 1945 experience of Soviet methods made Americans, as well as Englishmen, feel that Russian participation was a less attractive prospect than it had seemed to Roosevelt at Yalta. A trial bomb was successfully exploded at Los Alamos, New Mexico, on July 16. When the news reached Potsdam, where Truman and Churchill were holding their last wartime conference with Stalin, Churchill's immediate response was a sense of release from the nightmare prospect of a long-drawn agony in Asia. The Western Allies, he felt, had been presented with a wonderful opportunity of ending the war in the Pacific quickly, without appalling slaughter, and without the Russians.

Whether the President had it in mind to end the war by using the bomb before the Russians earned their promised loot by opening hostilities against the Japanese is another matter. He consulted Churchill before reaching a conclusion; but American technical skill and productive capacity had made such massive contributions to the manufacture of the weapon that the question of its use in a theater where American service chiefs were supreme was regarded as primarily one for the Americans, although the answer would vitally effect the standing of the Anglo-Saxon peoples as a whole in the eyes of all mankind. In accordance with Stalin's undertaking at Yalta to declare war on Japan within three months of Germany's defeat, the Russians would have to move on or before August 8 if they were to qualify for their reward. As an insurance against their entry the bomb would therefore be useless unless it were dropped before that date, although it could still be used later if a quick end to the war were needed to check a tendency to repeat in Asia the expansionist tactics which Stalin was exploiting with such success in Europe.

On July 18 the President decided at Potsdam that, in principle, his policy would be to use the bomb as soon as it was ready unless Japan yielded to an ultimatum. Thereupon he ordered that the wheels should be set in motion. On the same day Churchill advised him either to say nothing to the Russians or, "if he were resolved to tell," to make it clear to them that the first experimental bomb had been exploded only within the last few days. On July 22 Truman announced "casually" to Stalin, who seemed not to grasp the significance of the announcement, that the Western Allies had "a new weapon of unusual destructive force," and on that day or the next General Carl Spaatz, commanding the United States Strategic Air Force, was ordered to drop the first "special bomb" on either Hiroshima, Nagasaki, Kokura, or Niigata on August 3 or as soon afterward as the weather became suitable. According to the explanation given after the war, these orders were purely provisional and did not authorize Spaatz to use the bomb without confirmation from the President.

Meanwhile the men who would drop the bomb if it were used were making ready. As early as May the 509th Composite Group of the United States Army Air Corps, who had long been rehearsing the dropping of a "special secret weapon," began to leave their base in Utah for the island of Tinian in the Marianas. Early in June their commanding officer was promised a "working model" of the weapon "not later than August 6." But in the event a working model, in the form of a bomb shaped like the atom bomb but filled with high explosive, became available much earlier; it was the atom bomb itself which was ready by August 6, and was in fact dropped on that date. Meanwhile, too, the staff at Los Alamos had been ordered to go all out to prepare a trial bomb by the middle of July and one suitable for military use by August. Were these conjunctions fortuitous, or had the military authorities decided independently of the President by early June that, weather and Los Alamos permitting, they would forestall the Russians by dropping the bomb in the first week of August if they could work the oracle?[3]

By the morning of July 25 the chain reaction which would culminate in the dropping of the bomb had thus been started, but the holocaust could still be averted by a presidential veto. Next day the results of the general election held recently in

---

[3] General Groves testified in 1954 that he had felt almost from the start that Russia was the real enemy and believed from that time that "the project was conducted on that basis." But doubt has been cast on the accuracy of his recollection, and in any case his authority was limited. The key figure in the military hierarchy was General Marshall, whose opinion, in June 1945, was that the bomb ought to be used and that its effect on the war "could be decisive."

Britain were announced, and Churchill was succeeded as Prime Minister and British plenipotentiary-in-chief at Potsdam by the Socialist leader Clement Attlee, who had attended the conference from the beginning. On the same day, July 26, the Allies issued a declaration calling on the Japanese to surrender unconditionally or suffer "prompt and utter destruction," but not expressly mentioning a new weapon or the atom bomb. On July 28 the Japanese Prime Minister told a press conference that his government proposed to ignore the ultimatum, and on that day the Japanese radio announced that Japan would continue to fight. No further word had come from Japan when the American delegation left Potsdam on August 2, and in consequence the President gave the crucial order while on his way home for the dropping of two bombs on Japanese cities.

Yet when that fateful decision was made, the Emperor of Japan and his Prime Minister had been trying for more than a fortnight to convey peace proposals to the United States government by way of Russia, still nominally neutral. Their appeals had been intentionally delayed or played down by the Soviet Foreign Office, but the United States authorities had intercepted and decoded communications from the Japanese government to the Japanese Ambassador in Moscow which left no doubt of the Emperor's determination to make peace if the hurdle of unconditional surrender could be circumvented. "Japan is defeated. We must face that fact and act accordingly," was one such message, as paraphrased before release. But the government had also told the ambassador that they did not mean to surrender unconditionally "in any circumstances."

August 6 was the first day after the crucial order was received on which the skies over Japan were clear enough for visual bombing. On that day the first bomb was dropped on Hiroshima. More than seventy thousand dead or missing were reported when the count was made; but that was only the beginning. Japan did not surrender. Punctual almost to the hour, on August 8, the Russians declared war and began to stake out their sphere of influence in Manchuria. Airmen as well as scientists were shocked by reports of the suffering caused at Hiroshima. But a second bomb had arrived in Tinian, and the President had sanctioned the dropping of two bombs. On August 9 the second bomb was dropped, this time on Nagasaki. A few days later Japan did surrender. On August 14 America held a day of rejoicing overcast by the first hint of a suspicion that man's bright morning had turned to shadowed afternoon.

19

THE PRICE OF LIBERTY

AT THE END OF THE SECOND WORLD WAR THE BRITISH GOVERNMENT faced a recurrent question: Should Britain turn westward toward America or eastward toward Europe? Not convinced that the time had come for her to aim at a new balance of power by joining forces with Continental neighbors, Attlee and his colleagues accepted a large loan from the United States at a low rate of interest. Better attuned than their Conservative forerunners to an age in which shedding the load was a more popular catch phrase than the white man's burden, they also reduced their commitments by removing British troops and administrators from India and leaving Hindus and Moslems to settle their own quarrels.

America's foreign policy was soon decided by the Russians. In face of obvious preparations beyond the Elbe to make the world safe for Communism, the United States government renounced the intention of withdrawing its troops from Europe within two years of Germany's defeat, offered massive support to nations willing to stay outside the Russian orbit, and forged a network of alliances throughout the world. Almost simultaneously, the statesmen of the two great Anglo-Saxon powers thus carried through measures which would have stirred the orthodox to fury had they been suggested a few years earlier. When the revolutionary proposal which rang down the curtain on isolationism was debated in the Senate in the summer of 1948, only four Senators voted against the resolution.

By that year Communist governments directly inspired from

Moscow were firmly established not only in Rumania and Poland but also in Bulgaria, Czechoslovakia, and Hungary. From the Danube to the Baltic and from Kamchatka to the Oder, the avowed aim of the men in power was the destruction of Western political systems and modes of life.

The first act of open hostility in the Cold War between Russia and the West was the barring by the Russians of surface communications between Berlin and the Allied Occupation Zones in Western Germany. The Western Allies organized the transport of supplies by air, the inhabitants of West Berlin refused Communist offers of food and fuel at the price of absorption into the Russian sphere of influence, and the Western Allies gained a moral victory which they celebrated by merging their Zones into the West German Federal Republic under Dr. Konrad Adenauer.

In April 1949, a few weeks before the Russians abandoned their blockade after putting out peace feelers, the North Atlantic Treaty was signed in Washington. At the conference between Russian, British, French, and American representatives which formally ended the first stage of the Cold War, the Russians admitted privately that they had gambled and lost, and the Western Allies agreed among themselves that their ultimate aim should be the unification of Germany.

Meanwhile the division of Germany into two virtually distinct states had at least the advantage that a dangerous revival of Prussian militarism in the immediate future seemed unlikely. Toward the end of 1950 the Western Allies agreed in principle that German troops should take a hand in the defense of Western Europe.

But agreement in principle was one thing, and action was another. The French, still suspicious of Germany, insisted that a German contingent should be admitted only as part of a fully integrated army under supranational control. It was only after four years of delay, which tried American patience to the limit and led Secretary of State John Foster Dulles to threaten "agonizing reappraisals," that they withdrew their objections in return for a British undertaking to maintain four divisions and a tactical air force on the Continent until the end of the millennium.

Thus a British government at last felt able, in 1954, to give a pledge which, if given in 1921, might have allayed French fears and averted the tragedy of the Ruhr and the rise of Hitler. But American isolationism, as well as British insularity, had a lot to answer for in the meantime. And in 1954 the potential disturber of the peace was no longer a disarmed and defeated Germany, but a militant Russia with two hundred divisions said to be permanently embodied. Even when the British had promised their full share, inevitably at the cost of loosening their grip on the overseas possessions which were still among the most valuable strategic assets at the disposal of the West, the land forces of the North Atlantic Treaty powers were so small by Russian standards that Western Europeans felt bound to conclude that their security depended ultimately on the dubious assumption that the Americans and the British, who alone among nations outside the Russian orbit had the power to launch a nuclear war, would risk doing so in order to prevent the Russians from reaching Paris.

It was also obvious that a nuclear war would not be one-sided. While Russia and, less probably, the United States, with their wide tracts of undeveloped or partially developed territory, might hope to survive an all-out conflict, such densely populated countries as Belgium and the United Kingdom would stand little chance of doing so unless their defenses were impregnable. Since 1945 the Franck Committee's warning that a dangerous arms race was in prospect had been strikingly fulfilled. Treachery helped the Russians to evaluate American and British progress, but they did not need to look outside their own frontiers to find scientists capable of matching Anglo-American efforts. Not all were as recalcitrant as Pyotr Kapitza, a brilliant pupil of the pioneer nuclear physicist Sir Ernest Rutherford, who had been ordered by the Soviet government as early as the middle thirties to leave England and return to Russia, where he was afterward sentenced to forced labor for refusing to make atomic weapons. By the late summer of 1949 the Russians had made and tested their first atom bomb, and the American authorities were aware that they had done so.

A few months later Washington learned that Klaus Fuchs, a German-born scientist working for the British, had imparted to

Russian agents some of the secrets of the far more powerful hydrogen bomb whose development and construction American service chiefs had been urging on the government in recent weeks. On January 31, 1950, just four days after receiving news of Fuchs's defection, a special committee of the National Security Council advised President Truman to order a "crash program" for the construction of the hydrogen bomb. On the same day he did so.

In 1945 Dr. Franck had pointed out that Russia was not the only country which might make an independent bid for nuclear striking power if the Allies, by using the atom bomb against Japan, lost a chance of bringing nuclear weapons under international control from the start. Dr. Franck was right. The British were not satisfied that the Americans had observed the spirit of their undertaking to share atomic secrets during the war, and the evidence of the American General Groves that he had discouraged cooperation with the British suggested that there was something in their complaint. When an improved fission bomb was tested at Bikini in 1946, the voice of the British scientist who made the countdown was scrubbed from the official American film of the proceedings and replaced by a voice with an American accent. Thus the petty jealousies which had helped to prolong the war in Europe to the detriment of the Western Allies and the profit of the Russians continued, when the war was over, to put Anglo-American relations in jeopardy.

Such incidents might have been dismissed as insignificant trifles if evidence had been forthcoming after the war that the anticolonial policy of Roosevelt was dead. On the contrary, the signs suggested that it was still very much alive. France and Britain had important assets overseas which could be of immense strategic value to the West. It seemed to European observers that the United States government could have built a much more effective rampart against Communism by encouraging them to hold on to their possessions than it was likely to build by backing dubious nationalist movements which aimed at unseating them. When a disreputable Persian government defied its contractual obligations in 1951 by seizing the Anglo-Persian Oil Company's plant at Abadan, American mediators showed a proper regard for the claims of both sides, but the final outcome was the transfer of the company's property to an international consortium of oil companies in which American interests were prominent. Thereafter American taxpayers were compelled to pour vast sums into Persia in order to bolster up a régime whose corruption struck one American observer as startling even by Middle Eastern standards.[1] Conversely, when the British government encouraged the pro-Western Sultan of Muscat to reoccupy a part of his territories which had been filched from him, their action was condemned by the United States government as an act of aggression. And when, in 1955, the French faced in Algeria, which was not a colony but had been part of metropolitan France for half a century, a revolt financed by the Arab League with funds drawn partly from royalties paid in advance by American oil companies in Saudi Arabia, they were not reassured by hints that the United States government would feel happier about the safety of American bases in North Africa if they gave way.

If it was in the Middle East and Africa that American and Anglo-French policies seemed most out of alignment, there was logic in the argument that it was in the Middle East and Africa that the Russians would try hardest to drive a wedge between the Allies. To ordinary men and women who did not claim exceptional foresight the immediate danger seemed, however, to be in Europe. Even if anti-British sentiment in American service circles could be discounted, no one on the European side of the Atlantic could forget that Washington was more than three thousand miles from London and the Soviet Army less than five hundred miles from the Channel ports. Without consulting Parliament or the public, the Socialist government in Britain decided to make the atom bomb. In due course their Conservative successors decided, more openly, to make the hydrogen bomb.

Three months before President Truman sanctioned the American hydrogen bomb project, the General Advisory Commission of the Atomic Energy Commission in Washington recorded their

[1]Andrew Tully, *CIA: The Inside Story* (New York, 1962).

unanimous opinion that development and production of the bomb would be uneconomic and would lower the moral standing of the United States. They were on safe ground when they added that the job would take some time. Nearly three years elapsed before the experts were ready to test even an experimental bomb, too big and heavy to be carried in an aircraft and hence useless as a weapon. By that time President Truman's administration was on its last legs. Soon General Eisenhower would fill the office of President, and great power would be wielded by John Foster Dulles and his brother Allen Welsh Dulles, respectively Secretary of State and Director of the much-criticized Central Intelligence Agency.

Before the device was tested Vannevar Bush, who had been in charge of all American research for military purposes during the Second World War, begged the government to open negotiations with the Russians before crossing the threshold of a new and hideous world. His advice was rejected. On the night of October 31, 1952, final preparations were made at Eniwetok, in the Marshall Islands, for the birth of what some commentators called an artificial sun and others a man-made star. The islands were cleared of their inhabitants. All but a few of the thousands of scientists, technicians, soldiers, sailors, and civilian workers concerned with the experiment withdrew to a distance of forty miles. After the remaining experts had retired to a place of safety, the sixty-five-ton monster was set off with a bang which obliterated the islet on which it stood and blew a crater a mile long in the Pacific. Nearly one thousand, nine hundred and fifty-two years after the birth of Christ a new star had arisen in the firmament, but this star was in the West.

That sizable hole proved the grave of American hopes of attaining nuclear supremacy while the Russians were still groping for success. A practical weapon based on the Eniwetok monster had not yet been completed when Washington learned that the Russians already had such a weapon and had tested it. Soon afterward it became clear that the United States had also fallen behind in the development of intercontinental ballistic missiles, which had seemed likely at the end of the Second World War to replace manned bombers within ten years, but had later come to be regarded by American strategists as too inaccurate to deserve the highest priority. A good three years before the Russians fired their first Sputnik in 1957, frenzied cerebration by American scientists and service chiefs produced the concept of an ultimate weapon in which the inherent inaccuracy of the long-range rocket would be offset by a warhead so powerful that the target would be smothered with radioactive matter even if the missile fell ten miles from the point of aim.

The fact remained that America had, as yet, no intercontinental ballistic missile. Furthermore, the first test of a new series of super-bombs which might solve the problem of the warhead confronted the experimenters with unexplored vistas of human misery. The Eniwetok bomb had exploded with a force equivalent to that of the mere three million tons of conventional high explosive used in the whole of the Second World War. A bomb tested in the Pacific on March 1, 1954, was six or seven times as powerful. The bang was twice as big as the scientists expected, and even the direction of the wind belied their calculations. A Japanese trawler a hundred and twenty miles away, and well outside the predicted danger area, was showered with radioactive dust and limped into port a fortnight later with a doomed and suffering crew. During the next few days radioactive matter was detected in clouds and rain, in the lubricating oil of aircraft, and elsewhere in the sky over Asia, Australasia, North America, and Europe. A distinguished geneticist warned the public that many hundreds of children born in 1954 would suffer from the effects of cell-poisoning material liberated by bombs already exploded, and a member of the Atomic Energy Commission, who refused to allow his name to be published for fear of dismissal, disclosed information which led to the hotly disputed conclusion that continued tests at the current rate would poison life at the source for all mankind within a quarter of a century.

In the meantime many clashes had occurred between Communist forces and the Western powers, but no nuclear weapons had been used in war since 1945, and no Russian troops had been met in battle. The Korean War, which lasted from 1950 to 1953, cost the anti-Communist powers thirty thousand American and a much smaller number of British and other lives, but it did not cost the Russians any lives at all, except possibly those of a few specialists and airmen. The struggle began when the United States government, which was backing the ostensibly democratic but morally worthless Synghman Rhee in South Korea, persuaded the Security Council of the United Nations to agree, in the absence of the Russians, that North Korean Communists who had invaded South Korea should be made to withdraw. To all intents and purposes it ended when the Americans perceived that the aim of the Soviet leaders was to involve them in a far-reaching Asiatic war which would cost Russia nothing, and that they were in danger of being led into the trap by Russian guile and the zeal of their Commander-in-Chief on the spot.

Similarly, in Malaya and Indochina the Communist troops who fought the British and the French so bitterly were not Russian troops. As in the Spanish Civil War of the 1930s, but to an even greater degree, the outcome of the fighting was almost immaterial to the Soviet leaders as long as the struggle lasted long enough to drain the Western powers of their youth, embarrass their governments, and sow dissension in the Allied camp.

Nor were the Western powers eager to try conclusions with the Communist world once the first flush of their enthusiasm had worn off in Korea. When General Douglas MacArthur showed signs of widening the Korean War to embrace an all-out conflict between Communist China and the Chinese Nationalist forces of Chiang Kai-shek, President Truman recalled him and treated him as the dangerous political opponent which he was. When the American Admiral Arthur W. Radford urged that nuclear weapons should be used tactically in Indochina, strong objections were made and the idea was dropped. These dampers on excessive zeal were enthusiastically welcomed by an overwhelming preponderance of public opinion throughout the Western world, but they pointed more sharply than ever the contrast between Western determination to undertake only limited wars in the Far East, and the vast scale of American preparations for an all-out nuclear war with Russia in which the casualties would be reckoned in scores of millions or even hundreds of millions.[2]

Yet the paradox could be resolved, although only by another paradox. Majority opinion on both sides of the Atlantic agreed that possession by the West of enormous nuclear striking power was the best insurance against its use. But that argument had two weaknesses. The first was that the premium was too high. Since the Russians also wished to be insured, there seemed no limit to the extent to which East and West could go on stock-piling nuclear weapons, except that the resources of a modern industrial state were not inexhaustible, and that Russia was not only a modern industrial state but also a vast Asiatic empire whose living standards were far from sacred. The second weakness was that mutual deterrence could lead only to a stalemate which might content the West, but might not content the Russians. The Russians were doubtless no more eager than the West to launch a nuclear attack whose backwash might cost them several hundred million casualties even if they were successful. But they might wish to launch another kind of attack, especially a kind whose tactics they had mastered and which the Western powers, by reason of their lack of mutual trust and understanding, were peculiarly unfitted to withstand.

By the middle 1950s the pattern of Soviet aggression was so well established that Russia's next move could be predicted with considerable accuracy, if only in general terms. Somewhere in the world a militantly nationalist clique or junta, either eager for power or already in power and anxious to strengthen its hold by some spectacular achievement, would be chosen as the instrument of Russia's will to injure and confuse the West. Its leaders would

[2] In the spring of 1956 Lieutenant General James M. Gavin, then Assistant Chief of Staff for Plans and Operations, and later Chief of Research and Development, in the Department of the Army, told the Symington Committee (a Congressional committee concerned with the study of air power) that current planning for nuclear war rested on the assumption that deaths in Russia and neighboring countries would be of the order of "several hundred million." Some years later General Gavin's estimate was substantially confirmed by the United States Secretary of Defense, with the proviso that casualties would be much lower if aiming points were confined to military installations (e.g. missile-launching sites).

be encouraged by flattery and promises of substantial support to challenge one or other of the Western European powers on some convenient ground. They would be given enough arms and money to sustain a threat which the power concerned could not ignore, but not enough to sustain one which would bring the whole machinery of the Western alliance into instant action. Having set the wheel spinning, the Soviet leaders would sit back to await the luck of the game with the comfortable knowledge that their stake was inconsiderable and that their winnings might be anything from a minor setback for the Western powers to a major split between them. For the final rewards of their policy, already applied or about to be applied at numerous points on the periphery of the shrinking overseas possessions of their European enemies, the Russians were prepared to wait.

Among many baffling problems which faced the British government at the end of the Second World War was that of Palestine. On the eve of the war partition of the country between Jews and Arabs had seemed the only way out of the dilemma in which the British had placed themselves by promising during the First World War to set up a Jewish National Home in Palestine at the request of the powerfully supported Zionist leaders, and afterward accepting a mandate for the country from the League of Nations. When the Second World War was over, the problem was further complicated by an influx of illegal immigrants which the mandatory power was bound to resist in justice to Arab claims. Meanwhile the Zionist leaders had openly proclaimed that national sovereignty was their aim, and were actively seeking support in New York as well as London.

President Truman suggested after the war that large-scale immigration should be sanctioned and that a hundred thousand Jewish refugees from Europe should be admitted as a first step. The Socialist government which had come to office in Britain in 1945 responded by asking that an Anglo-American commission should consider the whole question of Palestine's future. The commission reported in favor of partition. Rejecting their advice, the Attlee government found it so difficult to hold the ring in Palestine that eventually they decided to renounce the mandate and clear out of the country, bag and baggage, in the spring of 1948.

The sequel was an Arab-Jewish war which unsettled the whole of the Middle East and left the Arab countries thirsting to wipe the new state of Israel off the map. The Egyptians, in particular, refused to recognize Israel as an independent sovereign state, regarded the armistice for which they themselves had asked as only temporary, and illegally prevented Israeli ships from entering the Suez Canal.

This state of affairs had an important bearing on the long-term problem of safeguarding and maintaining supplies of petroleum without which the ability of the Western powers to oppose the march of Communism would be immeasurably weakened. In 1914 the United States was supreme among oil-producing countries, and the Middle East produced less than a hundredth part of the world's output. By the early 1950s half the world's estimated oil reserves were in countries bordering on the Persian Gulf, and only about a quarter in the United States. Whether Middle Eastern oil was controlled by British or American companies seemed important to the American oil lobby and its counterparts elsewhere, but its importance was only relative. What mattered far more on a long-term view was, first, that control should not pass to the Russians or to rulers incapable of withstanding Communist pressure; secondly, that the westward flow of oil from the Persian Gulf to Europe should not be interrupted. Without the liquid gold stored up in the rich deposits of Kuwait, Persia, Saudi Arabia, and Iraq, the European allies of the United States would cease within a foreseeable time to be able to wage Cold War and perhaps even to maintain the standards of living to which their citizens had become accustomed.

As a vital link in the chain of communication between the Middle East and the Western world, the Suez Canal was thus a strategic point of immense importance to the West. No more than a small proportion of the oil extracted from Middle Eastern deposits was, or could be, piped to the Levant; the greater part was carried in tankers whose only alternative to the Suez route was the long haul round the Cape. In theory the right of the Western powers, as of all nations, to pass their tankers and other shipping through the canal was safeguarded by the international convention which bound all signatories to keep the canal open; in practice, they could still be deprived of it if the shores of the canal should pass into the hands of a power prepared to defy the convention, or the locks and waterways into those of a custodian unable or unwilling to maintain them. Insurance against these risks long seemed to successive British governments so important that the canal was guarded until 1955 by British troops at a cost to the taxpayer which rose in the 1950s to about fifty million pounds a year.

If this was not a very satisfactory arrangement for the British from the financial point of view, it was nevertheless the kind of arrangement to which they had become accustomed. Their position in Egypt had always been difficult, and at times anomalous. They had moved into the country in the nineteenth century with the express intention of withdrawing in favor of the first Egyptian administration which could satisfy them of its competence; but Egypt's long experience as an outpost of the Ottoman Empire had not taught her public men to shoulder their responsibilities, and for many years no such administration was forthcoming. When at last the British did part with political control of the country to an Egyptian government in 1936, the outlook was still so unpromising that they found it necessary to invite no less than thirteen Egyptian representatives to sign the treaty then made, so that no political party could afterward repudiate the bargain on the ground that its leaders had not been consulted.

Even after the signing of the 1936 treaty, Egypt thus remained a bad risk from the Western point of view. Insecurity was endemic in a country where vast wealth, and an utter disregard of the responsibilities which it entailed, went hand in hand with abject poverty. At all material times the Wafd was the strongest political party in Egypt, but the Wafd was neither democratic nor truly representative. It was a party of rich men, supported at the height of its power by the votes of less than fifteen per cent of the electorate. Moreover, Egypt was saddled not only with a corrupt and irresponsible ruling class, but also with an economy so unbalanced that the risk of financial collapse was never absent. Long-staple cotton was Egypt's only important commercial crop, accounting by 1952 for nearly nine-tenths of her export trade. Contributing rather more than a twentieth part of the world's output of raw cotton, Egypt was only a small producer compared with the United States, which contributed about two-fifths. The fact remained that the cotton crop was the main source of her revenue, and that failure to market it advantageously could bankrupt the country in a year. An incidental factor which was merely of minor importance, but which may have helped to keep alive American suspicions of British and French motives, was that Egypt and the Indian sub-continent were the only sources, outside Russia and Communist China, from which the Western European powers could obtain raw cotton in substantial quantities without paying for it in dollars and shipping it across the Atlantic.

After the Arab-Jewish war the position of the British troops which remained in Egypt to guard the canal under the 1936 treaty became more difficult than ever. Encouraged by a climate of world opinion which favored aggressively nationalist movements in all countries, the Egyptian government pressed for their removal and threatened abrogation of the treaty, although it was not due to expire until 1956. Claiming that their own army could defend the canal, the Egyptians called urgently for arms with the barely concealed intention of using them against Israel.

The Korean War, and the consequent preoccupation of the Western powers with the Communist menace, seemed to politically minded Egyptians to bring just the right conditions for them to press their claims still harder. At the same time, it encouraged Egyptian speculators to hold on to their cotton in the hope of a spectacular rise in prices, with the result that much of the 1950 crop remained unsold. In consequence the country's perennially unstable finances became more involved than ever. The Soviet government intervened with a well-timed offer to help train and equip an Egyptian army of two million men, accompanied by hints that the British and the Americans were too busy in Korea and elsewhere to look after the canal, even if the Americans had the will to do so. As one of their last acts before leaving office, the

Socialist government in Britain agreed to supply Egypt with substantial quantities of modern arms, and offered to withdraw their troops on terms which the Egyptians promptly declined in the hope of doing even better. Western hopes that an interallied force might replace the purely British force in the Canal Zone disappeared when the Egyptians also turned down proposals for a Middle East defense organization on the lines of NATO.

During the winter of 1951–52 the Egyptians did their best to make the position of the troops in the Canal Zone untenable by blowing up bridges, attacking road convoys, refusing customs facilities and withholding civilian labor. The British brought in labor from Cyprus, Malta, and East Africa, and raised the strength of their troops from 10,000 to 80,000. Unable to check the disorganization and corruption which continued meanwhile to spread in Cairo, the government and monarchy were finally swept away by the revolution which made Gamal Abdel Nasser virtual dictator of Egypt after a respectable figurehead, General Mohammed Naguib, had been pushed aside.

In spite of setbacks which included a blunt refusal by the new government to allow American participation in negotiations with the British, American statesmen remained hopeful that eventually the withdrawal of British troops would make the Egyptians so amenable that thereafter economic incentives would be enough to keep them on the rails. With American approval, the Conservative government which took office in Britain in 1951 made many attempts to bargain for withdrawal on terms which would allow the Western Allies to reoccupy the Canal Zone in an emergency. Finally, after a visit by the veteran Churchill and Foreign Secretary Anthony Eden to Washington in the summer of 1954, it was made clear to a restive House of Commons that the Conservatives intended to apply to Egypt the remedy which they had denounced as "a policy of scuttle" when the Socialists applied it to India and Palestine. All British troops would be withdrawn from the Canal Zone within twenty months of the signing of an agreement with the Egyptians, civilian contractors would maintain the base on terms which made the Egyptian government responsible for its security, and the British would return only in the event of an armed attack on Egypt, Turkey, or a member of the Arab League, and after consultation with the Egyptians. The government did their best to silence criticism by asserting that the Suez base had become highly vulnerable since the advent of the hydrogen bomb, and that the time had come for redeployment of British forces in the Middle East. Their critics, who included some thirty or forty back-bench Tories known afterward as the Suez Group or Suez Rebels, observed that there was no base which could not be wiped out by a hydrogen bomb, and that the abandonment of five hundred million pounds' worth of stores and buildings to the Egyptians was not a sell-out but a give-away.

The signing of the Anglo-Egyptian agreement on October 19, 1954, was nevertheless regarded in governmental and official circles on both sides of the Atlantic as the beginning of a new era and an incitement to fresh efforts in the cause of democracy and freedom. Undeterred by the arrest a week later of General Naguib and other prominent Egyptians, six of whom were hanged for alleged complicity in an attempt on Nasser's life, the Western powers continued their search for a successor to the abortive Middle East defense organization. Led from the rear by the United States government, which declined an active role but promised moral support, they persuaded Iraq and Turkey to sign a mutual agreement afterward widened to include Britain, Pakistan, and Persia and known as the Baghdad Pact. These gestures did not materially increase the capacity of the signatories to defend themselves, and the only immediate consequences of any note were a wave of fear and resentment in Israel, where the pact was interpreted as an incitement to Arab bellicosity, and an outburst of indignation in Egypt, where it was regarded as a breach of Iraq's undertaking not to conclude such agreements without reference to the Arab League. Thereafter Cairo poured out a stream of denunciation of Western imperialism, and also a stream of encouragement to the Arab nationalists who were defying French rule in Algeria. A secondary consequence was that the French made common cause with Israel against Nasser, and supplied her with arms as a counterweight to the weapons extracted by the Egyptians from the British.

The way was now clear for further Russian intervention on familiar lines. In the summer of 1955 Nasser began to drop hints to the Western powers that he was thinking of buying arms from countries behind the Iron Curtain, and a few months later both Egypt and Syria placed orders for substantial quantities of Czechoslovak and Russian weapons. Alarmed by this new development and by rumors of an impending Israeli attack on Egypt with arms provided by the French, the British and American governments showed such evident eagerness to keep Nasser out of the Soviet camp that he was encouraged to make large demands backed by the tacit threat to go elsewhere if London and Washington did not give him all he wanted. Suggesting that the Western powers might care to find at least part of the immense sum needed to carry out a projected enlargement of the Aswan Dam which had been proposed by a consortium of British, French, and German contractors, he simultaneously negotiated with the Russians, who offered to lend part of the money or alternatively to carry out the entire undertaking at a competitive price.

At first attracted by the prospect of enlisting Nasser on their side, the British and American governments became less enthusiastic in the light of a growing suspicion that he had only a vague intention of carrying out the project, and no intention at all of abandoning a position which enabled him to play off East against West. That Nasser, with all his faults, might be sincerely determined to keep his country out of the Cold War if he could manage it was an explanation which, even if correct, seemed hardly worth considering at a time when neutralism ranked, in the United States especially, as almost a worse crime than Communism. After sounding the State Department, the British government made up their minds in the summer of 1956 not to go on with the loan.

Almost at that very moment the Egyptian Ambassador in Washington, who had been recalled to Cairo for consultations, returned to the United States with instructions to speed up the negotiations. The Egyptian Minister of Finance also arrived in Washington, where he had several interviews with the State Department and the International Bank. The results were not encouraging to either side. Without further consultation with the

British government Secretary of State John Foster Dulles broke the news to the ambassador on July 19 that the deal was off.

With that rebuff, softened only by conventional assurances of American good will toward Egypt, Dulles ended any chance that the Western powers might still have had of keeping Nasser on their side. A week later, after a series of baffling statements by Soviet spokesmen had shrouded Russian intentions in impenetrable fog, Nasser seized the assets of the Suez Canal Company and announced his intention of using its revenues to finance the Aswan Dam project.

Prolonged and tortuous arguments followed as to the legality of Nasser's action. His supporters pointed out that nationalization with compensation was an act within the competence of governments, and that he had promised compensation. His critics retorted that the Egyptian Treasury was notoriously in no position to redeem the promise, and that in any case the right to nationalize did not extend to an international undertaking carried on by virtue of an unexpired concession which had the same force as a treaty between sovereign states.

Two men who had no doubt at all that Nasser must be brought to heel were the British Prime Minister, Sir Anthony Eden, and the French Foreign Minister, M. Christian Pineau. Mr. Dulles, who reached London on August 1 and left on August 3, did not differ from them on the main point, but sounded a note of caution. He agreed that Nasser must be made to disgorge, but thought that the Western powers must make sure that their case was unimpeachable in law before taking any action. He added that the United States did not exclude the use of force, but that force was "the last method to be tried."

Accordingly the British government called up about twenty thousand reservists and moved troops, ships, and aircraft to the Mediterranean in case they should be needed. Immediate intervention was ruled out, even if the British and the French had been willing to undertake it, since their combined airborne strength was less than one division and the nearest base to Suez at which a seaborne expedition could assemble was a thousand miles from the canal.

The Prime Minister continued for more than a month to believe that the Americans were prepared to see force used if all else failed, not only because their Secretary of State had said so, but also because they raised no objections during that time to precautionary moves of which they were informed in general terms. On September 3, however, he received a message from President Eisenhower to the effect that public opinion in the United States was against the use of force in any circumstances. Ten days later Dulles said publicly that the United States did not intend to shoot its way through the canal. He added on October 1 that the United States could not be expected "to identify itself 100 per cent either with the colonial powers or the powers uniquely concerned with the problem of getting independence."

Meanwhile Nasser had rejected proposals from France, Great Britain, the United States, and fifteen other powers for the administration of the canal by an international board on which the Egyptians would be represented. A plan for a "Users' Club," proposed by Dulles, lost what little chance of success it ever had when Dulles gave Nasser a plain hint that he could safely ignore it by publicly remarking that it had no teeth in it. Proposals to submit the issue to the Security Council of the United Nations were not pursued while other methods were being tried, and when the United Nations did consider the matter action was ruled out by a Russian veto. In the meantime the canal was working fairly satisfactorily under Egyptian control, but an overwhelming majority of the nations concerned were still of the opinion that control by a single power was not acceptable and that Nasser must be made to stand aside in favor of an international body.

The British and French Prime Ministers and Foreign Ministers met in Paris on September 26, when the French pressed for early action. They met again on October 16 to discuss reports that the Israelis were contemplating an attack on one or other of their Arab neighbors. The British asked the French to use their influence with the Israelis to dissuade them from attacking Jordan and thus forcing Britain to intervene in accordance with her treaty obligations toward that country. The statesmen agreed that in some ways an Israeli attack on Egypt would be less embarrassing.

What more was said, not only at the meeting but later by the French to the Israelis, was afterward the subject of much speculation. All that is certain is that, with or without French encouragement, the Israelis began to mobilize just under ten days later. On October 29 their forces crossed the Egyptian frontier. Late on October 30, after an Israeli communiqué had claimed that the invading troops were "on the approaches to the Suez Canal," the British and French governments issued an ultimatum calling on Israelis and Egyptians to cease fire and withdraw to a distance of ten miles on either side of the canal. On the same day British and French delegates twice vetoed United Nations resolutions condemning Israeli aggression.

The Franco-British ultimatum, afterward described by an official of the U. S. State Department as "the most brutal in modern history," was accepted by the Israelis but not by the Egyptians, with the result that the Israelis resumed hostilities after a brief delay. Accordingly the British and French governments put into effect the first stage of the plan they had framed for the purpose of seizing the canal from Nasser. This was not very appropriate, since their declared object was no longer to seize the canal from Nasser but to prevent it from becoming a bone of contention between Israelis and Egyptians; but the explanation afterward given was that it was the only feasible plan they had.

The bombing of aerodromes with which the Franco-British forces opened their offensive was so successful that they had complete mastery of the air within thirty-six to forty-eight hours of the first sortie, but it was not until November 5, after a further interval of a day and a night, that they followed up their attack by landing airborne troops near Port Said. That afternoon the Governor of Port Said asked for terms, but some hours later he changed his mind. Street fighting continued after the landing of the Franco-British seaborne forces next day, but at midnight the Allied Commander-in-Chief received orders to cease fire on the ground that hostilities between the Israelis and the Egyptians had ended.

In the meantime the Soviet government had hinted at reprisals with modern weapons such as long-range rockets if the Franco-British forces continued their attacks. Pressure on the pound from

New York and elsewhere would have been at least as potent a weapon if the British government had contemplated further action. British gold and dollar reserves fell by more than four hundred million dollars in September, October, and November, largely in consequence of speculation against sterling in the United States or on American account. During the same period Chinese balances were withdrawn and Indian balances reduced. In face of such strong suggestions from both sides of the ideological fence and from the uncommitted, the British needed no ballistic missiles to convince them that they were out of step.

The Suez operation remained, and remains, one of the most controversial episodes in British history. Its most interesting feature was not so much the marshaling of world opinion against British and French intervention, as the change in the attitude of informed Americans between the beginning of the crisis and its end. The United States government began by declaring in emphatic terms that Nasser must be made to disgorge and that the use of force was not ruled out. It ended by condemning the European democracies for using force to achieve, if not that object, at any rate one not less respectable. Moreover, the incident had a sequel. When Jordan, long a British sphere of influence, was torn by disorder less than six months later, it was an American fleet that was "rushed to the Mediterranean to protect the independence and integrity" of that country, and to keep on his throne a monarch whose family owed its elevation to such heights to British backing.

20

TOWARD A VERDICT

I

IN THE UNITED STATES, COUNSEL IN A COURT OF LAW ARE SAID TO try a case; in England the judge does so. In both countries the verdict, where the issue is important, is delivered by a jury.

There are no juries in the court of history. In that court, historians open the case, deliver the speeches, sum up the evidence and ultimately bring in their verdict. Not surprisingly, awareness of such wide responsibilities makes them reluctant, as a rule, to commit themselves until the last scrap of evidence becomes available for detailed study.

What will be the verdict of history on the tremendous happenings which this book recalls? Men and women who lived through the first half of the present century may feel that their lives were shaped by the interrupted struggle between Germany and the West for the mastery of Europe. Historians looking back from a remoter standpoint are perhaps as likely to regard the two German wars as little more than incidents in a mightier struggle between Britain and the United States for command of the sea and control of the world's markets and raw materials. The question they will then have to answer is whether the effects of that struggle were any less disastrous for one side than for the other.

From 1816 until 1914, Britain held the balance of power in the world. Not from a disinterested regard for universal peace, but because the trade and commerce which kept her merchants prosperous and her people fed could flourish only in a world undisturbed by major wars, she made it her business to avert a recurrence of the upheavals which had afflicted mankind between the onset of the French Revolution in 1789 and Napoleon's defeat at Waterloo in 1815. Her command of the sea was a powerful deterrent to potential troublemakers, but it would not have sufficed to localize conflicts between the great powers for nearly a hundred years without at least the rudiments of statesmanship. As the nineteenth century drew to a close and gave place to the twentieth, her statesmen found themselves on more than one occasion playing the part of the juggler who defies mischance by keeping six balls in the air at once.

In 1914 their skill deserted them, or their luck failed them. A ball fell. The balance of power was lost, and the world was at war.

In the heyday of British imperialism, and especially after the opening up of the Middle West, America prospered by exporting her surplus produce to the Old World and absorbing the Old World's surplus population. Her political philosophy was isolationist; her political practice was to steer clear of obligations toward her neighbors on the far side of the Atlantic while not depriving herself of the benefits of intercourse with them. Her attitude was not more cynical and selfish than theirs; nor was it less so. There are no altruists among the nations.

When the United States entered the First World War in 1917, her well-being was not directly threatened by any of the belligerents. Demands for food and raw materials and the rise in world prices were bringing such profitable business to American producers, large and small, that President Wilson had been elected for a second term precisely because he seemed, of all possible candidates, the most likely to keep the country neutral. By 1917 there was a risk that the Western Allies might be unable to meet their obligations to the United States Treasury if they did not gain a speedy victory, and the fear that Japan might profit by Allied preoccupations in Europe to become the dominant power in the Pacific was never absent from American calculations. But by far the biggest danger was that prolongation of the war might leave the whole of the Old World too poor to go on buying American oil, cotton, wheat, and copper. Thus the only rational aims which could justify the abandonment by President Wilson of his popular and well-tried policy of benevolent neutrality were first to bring the war to a speedy end, and secondly to restore the balance of power or put something better in its place.

The first aim was defeated when the President discovered that the mere threat of American participation was not enough to bring the belligerents to their senses, and that he would have to go through the lengthy business of shipping a large army to Europe with the aid of British carrying-capacity and command of the sea before he could make much impression on them.

As for the second aim, President Wilson had no use for the balance of power. Like his ultimate successor President Roosevelt, he believed that because it was old it was out of date, and because it was British it was un-American. Both Presidents hoped to replace it by a new internationalism in which British maritime supremacy and political know-how would yield to American control of raw materials and credit as the ultimate sanction in the cause of world peace. Such an arrangement, they thought, would better suit the interests of the United States and therefore of the world.

It seems scarcely necessary to await the verdict of history before suggesting that both Presidents were wrong. Woodrow Wilson was denied a clear run at the target, largely because he was unwilling to take the Senate into his confidence, perhaps also because he was before his time. But Franklin D. Roosevelt's policy was not immediately killed by his sudden death in 1945. By the end of the war in Europe, his aims were as near accomplishment as the reluctance of his perplexed followers to deviate from the path he had so confidently sketched could make them. The effect was to substitute for the balance of power a balance of terror, enormously costly to the American taxpayer and far more onerous to the rest of the world than the polite stranglehold long exercised by British statesmen.

It may be argued that the failure of Rooseveltism was due not to its inherent defects but to Russian intransigence. But a tree is judged by its fruits, and Russian aims were easily foreseeable. If British statesmen blundered before 1914 when they believed that they could keep the Central Powers on the rails without themselves raising a large army, their error was trivial in comparison with the vast miscalculation which led Roosevelt to believe thirty years later that Russia could safely be called in to fill the vacuum about to be created by the overthrow of Nazi Germany. Wilson showed a certain naïveté by assuming at the end of the First World War that, after undertaking to join the League of Nations and guarantee the Franco-German frontier, he could satisfy his isolationist critics by shipping the last remaining doughboy back to the United States. Roosevelt showed still more when he assumed that he, in turn, would be able to remove his army from Europe when the Second World War was over, and thereafter rule the nations by remote control from Washington as British statesmen had long ruled the nations by remote control from London. He forgot that the British had been able to do that only because many decades of confident imperialism tempered by paternalism had endowed them with a reputation for political sagacity and a string of bases conveniently dotted round the world.

Whether there was any point at which a bold stand by Old World statesmen could have pricked these illusions without destroying the hope of future cooperation with the United States is a vast and baffling question which historians will one day have to answer. Could President Wilson have been persuaded in 1916 to renounce a long-term naval program whose outcome turned out to be a bargain which left the two Anglo-Saxon nations without the means of safeguarding their Far Eastern interests at a moment of supreme psychological importance? Where Colonel House's arguments failed to shake the President, nothing within the power of the Western Allies would have been likely to convince him that British command of the sea was more of a benefit than a threat to the United States, and that Britain could be trusted to keep the Yellow Peril within bounds as long as he and his successors refrained from throwing a monkey wrench in the works. Even if the President had been open to persuasion, would the Senate and people of the United States have taken kindly to the suggestion that they did not need a powerful navy precisely because the British had one?

Again, it may seem in retrospect that the British and French governments ought to have done everything they could in 1917 to convince the President that he could do more for his country, and for them, by staying out of the war than by joining it. Apart from the obvious risk that he would insist on dictating peace terms to the belligerents, it was foreseeable that the immediate effect of America's entry would be to divert to her own armed forces supplies which might conceivably enable the Allies to win the war off their own bat. But would they have succeeded if they had tried, and were they likely to try in the circumstances of that time? Even if they did begin to suspect by 1917 that American participation would be detrimental to their long-term interests, still it was painfully obvious that, without it, they might suffer a defeat which would be even more disagreeable than a victory shared with the United States.

Once America was in the war, the Allies showed a lamentable lack of skill in their handling of the President, perhaps partly because France and Britain were both ruled by men distrustful of experts and therefore reluctant to take advice. But Woodrow Wilson was not an easy man to handle, and the fortunes of war put him in an exceptionally favorable position to give free rein to his ideas. Allied policy until 1918 aimed at preserving a reformed Austro-Hungary as an indispensable barrier between Russian and German rivalries. Wilson's decision in that year to foster disruption of the Austro-Hungarian Empire cut clean across that policy and was a blow struck at the heart of Europe. The acquiescence of the Allies was seen at the time, not merely in the light of afterknowledge, as a weak surrender to expediency. Yet could the Allies, in fact, have stopped the President from doing as he liked? Had they registered dissent when the United States government preached independence for the Slav minorities in Austro-Hungary, they would merely have advertised a lack of unity in the Western camp.

The fact remains that, by abandoning the Dual Monarchy to its fate in the closing months of the First World War, the Allied and Associated Powers made it almost certain that either Germany or Russia would fall heir to the Danubian States as soon as one of them was strong enough to keep the other out. Twenty-seven years later, after fresh mistakes had robbed them of a chance of redeeming some part of their error, Stalin accepted the invitation to swallow a morsel which had proved too tough for Hitler.

Right at the end of the First World War the Allies did have a chance of saving something from the wreck of Europe and advancing the proposition that Englishmen, Frenchmen and even Germans had at least as good a claim to self-determination as Czechs and Yugoslavs. Dazed and dazzled by near-defeat and imminent victory, they let it slip. They were so much perplexed by President Wilson's attempt to keep the pre-armistice negotiations in his own hands that, uncertain where their true interest lay, they allowed themselves to be blackmailed into letting him destroy ordered government in Germany and shatter their chances of arriving at a satisfactory peace settlement.

By a strange irony the amiable Colonel House, a firm believer in Anglo-Saxon solidarity, was the man deputed to hold the presidential pistol to the world's head. Rather than see the United States make a separate peace with Germany and cut off their supplies, the Allies agreed under extreme pressure to accept the President's Fourteen Points as the basis of their settlement with Germany, albeit with two reservations. Yet they knew, or at least they had been told by experienced diplomatists, that the Continental balance of power was not likely to be restored by anything but well-tried methods of diplomatic bargaining for which the Fourteen Points were not a substitute.

This was surely the point at which the Allies should have made their stand. The President could not, in fact, have made a separate peace without the approval of two-thirds of the Senate, and his hold on the Senate was slipping fast. With American farmers clamoring for an assured market, with American factories working at high pressure to fill orders from Allied governments, with the movements of General Pershing's army geared to Allied transportation systems, he could scarcely have put the machine into reverse by refusing supplies to the Allies without appalling consequences for himself and his supporters. The years ahead might have been less fraught with danger for Americans as well as Europeans if the Allied statesmen had suggested to Colonel House in those fateful days of late October 1918 that he should invite the President in the politest terms to think again. Yet even then they would have been handicapped by the time lost through their failure to loosen the President's grip on the armistice negotiations earlier in the month.

As it was, their surrender had fateful consequences. With his party's standing in the Senate and the House of Representatives fatally weakened by the Congressional elections of November, Woodrow Wilson sailed to Europe in December to show unregenerate European statesmen where their duty lay. To draft a settlement on which he and the Allied statesmen could agree took so long that no time was left to reconcile the Germans to its terms, or even to go through the formality of discussing them orally with German delegates. Instead of a stable peace, the European belligerents were left with the almost certain prospect of another war unless the victors could either bring themselves to offer the losers a new deal, or find a way of keeping them permanently in subjection. They were not helped to do either when the United States Senate repudiated the treaty which the Allies had brought themselves to sign rather than fall out with the President, turned its back on his promise of support should France again become a victim of aggression, and withheld American adherence from the League of Nations which he had insisted on their forming. But that was not the fault of the Senate or the American people, who had given the President no warrant for the assumption that his promises would meet with their approval.

II

After the First World War, both Europeans and Americans made the startling discovery that the Atlantic had grown wider since 1914. Alarmed by her narrow escape from foreign entanglements, the United States reverted when she turned down the Versailles Treaty to an aloofness which was all the more marked since the war had weakened old ties with Europe while fostering new rivalries.

A new and less satisfactory relationship between the Old World and the New was particularly noticeable in the cotton industry. Before the war the demand for cheap cotton goods from east of Suez had been so keen, and so successfully met by British textile factories, that the shipping of raw cotton from the Southern States to England, and thence of fabrics and finished articles to India and the Far East, had brought fortunes to Mississippi cotton growers and also to Lancashire cotton spinners and Hindu, Parsee, and Chinese merchants. After the Armistice the demand still existed, but patriotic calls and demands on shipping had forced British manufacturers to neglect their usual markets during the war years and sell their products to Allied governments nearer home. Unable in face of Japanese and American competition to regain all their lost ground after the war, they became less desirable customers in the eyes of their old suppliers, although that did not prevent them from figuring as dangerous competitors in those of their new rivals.

If the British committed the crime of becoming less dependable consumers of raw cotton yet still hankering after their old supremacy as suppliers of the finished product, on the other hand they seemed all set to do only too well as exploiters of Middle Eastern oil. Their hopes of finding yet-untapped deposits in Mesopotamia while continuing to develop their Persian concessions were eyed askance by American producers. At the same time, rumors that they meant also to develop Mesopotamia as a source of raw cotton did not increase their popularity in the Southern States. Thus there were economic as well as ideological grounds for American distrust of British imperialism and for American support for self-determination for non-European peoples. American propagandists were no more hypocritical or self-deluded than the general run of humankind when they supported the Congress Movement in India, attacked the British mandate in Iraq, and fought British influence in Egypt, whose chief commercial crop was long-staple cotton of the highest quality. They were only just about as much so.

In 1921 the United States emerged briefly from her isolation to conclude, after all, a separate peace with Germany and negotiate and sign the Washington Naval Treaty. President Harding and his political advisers believed that a due regard for policy and strategy was not incompatible with economy. Their objects were to curb Japanese ambitions and put the United States Navy on terms of equality with the Royal Navy and superiority over every other navy. They aimed at achieving both at little cost by letting it be known that they proposed to complete a program of naval construction which would give them an immensely powerful surface fleet by 1924 unless the other maritime nations agreed to support their policy of the "open door" in China and to an all-round limitation of naval armaments valid for ten years.

The naval restrictions proposed and accepted at Washington were viewed with disfavor by experts almost everywhere, but a minority of Englishmen who condemned British adherence to the treaty as a weak surrender to a mistaken policy were regarded in their own country as extremists. The fact remains that the treaty achieved neither of its main objects. Japanese ambitions were not curbed, and the myth of Anglo-Saxon naval supremacy in Far Eastern waters was exploded when Japan found herself strong enough by 1932 to defy the world. On the other hand, if the diplomacy of President Harding and Secretary Hughes at Washington failed to deter the Japanese, it did alarm a large number of Europeans who believed that they saw in the treaty evidence of a secret intention on the part of the English-speaking nations to make themselves joint masters of the globe.

European anxieties were increased after the early 1920s by the growing exclusiveness of American fiscal policy. Allied purchases of war material in the United States had been financed while British resources lasted largely by the transfer to American ownership of British foreign investments and gold reserves. Thereafter British borrowing power had kept the Allies going. American output and productivity had increased by leaps and bounds to meet the insatiable demands of the Allied and associated governments for food, clothing, and munitions. Once the postwar boom was over, the high standard of living thus created could be maintained only by a system of tariffs and immigration quotas which kept out cheap imports and cheap labor. At the same time, the concentration in the United States of a high proportion of the gold which served as the ultimate basis of all credit tended to put the brake on commerce between other nations. Since productivity and domestic consumption in the United States continued to rise until 1929, Europeans struggling to make a living in face of lost markets and shrunken credit had the mortifying experience of watching American prosperity climb to giddy heights behind a wall of restrictions which seemed expressly designed to keep America rich and the rest of the world poor.

Conversely, Americans were angered by the reluctance of the Allies to pay their war debts. The Allies, they argued, had borrowed the money, and there could be no doubt that they owed it. This was true. It was also true that every American citizen had been paid in full for goods supplied to the Allies, and that the remaining problem of inter-governmental debts was indissolubly linked in European eyes with that of the reparations which had yet to be extracted from the Germans. The British, in particular, were in the unlucky position of having sacrificed their foreign investments, their markets and their gold to keep the Entente powers in the field while the Americans remained neutral, yet of still being on the wrong side of the ledger because they had borrowed heavily for the benefit of partners whose credit in the United States was not as good as theirs. Their inability to enforce payment of the immense sum owed them by the Russians was recognized, at least in part, when the United States government reduced its claim on the Allies from twelve thousand million to seven thousand million dollars. There remained the difficulty that, irrespective of the ability or willingness of the Allies to meet their obligations, the debt could be paid only in the form of goods, which the Americans did not want, or of gold, of which they already had far more than was good for the world's economy.

A brighter prospect seemed to dawn for Europe when the Allies and the Germans agreed at Locarno in 1925 to sink some of their differences and not to go to war about the rest. But again the shadow of the New World fell across the Old. Nations battered by a decade of conflict and recrimination had only just begun to feel the benefits of a fresh start when the echoes of the Wall Street crash reverberated round the world, bringing the new-built edifice of hope and confidence tumbling down. A shock wave of economic anarchy came close behind. Britain, long the citadel of free trade, bowed to the storm by introducing a system of moderate tariffs which favored colonial exporters. While men starved in the midst of plenty, their leaders found no means of quickening the flow of goods from overstocked producers to needy consumers in face of American refusals to lower fiscal barriers and relax the tyranny of gold. In Germany, Hitler was swept to power on a swelling tide of disenchantment. The Allies were back where they were immediately after American repudiation of the Versailles Treaty, with the difference that Germany was no longer a nation crushed by defeat, but a militant and aggressive one whose masters had nothing to lose by trying novel cures for their economic ills. By adopting such unorthodox expedients as barter, impoverished Germany was able to finance an ambitious program of rearmament which the rest of Europe hardly dared to match for fear of ruin.

Even so, within little more than a year of Hitler's rise to power a decision to start rearming on a modest scale gave the British government an opportunity of showing Germany that they had at least the will to resist aggression; but they passed it by when they threw out the plan proposed by their advisers and fell back on a compromise. Hitler's remilitarization of the Rhineland two years later brought the French a chance of unseating him, but the crisis found the High Command of the French Army bankrupt of ideas. Moreover, many citizens of the European democracies believed, in spite of the solemn pledges given by the Germans at Locarno, that any attempt to stop Hitler by force from moving the troops about in his own country would be immoral and unethical.

In the late 1930s American observers watched with indignation attempts by the British and French governments to conciliate Hitler at the expense of the Czechs. At the same time, the United

States government took up a position on the sidelines by publicly opting for neutrality. Neville Chamberlain, the British Prime Minister, was regarded in America as a weak-kneed champion of democracy because he seemed unable to stand up to Hitler, but his attitude was a logical consequence of his convictions. He believed that there was no chance of wholehearted American support for France and Britain. He also believed, at least for a time, that the French did not mean to fight in any circumstances. He himself was not willing to lead his fellow countrymen into a war which threatened to strip them, for the second time within a generation, of their wealth and means of livelihood while other nations prospered. He concluded that his only course was to appease the Germans until his rearmament program put him in a position to talk to Hitler on equal terms. He was confident that, when that stage was reached, he would be able to handle the Führer without war and without asking favors of the Russians, whom he distrusted even more thoroughly than he did the French.

Equally confident that he had nothing to fear from the democracies on either side of the Atlantic, in 1939 Hitler walked into Poland in spite of British protests and of warnings from his military advisers that dire trouble lay ahead.

German successes early in the war were due at least as much to the defects of the Allied High Command as to the virtues of the Nazi war machine, whose biggest asset was the Führer's readiness to take risks which the German General Staff would not have dared to take without his urging. German generals were astounded when the Allies neglected their opportunity in 1939 of moving into the Rhineland and beyond while the German Army was preoccupied in Poland. Hitler's seizure of Norway in the following April was a triumph of boldness over irresolution. The headlong advance of Rundstedt's armor from the Meuse to the Channel coast in May might have led the German Army to disaster if Gamelin had been as quick to see a chance of turning the tables on the enemy in 1940 as he was when in 1914 he helped to shape French plans for the Battle of the Marne.

Yet these successes were enough to establish the legend that Germany's armed forces were invincible. After the fall of France, few people remembered that the British Expeditionary Force had shown itself at least equal in fighting value to the troops which opposed it, or that its successful withdrawal to the Dunkirk bridgehead was about as difficult a feat as an army could undertake in face of continuous pressure from the enemy. The retreat to Dunkirk was a defeat for the High Command which allowed its forces to be split in two and the French Ninth and Second Armies to be overwhelmed, but it was not a defeat for the British Expeditionary Force or the French First Army.

With Dunkirk in their minds, the British people took a gloomy view of their chances of escaping invasion and subjugation until Winston Churchill rallied them. The United States Ambassador in London reported unfavorably on their prospects, and even the indomitable Churchill made a point of insuring against setbacks by stressing difficulties and dangers. When the British succeeded in bringing back to England nearly a quarter of a million of their troops who had expected to spend the rest of the war in German prison camps, and in rescuing more than a hundred thousand Frenchmen into the bargain, the world believed that a miracle had occurred and praised the weather. When they won the battle of Britain, it seemed that David had prevailed over the Philistine with a sling and with a stone.

But the withdrawal from Dunkirk and the Battle of Britain were not miracles. They were military events whose outcome was determined by military factors. No assistance from the weather could have enabled the British to ferry three hundred thousand men across the Channel under the noses of the Germans without sea power and air power. The British were able to get their troops away from Dunkirk because they had overwhelming naval superiority, enough ships and enough seamen to undertake the business at short notice, and the means of providing at least the bare minimum of air cover which seemed necessary to make the project feasible. They won the Battle of Britain because their air defense commander had been preparing for just such a conflict for at least four years, because his forces were better organized and better led than the enemy's, and because the British aircraft industry rose to the occasion by stepping up its outcome of fighter aircraft at the crucial moment.

But romance has always had a better press than reality. By the summer of 1940 a new image of Britain was beginning to take possession of men's minds. The England of Pitt and Wellington, which was also the England of Winston Churchill and even Neville Chamberlain, was seen no longer as the center of a vast empire on which the sun never set, but as a small, weak country struggling against overwhelming odds.

Foreigners accepted the new image with alacrity because it enabled them, at one and the same time, to indulge feelings of chivalry and to take a psychological revenge on a nation whose easy assumption of superiority and patronizing airs they had long resented. Englishmen shocked by the violence of the German air attacks during the winter of 1940–41, and many of them exhausted by sleepless nights, came in time to accept it too. It received apparent confirmation when the Japanese walked into Singapore. Yet the true lesson of the Singapore fiasco, as of Pearl Harbor, was not that the Anglo-Saxon race was in decline, but that the political and strategic assumptions which flowed from the Washington Conference were unsound.

The picture seemed strengthened, too, by Hitler's invasion of Russia, for the vastness of the forces deployed there made the British effort in North Africa and elsewhere seem tiny in comparison. Yet statistics from the Russian front told the world nothing it ought not to have known already. All they showed was that the Führer was able to send a large army into Russia at the cost of withdrawing troops and squadrons from the West, and that the Russians were able to raise a still larger one but were nevertheless incapable, on their own showing, of turning the Germans out without British help.

The persistence of a David-and-Goliath image did not help the fortunes of the British people, or, in the long run, those of the American people either. From the moment when Russia and the two English-speaking nations became linked in the struggle against Germany, Britain was cast for the role of junior partner. Her spokesmen saw to it that her views were not overlooked, but they had to fight for every point at conferences where a speaker's arguments tended to be weighed by the number of divisions his country could put into the field. Neither the American people, nor even American service chiefs and officials, were always conscious of the true extent of the British contribution on land, at sea, and in the air. This might not have mattered very much if it had not gone some way to foster an impression that Britain was content to allow the Russians to bear practically the whole burden of the war with Germany until the United States developed her full strength. It was bad psychology on the part of the British and American governments not to stamp on every reference to their projected invasion of northern Europe as a Second Front at times when one or both of them were actively maintaining fronts against the Rome-Berlin Axis in the Mediterranean and Atlantic theaters and in German skies.

The British and American tendency to follow the Russian lead by reckoning too exclusively in terms of numbers had adverse effects, too, on Anglo-American organization and strategy. When the Allied Army of Liberation went ashore in Northern France in 1944, the Royal Navy and the Royal Canadian Navy provided three-quarters of the warships and light naval craft which covered the landings, but it was foreseen that eventually there would be more American soldiers in the theater than British and Canadian. American troops would necessarily be commanded in the field by American officers. At the same time, it was clearly in the interests of all that the best use should be made at the topmost level of the most suitable men, irrespective of nationality. The distribution of appointments at Supreme Headquarters was intended to achieve that aim insofar as it was compatible with a reasonable balance between British and American interests; but in practice the cult of the big battalions exerted such influence that the key positions of Supreme Commander and Chief of Staff both went to American soldiers, while a British airman held the rather ill-defined post of Deputy Supreme Commander. The objectionable feature of this arrangement was not that it might have aroused national prejudices if Generals Eisenhower and Bedell Smith had been less tactful and less popular, but that an organization which found no room near the top for a British general of first-class caliber hardly seemed to be making the best use of the available resources. The world was treated to the strange spectacle of a headquarters staff which was supposed to represent the cream of British and American strategic thought, yet which did not include a single soldier with an international reputation as a strategist, although the British Army had at least three or four such men on the active list.

For the first twelve weeks after the landings in Normandy the land battle was directed by a coordinator, General Montgomery, in accordance with an over-all plan which took the Army of Liberation almost to the gates of Germany within that time. Thereafter it was directed by the Supreme Commander. General Eisenhower's over-all plan, insofar as he had one, was to advance on a broad front and trust to superior equipment and the skill of his commanders in the field to get the better of the enemy at all points. Whether this was inherently a good plan or a bad one is debatable, but in either case, the fact remains that the Supreme Commander was not in a position to get his supplies up fast enough in the latter part of 1944 to secure a rapid victory by such means. To make matters worse, the German offensive in the Ardennes took Supreme Headquarters by surprise, and delayed the Allied advance by many weeks. When victory did come in sight in the spring of 1945, General Eisenhower felt obliged by the terms of a bargain made with Stalin to limit his aims in order to conform with Russian movements. He emphasized after the war that the factors governing all his decisions as Supreme Commander were military, not political.

Still worse consequences flowed from President Roosevelt's conviction that the Russians were more reliable Allies than the British, and could be trusted to behave well in Central Europe while the British could hardly be trusted to behave well in their own empire. At the Teheran Conference in 1943 the British faced united opposition from the Russians and the Americans to their proposal that a projected landing in the South of France should be abandoned in favor of a drive toward the Hungarian Plain from the head of the Adriatic. Stalin interpreted Roosevelt's support for his case as an invitation to grab as much of the Danubian

Basin as he could, and in due course the work begun by Woodrow Wilson in 1918 was completed in a fashion not foreseen by that architect of Central Europe's ruin.

Accordingly, the end of the war in Europe brought the Russians and the Western Allies face to face along a line from the Baltic to the Danube. Outwardly, both sides were still bent on cooperation and peaceful co-existence. Inwardly, Stalin's obvious determination to tolerate only Communist governments in Rumania and Poland was already raising for Roosevelt's successor doubts from which the British had never been quite free. A few months later, when President Truman ordered after consultation with the British government that the atom bomb should be used against Japan, some observers even saw in his decision a move to end the war in the Far East before the Russians could intervene in accordance with a promise made to Roosevelt at Yalta. The two bombs dropped by the Americans, they claimed, were aimed not so much at Hiroshima and Nagasaki as at Moscow. They were not so much the closing shots of the Second World War as the first shots in the Cold War against Russia.

By the summer of 1948, at any rate, the Cold War and the Iron Curtain were realities. The Communist grip had tightened over every one of the countries overrun by Russian troops in 1944 and 1945, with the borderline exceptions of deviationist Yugoslavia and perhaps Albania. The Russians were ready and willing to defy the Western Allies by refusing them access to Berlin.

A year after the date by which Roosevelt had hoped to remove the last American soldier from Europe and revert to the comfortable isolationism of the pre-slump years, the Senate dealt a knockout blow to all such fancies by giving the administration sweeping powers to associate itself with defensive arrangements in foreign countries. Under the Marshall Plan the United States had already offered massive economic aid to countries willing to stay outside the Russian orbit. More recently Britain, France, Belgium, Holland, and Luxembourg had taken the first step toward the North Atlantic Treaty by signing a defense pact which they hoped to make effective with the help of American equipment and American participation.

Exactly a generation after the Woodrow Wilson era, the United States thus set forth to check the rising tide of Communism which threatened to engulf the capitalist world in which her citizens could live and prosper. In much the same spirit of more-or-less enlightened self-interest, but more haphazardly and with a warier eye to the exchequer, Britain had once set forth to drive back the ebbing tide of lawlessness and tyranny which threatened to recede too slowly from the less civilized parts of the globe to keep pace with the expansion of her trade. As compared with the miscellaneous band of merchants, speculators, soldiers and administrators who consolidated and extended the rambling British Empire in the nineteenth century, American statesmen and officials who labored to make the world safe for capitalism in the twentieth were burdened, however, by at least one major handicap. British empire-builders in the Victorian heyday could offer backward or neglected peoples not only the advantages of association with a great trading community and an external security backed by unchallenged command of the sea, but also settled government and protection from local tyrants. Their successors, forbidden by their political philosophy to look kindly on imperialism, could offer only material benefits and an external security whose ultimate sanction was the two-edged sword of the nuclear deterrent.

There was no doubt which was the more attractive of these last inducements. European nations willing to qualify for American favors by signing defense pacts were not always so prompt in contributing to their own security. Among more distant countries not immediately threatened by the proximity of Russian armies, some chose neutralism, while others joined the scramble for subsidies with the tacit proviso that none of the money should be spent in ways which did not directly benefit the men in power. National defense, which soon came to mean the defense not merely of the United States but of half the world, became America's biggest industry, a boundless source of revenue for producers of every kind of war material from candy for the troops to global bombers, but a severed artery for the taxpayer and the Treasury. Before long disillusioned statesmen were seeing in disunited Europe a potential field for agonizing reappraisals, and were wondering whether the Korea of Synghman Rhee and the micro-China of Chiang Kai-shek really were worth the millions of dollars spent on them.

At the same time, the problem of defending the non-Russian world against Russia showed an obstinate resistance to change, despite the transformation wrought by the nuclear bomb, the world-encircling bomber and the long- or intermediate-range ballistic missile. In the Middle East, the British had been familiar with it for at least a century or so. Britain's persistent interest in the string of Arab and non-Arab countries from Afghanistan through Persia, Iraq, and Arabia Deserta to the Libyan Plateau had been dictated from the middle of the nineteenth century and earlier not solely, or even mainly, by hopes of commercial gain but, above all, by the fear of Russian penetration and expansion to the shores of the Arabian Sea, the Persian Gulf and the Red Sea. To safeguard the Northwest Frontier, the Suez Canal and, more recently, the strategically vital oilfields of Mesopotamia and Persia had long been the great aims of British Middle Eastern policy; but all these preoccupations were comprehended in the abiding problem of containing Russia.

Even so, this had never been an exclusively British problem. French interests in the Arab countries, to say nothing of German ambitions on the eve of the First World War, had led to bitter rivalries, and also to such working arrangements as the San Remo oil agreement of 1920, which gave France a stake in Middle Eastern oil. The Cold War made containment of Russia within her southern boundary a problem of vital concern to every nation opposed to Communism, while the addition of Kuwait and Saudi Arabia to the list of Middle Eastern oil-producing countries enlarged its scope by increasing the number of strategic points whose defense was vital. For the framers of American foreign policy and strategy, especially, the undisguised ambition of every Russian ruler since the middle of the nineteenth century to extend his influence southward to the Indus Valley and the Tigris was a threat which might have been expected to stand high among their preoccupations.

Nevertheless, it was natural that most eyes should be focused on

Europe, where vast Russian armies were already at the gates of the Western world. It was also natural that American statesmen should think twice before grappling with the huge perplexities which the Middle Eastern problem posed for them. No one who took a broad view of the outlook in the 1950s could doubt that the capacity of the anti-Communist nations to resist Soviet encroachment in the Middle East would turn on the extent to which they succeeded in upholding Western influence in the Arab countries, or that strategic bases and spheres of influence were the keys of power in undeveloped territories. But what flowed from those conclusions? For as long as anyone could remember, American statesmen and propagandists had fought British and French domination of the Arab world as contrary to the principle of self-determination, a denial of American claims to the "open door," and a threat to American oil interests. Should the United States now reverse that policy, plead guilty to abandoning cherished principles, and support the very powers whose imperialist ambitions she had long condemned? Or should she seek spheres of influence and bases of her own at the cost of exacerbating transatlantic rivalries, and incidentally at the risk of seeing her public men accused by their fellow citizens of fostering dollar imperialism and surrendering to the much criticized oil lobby?

Not surprisingly, American statesmen fell back on a series of compromises. Outside the Arab countries, the transfer of the Abadan refineries from the Anglo-Persian Oil Company to an international consortium backed by American interests saved Persian oil for the West, but left ruffled feelings on the European side of the Atlantic. In Saudi Arabia the United States government ostentatiously refrained from intervention in the domestic concerns of a country whose rulers would have been none the worse for a dash of old-fashioned imperialist supervision. American commentators complained that the government allowed money to pour into both countries without insisting that a reasonable proportion should be spent on the welfare of the people, but they might have been still more scathing had American officials aimed openly at political domination. Thus it was not until the Suez crisis dealt a staggering blow to Western influence in the Middle

East that the American dilemma was revealed in all its stark simplicity. The revelation was all the more startling since the Suez incident also gave ordinary men and women on both sides of the Atlantic their first blood-chilling glimpse of the inability of their leaders to bring their outlook on an issue of paramount importance to a common focus.

If any aspect of Suez was more striking than the heartfelt agreement with which the nations condemned France and Britain when it appeared that their intervention could conceivably lead to war with Russia and had already brought a massive attack on sterling, it was the unanimity with which those not pro-Communist or neutralist concluded when Nasser seized the assets of the Suez Canal Company that he must be dislodged at almost any cost.

Their attitude, if not surprising, seems in retrospect less obviously right than it did when the affair was at its height. Nothing which came to light afterward justifies the assumption that disaster would have come to the West if Nasser had been left in undisturbed possession. On the contrary, there is a good deal to suggest that the Western Allies overestimated the extent to which Nasser was still under Soviet influence when he seized the canal, that in fact he had already lost faith in Russian promises, that his action was, in reality, the gesture of mingled acquisitiveness, resentment and near-despair which anyone unaware of his recent flirtation with Moscow would have taken it to be. There was no doubt that sooner or later the Allies would have to stand up to the threat of Russian encroachment in the Middle East, but did Nasser's act of nationalization stamp him unmistakably as the tool of Moscow, and did it create the right conditions for a trial of strength?

The fact remains that the anti-Communist powers did take that view of Nasser, and that they did choose that moment for a showdown which they hoped would prove that Moscow was bluffing. In general Secretary of State John Foster Dulles appeared to encourage them to do so in accordance with his well-known policy of brinksmanship. Nasser, he said at the beginning of the crisis, must be made to disgorge.

On the other hand, there were times when Dulles seemed hesitant and overcautious. There were even times when he showed a confusion of thought and a lack of precision surprising in a successful lawyer. He commended a plan for a Users' Club to the Western Allies on the ground that Nasser would like it even less than he liked their own plan for an international board of control, but nevertheless appeared to think that his plan might be accepted. If his object was to score a triumph for the West and humiliate Nasser by forcing the Egyptians to accept a plan obnoxious to their leader, then he defeated it when he announced publicly that there were no teeth in his proposals, thus giving Nasser the plain hint that he could safely disregard them. If, on the other hand, his intention was to put Nasser in the wrong by causing him to reject proposals which the rest of the world regarded as reasonable, then the maneuver became pointless when Nasser turned down a plan which Dulles himself described as more acceptable than his own. The plan for an international board of control on which Egypt would be represented was backed by eighteen nations, the United States included. When Nasser rejected it, no more was needed to show that he meant to keep the canal if he could and that only force or the threat of force was likely to dislodge him.

Meanwhile Dulles knew that the British had called up reservists and that they and the French were preparing to put troops into the Canal Zone if the need arose. He would have known it even if such moves could have been concealed from the Central Intelligence Agency, of which Allen Dulles was director, for the British government had given him from the first as much of the picture as he cared to have. His reluctance to enter into details was understandable in view of the special position of the United States as wielder of the nuclear deterrent, but that made it more than ever necessary that he and his European counterparts should understand each other. From the moment when Nasser refused to turn over the canal to an international board of control, it became imperative that the anti-Communist nations should either leave him in possession and content themselves with formal protests, or agree promptly on a plan of action which all were willing to put into effect, and if necessary back by force, should further negotiations fail. In the absence of such a plan, their continued insistence that Nasser must be made to stand aside in favor of some international body became an empty bluff which contradicted the rule that statesmen should never make threats or promises which they are not prepared to carry out.

If the anti-Communist nations reached no such agreement, the blame did not rest solely with the British and French governments. They at least took realistic steps to back the insistence of eighteen nations that Nasser must be *made* to part with control of the canal. What steps did Dulles take?

From the beginning of September, when the crisis had already entered on its second month, Dulles was burdened by the knowledge that public opinion in the United States was hardening against the use of force. Thus it became more than ever necessary that he should make his country's intentions crystal-clear. Yet his statements continued to be clouded by a baffling imprecision. The United States, he said, did not intend to shoot its way through the canal, and could not be expected to identify itself completely with either "the colonial powers" or the powers "uniquely concerned with the problem of getting independence." But no one had ever suggested shooting a way *through* the canal, none of the powers had colonial interests in Egypt, and Egypt had long since achieved her independence. Did Dulles think that the canal was closed and that Egypt was a colony? The French, it was true, were struggling to avoid being turned out of Algeria by Arab Nationalists financed partly from the proceeds of Saudi Arabian oil royalties, but Algeria was a province of metropolitan France, to describe Algerians as uniquely concerned with independence would have been a gross abuse of words, and in any case the context was confusing.

According to a statement attributed to his brother, John Foster Dulles was warned on some unspecified occasion before the Franco-British intervention that a "three-nation attack on Suez" was in prospect. It is not necessary to accept the evidence for that statement to be convinced that the State Department must have received notice from its intelligence sources, at least some days before the issue of the Franco-British ultimatum, that an Israeli attack on Egypt was extremely probable. The State Department knew, too, that Franco-British forces were assembling within striking distance of the Canal Zone. It follows that Dulles must have believed either that the British and the French meant to intervene in the event of an Israeli attack, or that they did not mean to intervene. If he thought that they did mean to intervene, why did he not avert the disaster which, on that assumption, he must have foreseen, by warning them that the United States would disavow them unless they changed their minds? If he thought that they did not mean to intervene, what did he expect to happen? How did he propose to meet the situation that would arise if Nasser were overwhelmed by an Israeli attack which was almost certain to succeed unless checked by intervention of one kind or another?

Irrespective of the answers which may one day be given to these questions, it seems clear that the tragedy of Suez had deeper causes than the rashness of European statesmen whose judgment was impaired by their assumption that Nasser was, at one and the same time, a Soviet stooge and a second Hitler or a second Mussolini. To some extent, perhaps above all, it was a product of the confusions to which John Foster Dulles was exposed by the tripartite conflict between his emotional conviction that Nasser was a bad man for whom toppling was too good, his instincts as an anti-imperialist to whom armed intervention in a country struggling to consolidate its independence seemed a monstrous wrong, and his acquired habits as arch-apostle of a new creed of bluff, brinksmanship and toughness.

If that was the lesson of Suez, it did not go unheeded. When a fresh bout of trouble in the Middle East a few months later took an American force to the Levant to look after the internal affairs of Jordan in loose partnership with the British, the expedition was regarded by some observers as another milestone on the British Empire's road to ruin, by others as evidence that the recent breach between the Anglo-Saxon powers was mending. It could also be interpreted as a sign that the United States had taken a fresh look at imperialism and was ready to accept a first installment of the white man's burden.

BIBLIOGRAPHY

Aldington, Richard: *Lawrence of Arabia* (1955)
Aloisi, Baron: *Journal* (Paris, 1957)
Amrine, Michael: *The Great Decision* (1960)
Astor, Michael: *Tribal Feeling* (1963)
Attlee, Earl (Clement Richard Attlee): *As it Happened* (1954)
Avon, Earl of (Sir Anthony Eden): *Full Circle* (1960)
        Facing the Dictators (1962)

Baldwin, Earl (A.W.): *My Father* (1955)
Baldwin, Hanson W.: *Great Mistakes of the Second World War*
        (1950)
        The Great Arms Race (1958)
Beaverbrook, Lord (William Maxwell Aitken): *The Decline and
        Fall of Lloyd George* (1963)
Beloff, Max: *The Foreign Policy of Soviet Russia 1929–1941*
        (1949)
Blackett, P. M. S.: *The Military and Political Consequences of
        Atomic Energy* (1952)
Blake, Robert: *The Unknown Prime Minister* (1955)
Blumentritt, Guenther: *Von Rundstedt, The Soldier and the Man*
        (1952)
Boyle, Andrew: *Trenchard, Man of Vision* (1962)
Bradley, General Omar: *A Soldier's Story* (New York, 1951)
Brook-Shepherd, Gordon: *Anschluss, the Rape of Austria* (1963)
Bryant, Sir Arthur: *The Turn of the Tide* (1957)
        Triumph in the West (1959)

Bullitt, William C.: *The Great Globe Itself* (1947)

Bullock, Alan: *Hitler, A Study in Tyranny* (1952)
    The Life and Times of Ernest Bevin (vol. i, 1960)

Butcher, Captain Harry C.: *My Three Years with Eisenhower*
    (New York, 1946)

Butler, Sir James: *Grand Strategy, September 1939–June 1941*
    (History of the Second World War) (1957)
    Lord Lothian (Philip Kerr) (1960)

Butler, Rohan, see Woodward, E. L.

Byrnes, James F.: *Speaking Frankly* (1947)

Callwell, Major-General Sir C. E.: *Field-Marshal Sir Henry Wil-
    son, His Life and Diaries* (1927)

Chandos, Viscount, see Lyttelton, Oliver.

Childers, Erskine B.: *The Road to Suez* (1962)

Churchill, Sir Winston: *The Second World War* (1948–54)

Ciano, Count, see Muggeridge, Malcolm.

Clark, General Mark: *Calculated Risk* (1951)

Cole, Hubert: *Laval, a Biography* (1963)

Collier, Basil: *The Defence of the United Kingdom* (History of
    the Second World War) (1957)
    The Battle of Britain (1962)

Connell, John: *The Most Important Country* (1957)

Deakin, F. W.: *The Brutal Friendship* (1962)

Deane, John R.: *The Strange Alliance* (1947)

Dempster, Derek, see Wood, Derek.

Derry, T. K.: *The Campaign in Norway* (History of the Second
    World War) (1952)

Dugdale, B. E. C. (Mrs.): *Arthur James Balfour, 1906–1930*
    (1936)

Eden, Sir Anthony, see Avon, Earl of

Ehrman, John: *Grand Strategy, August 1943–August 1945* (His-
    tory of the Second World War) (1956)

Eisenhower, General Dwight D.: *Crusade in Europe* (New York,
    1958)

Ellis, Major L. F.: *The Campaign in France and Flanders, 1939–
    1940* (History of the Second World War) (1956)

Feiling, Keith: *Life of Neville Chamberlain* (1946)
Flandin, Pierre-Etienne: *Politique française, 1919–40* (Paris, 1948)
Fleming, Peter: *Invasion 1940* (1957)
Fuller, General J. F. C.: *The Second World War* (1948)

Gamelin, General: *Servir* (Paris, 1946)
Garnett, David (Editor): *The Letters of T. E. Lawrence* (1938)
Garthoff, Raymond L.: *Soviet Strategy in the Nuclear Age* (1958)
George, David Lloyd (Earl Lloyd-George): *War Memoirs* (1938)
    The Truth about Reparations and War Debts (1932)
Gilbert, Martin, and Gott, Richard: *The Appeasers* (1963)
Goold-Adams, Richard: *The Time of Power* (1962)
Gott, Richard, see Gilbert, Martin
Goutard, Colonel A.: *The Battle of France, 1940* (1958)
Grinnell-Milne, Duncan: *The Silent Victory* (1958)

Halifax, Earl of: *Fullness of Days* (1957)
Hart, Captain B. H. Liddell: *The Other Side of the Hill* (1951)
Henderson, Sir Nevile: *Failure of a Mission* (1940)
Herriot, Edouard: *Jadis* (Paris, 1952)
Hewins, Ralph: *Mr. Five Per Cent* (1957)
Hinsley, F. H.: *Hitler's Strategy* (1951)
Hitler, Adolf: *My Struggle (Mein Kampf)* (1939)
Hoare, Sir Samuel, see Templewood, Viscount
Hope, Stanton: *The Battle for Oil* (1958)
House, Edward Mandell, and Seymour, Charles (Editors): *What Really Happened at Paris* (1921)
Hull, Cordell: *Memoirs* (1948)

Jungk, Robert: *Brighter Than a Thousand Suns* (1958)

Kelly, Denis, see MacLeod, Roderick
Kemp, Norman: *Abadan* (1953)
Keynes, J. M.: *The Economic Consequences of the Peace* (1919)
King-Hall, Stephen: *Our Times, 1900–1960* (1961)
Kirkpatrick, Sir Ivone: *The Inner Circle* (1959)

Lee, Asher: *The Soviet Air and Rocket Forces* (1959)
Lewinsohn, Richard: *The Man Behind the Scenes* (1929)

Lloyd-George, Earl, *see* George, David Lloyd

Lodwick, John: *Gulbenkian* (1958)

Longrigg, S. H.: *Oil in the Middle East* (1954)

Lyttelton, Oliver, Viscount Chandos: *The Memoirs of Lord Chandos* (1962)

McKee, Alexander: *Strike from the Sky* (1960)

MacLeod, Roderick, and Kelly, Denis (Editors): *The Ironside Diaries* (1962)

Macphail, Sir Andrew: *Three Persons* (1929)

Manstein, Field-Marshal Erich von: *Lost Victories* (1958)

Martienssen, Anthony: *Hitler and his Admirals* (1948)

Merriam, Robert E.: *The Battle of the Ardennes* (1958)

Middleton, Drew: *The Sky Suspended* (1960)

Miksche, F. O.: *The Failure of Atomic Strategy* (1959)

Minney, R. J. (Editor): *The Private Papers of Hore-Belisha* (1960)

Montgomery of Alamein, Field-Marshal Viscount: *Normandy to the Baltic* (1947)
  El Alamein to the River Sangro (1948)

Morison, Samuel Eliot: *The Battle of the Atlantic* (Boston, 1947)
  American Contributions to the Strategy of World War II (1958)

Morrison of Lambeth, Lord (Herbert Morrison): *Autiobiography* (1960)

Muggeridge, Malcolm (Editor): *Ciano's Diary, 1939–1943* (1947)
  Ciano's Diplomatic Papers (1948)

Namier, Sir Lewis: *Diplomatic Prelude, 1938–1939* (1948)
  Europe in Decay (1950)
  In the Nazi Era (1952)

Neumann, Robert: *Zaharoff the Armaments King* (1938)

Nicolson, Harold: *Peacemaking 1919* (1933)
  Curzon, the Last Phase (1934)

O'Brien, T. H.: *Civil Defence* (History of the Second World War) (1955)

Owen, Frank: *Tempestuous Journey* (1954)

Postan, M. M.: *British War Production* (History of the Second World War) (1952)

Roosevelt, Elliot: *As He Saw It* (New York, 1946)
Roskill, Captain S. W., R.N.: *The War at Sea* (History of the Second World War) (vol. i, 1954)
Rowse, A. L.: *All Souls' and Appeasement* (1961)

Saundby, Air Marshal Sir Robert: *Air Bombardment* (1961)
Schellenberg, Walter: *The Schellenberg Memoirs* (1956)
Schmidt, Paul (edited R. H. C. Steed): *Hitler's Interpreter* (1951)
Schröter, Heinz: *Stalingrad* (1958)
Seymour, Charles: *The Intimate Papers of Colonel House* (1926-28) see also House, Edward Mandell
Sherwood, Robert E.: *Roosevelt and Hopkins, an Intimate History* (New York, 1948)
Shirer, W.: *The Rise and Fall of the Third Reich* (1960)
Shulman, Milton: *Defeat in the West* (1947)
Simonds, Frank H.: *How Europe Made Peace Without America* (1927)
Spears, Major-General Sir Edward: *Assignment to Catastrophe* (1954)
Speidel, Hans: *We Defended Normandy* (1951)
Steed, R. H. C., see Schmidt, Paul
Stettinius, Edward R.: *Roosevelt and the Russians* (1950)

Temperley, H. W. V.: *A History of the Peace Conference of Paris* (1920-24)
Templewood, Viscount (Sir Samuel Hoare): *Nine Troubled Years* (1954)
Trevor-Roper, H. R.: *The Last Days of Hitler* (1956)
Tully, Andrew: *CIA, The Inside Story* (New York, 1962)

Welles, Sumner: *The Time for Decision* (1944)
Wheatley, Ronald: *Operation Sea Lion* (1958)
Wheeler-Bennett, J. W.: *The Nemesis of Power* (1953)
Wilmot, Chester: *The Struggle for Europe* (1952)

Wood, Derek, and Dempster, Derek: *The Narrow Margin* (1961)
Woodward, E. L., and Butler, Rohan (Editors): *Documents on British Foreign Policy 1919–1939* (First, Second and Third Series, 1946–1952)

Young, Desmond: *Rommel* (1950)
Young, G.W.: *Stanley Baldwin* (1952)
British Official Publications not Listed Above

Documents on German Foreign Policy 1918–1945 (1949–   )
Parliamentary Debates (Hansard)

INDEX